THE COMPLETE
HISTORY
OF THE
SAS

Published in 2021 by Welbeck

An Imprint of Welbeck Non-Fiction Limited, part of
Welbeck Publishing Group
20 Mortimer Street London W1T 3JW

Text © 2003, 2007, 2021 Nigel McCrery
Foreword on page 7 © 2021 Andy McNab
Design © 2021 Welbeck Non-fiction Limited

A CIP catalogue record for this book is available from
the British Library

ISBN 978 1 78739 687 6

Printed and bound by CPI Group (UK) Ltd, Croydon CR0 4YY

10 9 8 7 6 5 4 3 2 1

Some of the material in this book previously appeared in
The Complete History of the SAS, Carlton Books, 2007

THE COMPLETE HISTORY OF THE

SAS

The Story of the World's
Most Feared Elite Fighting Force

NIGEL McCRERY

Consultant Editor Barry Davies BEM
Foreword by Andy McNab CBE DCM MM

WELBECK

FOR TIM

For remaining upbeat and cheerful despite going through so much. You have my complete admiration.

AND FOR

DEB, CLARE and LAURA

Who always stand by his side.

Thanks to:

Pete Winner (Soldier I)
John Geddes
Amy Scholey
Lynne Scholey
Roland Hall (Editor)
Odette Price

CONTENTS

PREFACE

THE BRITISH SAS is a household name, not only in the United Kingdom but throughout the world. Ever since black-clad figures suddenly appeared on television screens during the Iranian Embassy siege in 1980, the Regiment has become legendary. For some, that was the first they had heard of the SAS. For others, it was the first time they had seen the soldiers they had heard so much about in action. It was an action that changed the face of modern reporting, changed the face of modern policing and changed the way that anti-terrorist organizations work around the world. This is the story of the SAS...

Barry Davies, B.E.M.

FOREWORD

HUNDREDS OF BOOKS have been written about the Special Air Service Regiment in its 80-year history, from the time of the 'Originals', the very first band of SAS operators, selected by its founder David Stirling in 1941 to attack General Erwin Rommel's Afrika Korps, right up to the post 9/11 wars in Iraq and Afghanistan. And as a lot of the books have shown, special forces operations have never been a science; in fact, the very first operation conducted by the Originals was a failure.

There are too many unknowns. Once in the battlespace, the kit could suddenly no longer work, the intelligence might be wrong, the enemy will never react in the way you expect them to. The Regiment's official motto is 'Who Dares Wins', but it could just as well be 'Check and Test'.

But no matter what the battlespace has thrown at the Regiment throughout history, the professionalism of its 'Bayonets' – the soldiers in the SAS Sabre squadrons – has never diminished.

The reason is simple. Our founder, David Stirling, was determined to build a unit of dedicated men capable of self-discipline and outstanding ability. He is quoted as saying, 'We believe, as did the ancient Greeks who originated the word "aristocracy", that every man with the right attitude and talents, regardless of birth and riches, has a capacity in his own lifetime of reaching that status in its true sense. In fact, in our SAS context, an individual soldier might prefer to go on serving as an NCO rather than leave the Regiment in order to obtain an officer's commission. All ranks in the SAS are of "one company" in which a sense of class is both alien and ludicrous.'

This ethos remains within the Regiment today, and that is why people like me give up the rank and privileges they have earned in their own units to restart their military career as SAS troopers. I would call that more than 80 years of true social mobility.

David Stirling's gold standard ensures that there is no difference between the Originals in 1941, those who stormed the Iranian embassy in London in 1980, or the Bayonets who are fighting in the Sabre squadrons today. All troopers are still chosen because they fulfil Stirling's three requirements of dedication, self-disciple and ability.

But who are these people who volunteer to attempt selection, knowing that the vast majority of candidates never even make it past the first few weeks of the seven-month process?

Volunteers come from all three UK services and their reserves, as well as personnel from many other countries, notably Australia and New Zealand. The wider the range of expertise and experience, the more effective the Regiment will be in the fight.

The first month of selection consists of the volunteer putting a bergen (rucksack) on their back, a rifle in their hands and tabbing (TAB: Tactical Advance to Battle) anything up to 38 miles over the peaks of the Welsh Black Mountains and Brecon Beacons. During this first phase, the directing staff don't even want to know who the volunteers are. Known only by a colour and number, each candidate tabs with no idea of the distance they will have to cover, nor the time allowed for covering the distance. This isn't just a fitness test: it's about dedication. No matter the distance, the terrain or the weather conditions, a determined volunteer pushes his or her body to the limits and tabs as quickly as they can, every single day.

My intake initially consisted of 220 volunteers. By the end of this first phase, there were 24 of us left.

The remaining six months of selection are dedicated to evaluating Stirling's other two gold standards: self-discipline and ability.

Living tactically for a month as an SAS patrol in the rainforest, volunteers learn how to live in an alien environment while conducting special forces operations. The pressure to perform is intense, but volunteers are never told how good or bad their performance is while under the canopy. To add to the pressure, live ammunition is used. There have been casualties during the jungle phase. But it is about much more than just assessing how good you are at operating in rainforests. It's about the amount of self-discipline you can muster while working as a small group. You have to prove that not only are you at the top of your game, but you're also helping others to be at the top of theirs, to ensure the patrol is as efficient as it can possibly be.

At the end of the jungle phase, the directing staff are asked a simple question: 'Would you have this volunteer in your patrol?' It's critical; when the instructors go back to their squadrons, a volunteer who passes may well be in their patrol. Only if the majority of instructors say yes, has that candidate passed the jungle phase. One volunteer in my intake failed for not helping others to learn Morse code when they needed to. As an experienced Morse operator, he should have been helping his fellow patrol members learn his skill without being asked to. Of the 24 who went to the jungle, eight passed and all were eventually badged. But this isn't always the case. There have been occasions where an entire selection has failed and been RTU'd (Returned To Unit) because the gold standard hadn't been reached.

The general perception of an SAS trooper is that they have come from the infantry, but many also come from the corps: engineers, logistics, mechanics and other technical trades from the three services. These volunteers make the grade not just because they have the required determination and self-discipline, but also because they have the required level of ability. That ability enables them to learn quickly and adapt to any situation. I remember a Royal Marine corporal doing extremely well during his two weeks' weapon training phase. As you would expect, he was incredibly capable when it came to using weapons he was familiar with – as a Marine he had been using them every day of his career. Alongside him was a tank mechanic from the Royal Electrical and Mechanical Engineers (REME). Unsurprisingly, the mechanic struggled when using these same weapon systems. His trade was all about spanners. Of course, the Royal Marine looked to be far more proficient at weapon skills when standing next to the mechanic completing the tasks, but his ability quickly diminished when the pair moved on to different weapon systems used by the Regiment, ones with which neither one of them was familiar. The Marine was RTU'd due to his lack of ability to learn and adapt easily, whereas the mechanic passed the module having mastered all weapon systems. It isn't about what you know, it's about being able to learn what you don't.

David Stirling's 80-year-old requirements to become an SAS operator are the thread that binds together all of the amazing stories you will find in this book of our Regiment's history: dedication, self-discipline and ability.

Andy McNab CBE DCM MM

INTRODUCTION

THERE HAVE BEEN many books written about the SAS, most without the Regiment's approval, yet the public desire to glean new information about any aspect of SAS operations continues unabated. Writing the latest stories of this unique regiment presents a problem, for the SAS has now gagged most of its members. However, wars have become part of the public domain and every now and then a new tale will surface. During the research for this book, I have visited Hereford many times, talking to members both past and present. Some have greeted me with smiles, while others have shown nothing but disdain. Notwithstanding, one characteristic bonded them all: they are normal, healthy human beings and not the psychopaths many would have you believe.

The SAS is part of the British Army and, regardless of military disbandment, amalgamations and a steady erosion of service manpower, the Regiment has survived since its inception in 1941. True, it was reduced to little more than a territorial unit after the Second World War, but its time in the wilderness was short. There has always been, and always will be, a role for those who 'dare', especially those who 'dare and win'. For this reason, and despite the Regiment's misgivings about publicity, its history is one worth writing, for it would be wrong to let such deeds and heroism go unrecorded.

Since the 1940s, the SAS has suppressed insurgencies, fought in major wars and confronted terrorism energetically. Yet, from the very beginning, its soldiers have remained hidden, often shrouded in myth and half-truths. And this is still true of their more recent operations in Iraq. The SAS family is truly a group of special people: for when people of the right calibre accept a common philosophy based on the individual spirit acting in tune with his or her fellow soldier to form a whole, then excellence can be the only result.

Research for this book has taken many forms and required the reading of more than 30 books about the SAS family. By far the best information was gleaned from SAS author and historian Barry Davies. Barry has amassed a huge database concerning all aspects of the Regiment, and his picture library of the SAS is undoubtedly the finest in private hands. Many operations and individuals are mentioned more than once throughout the book, but where possible I have tried to keep repetition of stories to a minimum.

Unlike previous books, I have written this one using a familiar style, hoping to retain the original character of the conversations on which it was based. Inevitably, a number of personal opinions have crept into the book: should you discover these, please view them for what they are, as they do not reflect the official opinions or policies of the SAS.

Nigel McCrery

1

THE 'ORIGINALS'

I T IS DIFFICULT to be totally accurate about anything relating to the early SAS as records during its formation are scant, to say the least. Names of those who volunteered or joined have to be gleaned from a wide variety of sources, in many cases the actual soldiers themselves, who in later years wrote of their experiences. As a group, these became known as the 'Originals'.

The 'Originals' were the first SAS soldiers, and to claim to have been an original member of the SAS one must have been on the very first operation. The list of those soldiers recruited into L Detachment SAS by David Stirling numbers more than 70, yet only some 65 (the figure varies by one or two, depending on the source quoted) actually took part in Operation Squatter. Two of the 'Originals', Ken Warburton and Joe Duffy, were killed during parachute training prior to the operation, and it is logical to suppose that a handful remained behind in camp during Operation Squatter or arrived immediately after it. Some, such as 'Sandy' Scratchley and 'Bill' Cumper, are on the original list, and yet they did not arrive at Kabrit until after Operation Squatter. One early member, to whom everyone refers simply as 'Kaufman', seems to have been the camp scrounger and storeman. There is also no mention of Dave Kershaw before or on the first operation, yet he is proclaimed as an 'Original' by Reg Seekings and Johnny Cooper, among others.

Operation Squatter did not go well – indeed, was little short of a total disaster – so identifying the 'Originals' and those who made it back alive is a matter of simple research and elimination.

Records show that the men were divided into five groups under the command of David Stirling, 'Jock' Lewes, 'Paddy' Mayne, Eoin McGonigal and Charles Bonnington. Each group of 10 was subdivided into two five-man raiding patrols, which were dropped separately by five Bombay aircraft supplied by 216 Squadron RAF. This was the first Allied airborne landing in North Africa. Once again, figures do not tally exactly, as the RAF reported dropping 65 troops from its aircraft on the night of 16–17 November 1941. Of these, it is reported that 22 returned to Kabrit camp; the figures vary from account to account. The list below is compiled from those mentioned as 'Originals' and believed to have taken part in Operation Squatter, and who are also identified as participating in later actions, meaning they must have survived the first operation.

1. Albert Youngman
2. Alf Dignum
3. Arthur 'Phil' Phillips
4. Sidney James 'Barney' Stone
5. Bill Fraser
6. Bob Bennett
7. Bob Lilley
8. Bob Tait
9. Robert White
10. Charles Sidney Cattell
11. David Stirling
12. Eoin McGonigal
13. Harry Poat
14. Jim Almonds
15. James 'Jim' Blakeney
16. Jimmy Storie
17. Jack Byrne
18. John 'Jock' Cheyne
19. 'Jock' Lewes
20. Joe Duffy
21. Johnny Cooper
22. Mick D'Arcy
23. 'Paddy' Mayne
24. Pat Riley
25. Reg Seekings
26. Roy David Davies
27. Roy Dodd
28. Stanley Bolland

The remaining 'Originals' went on to carry out many successful raids deep behind enemy lines. This handful of soldiers did so much for their country and yet their deeds go unsung. This is true of Sergeant Jack Byrne, for example. It was not until his medals were put up for auction in 2007 that that story surrounding his military life came to public knowledge.

Jack Byrne

Born in Preston and brought up in a tough Lancashire orphanage, Jack Byrne enlisted with the Gordon Highlanders in 1939, aged 19, and fought throughout the war. While details of some of his escapades are still rather sketchy, what little is known of this former soldier is exceptional.

Why an Englishman should join a Scottish regiment is known only to Jack himself, and why a Scottish regiment accepted him is again a mystery. However, having joined the Gordon Highlanders, Jack was part of the British Expeditionary Force (BEF) tasked in May 1940 with fighting a rearguard action, allowing the remnants of the BEF to evacuate from Dunkirk. Jack has little to say about the exploits of the Gordon Highlanders, other than this: 'After every battle or skirmish we buried the bravest and the best of us, the men whose dash and daring won the victories which cost their lives.' During the vicious fighting, Jack was wounded by shrapnel, but he continued to fight until he was bayoneted in the groin by a German soldier and left for dead. Amid the chaos of Dunkirk, a guardian angel decided to look after him; two French civilians found Jack, who then carried him to the beach, from where he was eventually evacuated. The rearguard action of the Gordon Highlanders at Dunkirk is a tribute to our heroic Scottish brothers.

Jack recovered in England and then joined 11 (Scottish) Commando; after fighting in Syria, he found himself in North Africa, where he was recruited into 'L' Detachment SAS. Two months later, on the night of 16–17 November, he took part in the first SAS operation, codenamed Squatter, being assigned to Bill Fraser's patrol which was part of Lieutenant Charles Bonnington's section. Unfortunately, due to bad weather, the operation was an unmitigated disaster; luckily, Jack survived.

Even with their numbers dramatically depleted, Stirling decided to send out another patrol. This time they would be taken to and from the area by a Rhodesian patrol of the Long Range Desert Group (LRDG). The patrol consisted of just five men: Lieutenant Fraser in command, Sergeant Bob Tait, Sergeant Jeffery du Vivier, 'Phil' Phillips and Jack Byrne. The LRDG took them within a few miles of the airfield, from where they proceeded on foot.

Each man wore a pistol for personal protection. In addition to this, they carried eight Lewes bombs apiece, a compass, a pair of binoculars, a water bottle and some emergency rations made up of chocolate, raisins, cheese and biscuits. Jack also carried a tommy gun for fire support. The Lewes bombs were all primed with a two-hour time pencil and also fitted with an emergency 14-second pull switch. For camouflage, the men wore boiler suits over their battledress; these had been washed and bleached by the sun to blend in with the desert sand.

For the rest of that night and the following day, they lay up undetected, and just before sundown observed four German aircraft landing. As soon as it was dark Fraser led his group to the airfield and discovered numerous aircraft parked in small clusters; they went to work placing Lewes bombs on every aircraft, including eight new Me109s that had recently arrived. Suddenly the bombs started going off and bright red flames leapt into the night sky. Elated, the five made their way from the airfield back to the rendezvous (RV) with the LRDG. They were there by 05:00, and by dawn the Rhodesians had them on their way home. As day broke they met some armoured cars of the King's Dragoon Guards and stopped to tell of their escapades; Bill Fraser estimated they had destroyed 37 aircraft.

The raid did not end well. Once the armoured cars had departed, the LRDG decided to brew up for breakfast, putting out air markers to identify itself. Shortly afterwards, two

British Blenheim fighter-bombers spotted them and came in for the attack. Despite the clear warning – and men standing out in the open waving – two of the Rhodesians were killed, blighting an otherwise perfect operation.

In December, Stirling ordered more attacks on the same airfields. This time Jack was in 'Jock' Lewes's patrol. Once again the LRDG was to ferry them to and from their target. Despite the successes on the airfields, not every aspect of the operation went according to plan, and on several occasions the pickup RV with the LRDG was missed. Working behind enemy lines posed many difficulties, not just to the SAS but also to the LRDG; enemy action and breakdowns all had a part in missed RVs or late pickups. In such a case it was up to the SAS patrol to either walk back or wait until help arrived. On more than one occasion Jack had to walk several hundred miles with little more than a single bottle of water.

After an attack led by Paddy Mayne on Berka airfield, Jack was taken prisoner while walking back through the desert. Shortly afterwards he was shipped to a prisoner-of-war camp near Tripoli and later to Crete, before being sent to Stalag Luft III. The main reason for sending him to an RAF prisoner-of-war camp was his SAS wings; the Germans had thought he was a flyer. After several abortive escape attempts he was transferred to Stalag Luft VI near Königsberg in East Prussia. Jack had been warned that any further escape attempts would mean his being shot, but escape he did. On 17 July 1943, he made another bid for freedom and seven days later, on 24 July, he managed to get to Danzig and steal aboard a ship bound for neutral Sweden. He was eventually flown to Leuchars in Scotland.

Despite ill health, Jack managed to get himself fit once again and joined the Commandos in time for the invasion of Europe. Again he was wounded, and again he survived. After the war, and still a young man, Jack joined the Kenya Police, but at the beginning of the Malayan Emergency he went east. Once again his life was full of adventure, until he was badly wounded when shot at point-blank range by one of the guerillas. Again he survived. He returned to England, got married to Mary Hayes and had three daughters. He built up a drapery business in Shropshire and owned a wool shop in Teagues Crescent, Trench, Telford.

In 1986 he published a book entitled *The General Salutes a Soldier*, telling of his SAS past and his escape. It was originally written while he was recovering in hospital after being shot in the knee after the Normandy landings in 1944, which means the account is accurate. Unfortunately the book was not well promoted, and it was not until after his death that his full story emerged. Jack Byrne was awarded eight service medals, including the Distinguished Conduct Medal for his escape – then the second-highest award for gallantry in action after the Victoria Cross. His medal collection, which was the tangible proof of his extraordinary life story, eventually sold for £77,000 – a tribute to a real SAS hero. Jack Byrne died in 2007 aged 85.

2

1940s

THE EARLY HISTORY OF
THE REGIMENT

THE SPECIAL AIR SERVICE was established in July 1941, founded by the individual thinker Lieutenant David Stirling No. 8 (Guards) Commando. The unit was to work behind enemy lines collecting intelligence, attacking airbases and planning ambushes. They served in most theatres and after initial scepticism proved very effective, participating in some 40 operations before the end of the war. However, this kind of warfare did come at a high cost. By the time the Second World War ended, the SAS had suffered 330 casualties. However, in exchange, they had killed or wounded 7,733 enemy combatants and captured a further 23,000.

The allied campaign in North Africa during the Second World War was fought to restrict German access to the Suez Canal and prevent them from capturing the Arabian oilfields. For the first part of the conflict, a small British and Commonwealth army faced the Italians who, while superior in numbers, were poorly equipped. However, it was not long before Hitler sent the famous Afrika Korps under the command of General Erwin Rommel, the 'Desert Fox'. As both armies grew in size, the pace of battle slowed to a virtual stalemate.

For the British, the most crucial aspect of the war in the North African desert in 1940 was the maintenance of its military supply lines, most of which terminated along the coast at a network of depots, airfields and ports. This network supplied its vast desert army, which included a unit called Layforce. Named after, and commanded by, Brigadier Robert Laycock, Layforce was a Commando brigade attached to General Wavell's Middle Eastern Army. On paper, it was an impressive force, comprising some 2,000 men of 7, 8 and 11 Commandos. One of them was a young Scots Guards lieutenant by the name of David Stirling, who had been involved in a number of unsuccessful large-scale raids on enemy targets along the coast around Cyrenaica. Stirling understood the benefits of attacking targets from behind enemy lines, but he felt sure the raids would have a greater chance of success if they were executed by small groups of men, thus using the element of surprise to its best advantage. Stirling had been lying in a hospital bed, having suffered a severe injury during a parachute drop, when he first conceived the idea of the SAS.

In the belief that a small band of dedicated men could operate successfully behind the enemy's lines, he managed to present his plan to Major-General Neil Ritchie, who at the time was Deputy Chief of the General Staff. His idea, set out in a memorandum, finally reached the desk of the Commander-in-Chief in the Middle East, General Sir Claude Auchinleck, and the SAS was born.

As the founder of the SAS, Stirling's main strength came from his ability to select and enlist men who were both daring and had vision. One such man was 'Paddy' Mayne, one of Stirling's first recruits into the SAS. The nickname 'Paddy' came with his Irish ancestry, and before the war he was well known for his accomplishments in the world of sport. In battle, he possessed qualities of leadership that set him apart from most men, and he gained a reputation for personal bravery, which some, at times, characterized as wild recklessness.

In July 1941, L Detachment of the SAS Brigade, as it was precisely know, came into being. HQ Middle East dreamed up the name in an effort to convince the Germans that they had formed a whole new airborne brigade. Whether the ploy worked or not is unknown, but the reality was that L Detachment comprised just 67 men, most of whom had been recruited from Layforce. This 'Brigade' had no weapons, no tents and no supplies. As there was no parent unit, Stirling reported directly to General Auchinleck; it was the first move in securing the independence of the SAS.

The men of the unit begged, borrowed or stole whatever they needed, while Stirling and Mayne got on with planning a tough training programme. Initially, much of this training involved jumping backwards off moving trucks to simulate parachute landings. However, this activity was quickly curtailed following several accidents that severely reduced the unit's ability and numbers. The other aspect of SAS training was an introduction to the Lewes bomb, a device designed by Lieutenant 'Jock' Lewes with the express purpose of destroying parked aircraft. The bomb, basically a mixture of plastic explosive (TNT 808), thermite and diesel oil, was attached to the aircraft on or near the engine and initiated by a time pencil and detonator.

It was around this time that the SAS's famous insignia materialized. There has been many a discussion on what the emblem depicts: some say it's the flaming sword Excalibur, while others refer to it as a winged dagger. Whatever it symbolized, it was attached to the unit's equally famous beige berets – adopted after a white beret was first tried, with disastrous results. Introducing an entirely new insignia in the British Army is not easy, but Stirling met General Auchinleck in person at Shepheard's Hotel in Cairo and the emblem was approved.

Into Action: Operation Squatter

By November 1941, L Detachment of the SAS was ready to carry out its first operation. The Regiment's first raid was in support of Operation Crusader, and its mission was to attack a German airfield in Libya. On the night of 17–18 November, a force of 65 men boarded five Bristol Bombay transport aircraft provided by 216 Squadron. This force was divided into five sections, commanded by David Stirling, 'Paddy' Mayne, Eoin McGonigal, 'Jock' Lewes and Lieutenant Bonnington. The targets of the raid were German airfields in the area of Tmimi and Gazala. It was widely believed that the Luftwaffe had received reinforcements in the form of the latest type of Messerschmitt 109 fighter aircraft. The raids were designed to destroy these aircraft prior to General Auchinleck's planned offensive, due to commence two days later. Entry was by parachute, dropping some 12 miles from the target.

The five aircraft took off from Bagoush airfield on schedule. Although conditions on take-off were clear and still, as the aircraft proceeded towards their drop zones there was a sudden change of weather. Thick cloud, heavy rain and high winds hampered navigation. In order to pinpoint their position, the aircraft were forced to drop down to 200 feet, where they encountered heavy flak from the German defences. The drop was disastrous, with storms and high winds scattering the men over a wide area on landing and several injuries were sustained – Stirling himself was knocked unconscious. One of the Bombay transports used was lost together with its crew and troops. As a result, the operation was abandoned, and the soldiers had to make their way individually to a prearranged RV with the LRDG. Only 22 of the original members of the attacking force returned.

The problems encountered on this first operation prompted a radical rethink about transporting troops to the target in future SAS operations. Stirling resolved never to use parachute drops again, and instead decided to use vehicles, starting with those of the LRDG.

Like so many ad hoc British units, the LRDG came into existence during the Second World War and, like the SAS, was the product of a group of eccentric individuals. During the 1920s and 1930s, Major Ralph Bagnold, Royal Corps of Signals, and a group of friends had undertaken a series of journeys with the aim of resolving the considerable problems of living in and travelling through the desert. His studies resulted in a paper advocating the formation of a military desert reconnaissance force. The provisional war establishment of the LRDG was authorized in July 1940, originally for 11 officers and 76 men. This number was increased to 21 officers and 271 men in November of that year, and by March 1942 the LRDG numbered 25 officers and 324 men. Operating in open-topped Chevrolet trucks, the LRDG carried out reconnaissance, intelligence-gathering and courier duties. These tasks involved long drives across the featureless desert terrain, followed by observation of enemy posts and convoys. There were also behind-the-lines raiding activities, which forced the Italians to divert troops from the front to safeguard their rear areas.

The SAS used LRDG trucks for transport from late 1941 until early 1942, though Stirling's men caused problems for the LRDG because their aggressive activities provoked greater enemy reaction. Despite this, cooperation between the SAS and LRDG remained excellent. However, Stirling believed that the SAS should have its own form of transport, and in July 1941 it materialized in the form of the Willys jeep. In a much-modified form, the jeep was used by the SAS throughout the war. Light, agile and robust, the jeep was ideally suited to the desert terrain because of its four-wheel drive. The jeep had a top speed of 60 mph and a range of 300 miles, although it could be greatly extended by carrying additional fuel in separate containers. During the North Africa campaign, the SAS jeeps were normally overloaded with extra water, fuel and ammunition. They were also burdened with considerable firepower in the form of 0.5-inch Browning heavy machine guns and rifle calibre Vickers 'K' guns, originally intended for use in aircraft, of which a supply was found sitting in a disused hanger. So equipped, the jeeps were not used simply as a means of transport but also as a weapon. On many occasions they were driven, guns blazing, directly on to the enemy airfields to wreak havoc on the rows of parked aircraft.

Success at Last

Despite the shaky start, Stirling continued with his planning, and a month later the SAS had their first successful raid in December 1941 – just what they needed to prove their worth. The high command were scrutinizing the unit to see if they could work behind enemy lines and harry the enemy lines of communication and airfields. Transported by LRDG trucks, the mission targeted several Libyan airfields near the coast. Once they had arrived at their targets, the SAS crept onto the runways and planted time-delayed explosives on as many aircraft as possible before retreating as quickly as possible. The method proved very effective, with 61 Axis aircraft being destroyed and the SAS getting away without a single casualty. The SAS raided airfields at Sirte, Nofilia, El Agheila, Agedabia, Tamit and Marble Arch (the latter gained its name from a large arch erected in the desert by Mussolini to mark the border of the Italian colony of Tripolitania). The raid on the airfield at Agedabia, a small town situated on the Libyan coast, south of Benghazi, went particularly well. It was launched on 21 December by a force of five members of L Detachment SAS, comprising Sergeant Bob Tait, Sergeant du Vivier, Private Byrne and Private Phillips, under the command of Lieutenant Bill Fraser. Having been dropped off by an LRDG patrol 10 miles south of its objective, the men marched throughout the night and reached a lying-up place from which they were able to observe the airfield throughout the following day. Each man carried a water bottle, a compass, a revolver, eight Lewes bombs and a tin of chocolate, plus other rations consisting of raisins, cheese and broken biscuits. After nightfall on the following day, Fraser and his men succeeded in penetrating the defences of the airfield, which was heavily wired and well guarded, placing Lewes bombs on 37 Fiat CR42 fighter-bombers. The raid was a great success: all the bombs went off and all the aircraft were destroyed. During the confusion caused by the explosions, the patrol withdrew without any losses and made its way to an RV, where an LRDG patrol was already waiting for them. However, though no casualties were suffered during the raid itself, two members of the unit were killed when two RAF Blenheims strafed their vehicles, despite the fact that the correct air recognition signals had been displayed. The rest, worn out and bedraggled, managed to reach the LRDG and SAS base at Jab Oasis on December 23.

In early January 1942, L Detachment of the SAS absorbed the 1st Company of Free French Paratroopers under the command of Commandant Bergé. In March of the same year, the Special Interrogation Group (SIG) also came under L Detachment's control. SIG was a small unit made up of German-speaking Jews, formed and commanded by Captain Herbert Buck MC. They operated in the guise of German soldiers – including wearing German uniforms. Their fate, if captured, was certain death.

Stirling's concept of small raiding parties continued to be a great success when, on the night of 23 January 1942, the SAS struck at a German oil supply depot in Buerat, west of Sirte. They destroyed 18 enormous fuel transporters, each loaded with 4,000 gallons of fuel. At the same time they attacked the dock facilities and accompanying warehouses, filled with everything from foodstuffs to heavy machinery – all just prior to a major offensive by Rommel.

The Berka main and satellite airfields in Libya were also the targets of L Detachment SAS, on more than one occasion. In March 1942, Captain 'Paddy' Mayne mounted an operation involving a number of attacks on Benghazi and the airfields in the area, with the Berka satellite airfield being the objective of a four-man patrol led by Mayne himself. The other members were Corporal Bennett, Corporal Rose and Private Byrne. Travelling with an LRDG patrol via the Siwa Oasis, Mayne and his men reached a mountain (like another mountain in Oman, where the SAS was to win further battle honours in the 1950s) called the Djebel Akhdar. From here, they could observe the area of coastal plain on which Benghazi and the airfields were located. Under the cover of darkness on the following night, they left the wadi in which they had been lying up and made their way down the escarpment to their target. Moving on to the airfield, they placed Lewes bombs on 15 aircraft, a number of fuel dumps and 12 large aerial bombs before withdrawing and making their way during the rest of the night to an RV, where they were collected by the LRDG.

Another raid on the Berka airfields took place on 13 June 1942. This coincided with a raid on the Berka satellite airfield by the RAF, whose bombers arrived overhead as Mayne, Corporal Lilley, Corporal Warburton and Private Storey were moving across the airfield towards some aircraft. There was little they could do but seek what cover there was on the airfield until the raid was over. With the enemy on full alert, Mayne planted some bombs on a fuel dump and withdrew, avoiding the enemy patrols that were already scouring the area, and led his men to the RV with the LRDG. There, he met Major Stirling, who had attacked a nearby aircraft repair base at Benina, and Lieutenant André Zirnheld with a patrol of L Detachment's Free French troops who had attacked the Berka main airfield, destroying 11 aircraft. The Benina aircraft repair base had been targeted twice before, on each occasion by Stirling, accompanied by Sergeant Johnny Cooper and Sergeant Reg Seekings. On the first two occasions, they found the base deserted, but this time they achieved success. During an RAF bombing raid on Benghazi, they made their way past the sentries and succeeded in placing Lewes bombs on a number of aircraft, some new aircraft engines still in their crates and some machinery. As a *coup de grâce*, Stirling attacked the enemy guardroom with grenades as he and his men withdrew.

Not content with the results achieved that night, however, Stirling decided to mount a further raid on the area. On the following night, accompanied by Captain Mayne's patrol, plus a number of other individuals, they drove down the escarpment in a borrowed LRDG vehicle. Having bluffed their way through a German checkpoint, Stirling and his party encountered a number of Italian troops, and although the Italians opened fire, they were unsuccessful in halting the SAS vehicle as it sped past. Shortly afterwards, a number of enemy vehicles were spotted by a petrol filling station and these soon had Lewes bombs planted on them. By now the entire area was alive with enemy troops, and Stirling decided to withdraw. Heading across the desert, successfully avoiding enemy patrols dispatched to intercept them, the SAS succeeded in reaching the Djebel Akhdar. As they reached the top of the wadi, which led up the escarpment, Corporal Bob Lilley noticed that a time pencil fuse attached to one of the remaining Lewes bombs was burning. Thanks to his split-second warning, all the occupants of the vehicle succeeded in baling out just prior to it exploding. Deprived of transport, Stirling and his men had to complete the journey to the RV with the LRDG on foot.

One of the longest surviving members of these raids, Bob Bennett remembers one particular event clearly, even years later. It is of watching fellow troopers ripping open aircraft doors and firing into the planes, killing the men inside before planting their explosives. Finally, reaching the last aircraft, they realised they had run out of bombs. Incensed, one of Bob's fellow troopers destroyed the cockpit of the aircraft, using only physical force to destroy it totally.

So effective did the unit become, that by the end of the North African campaign, the Regiment had destroyed over 400 grounded Axis planes. Not only did they impress the British high command: the famed German 'Desert Fox', Field Marshall Erwin Rommel, even expressed his admiration for the Regiment's audacity and skill. Hitler, however, wasn't so happy and ordered that any SAS officer taken prisoner of war (POW) should be interrogated by the notorious Gestapo. He then issued the infamous 'Commando Order', which meant any member of the SAS captured was to be executed immediately – and, alas, many were.

Convoys Under Attack

The Luftwaffe's airfields in Crete became increasingly important for supplying the Afrika Korps as well as for operating photoreconnaissance and attacking Allied convoys. To complete these operations the Luftwaffe used the Ju 52 and Me 323 for transport purposes and the Ju 88 and the Ju 86 for bombing and photographic purposes, as well as the Bf 109 as fighter cover. German airfields around Cyrenaica, along Libya's eastern coast, were also able to attack British convoys as they attempted to reach Malta. Stirling planned a number of raids against these airfields for the night of 13 June. Most of the targets were in the Benghazi sector, the Derna area, Barce and Heraklion airfield in Crete. Each raiding party consisted of five men and, for the attack on Derna, which was by far the hardest target, Stirling enlisted the help of SIG. The idea was to use the SIG personnel to transport the SAS directly to the Derna airstrips using German vehicles. Unfortunately, one of the anti-German sympathizers attached to SIG betrayed them, and all three teams were lost. Things went better at Benghazi, where the SAS team destroyed 16 aircraft and an additional 30 brand-new aircraft engines. Most of the repair shops and ammunition dumps were also severely damaged.

The raid on Crete comprised a mixed bag of Free French paratroopers who had joined L Detachment SAS at the beginning of 1942, under the command of Bergé. A newcomer to the SAS, Captain George Jellicoe (2nd Earl of Jellicoe) accompanied him along with a Greek guide named Lieutenant Costi. After landing at night by inflatable boat from the Greek Navy submarine *Triton*, the party marched for two nights over the mountains to the enemy airfield at Heraklion, where some 60 Junkers Ju 88s and a number of Stuka dive-bombers were assembled. The party had some difficulty moving on to the airfield due to the quantity of barbed-wire defences and numerous guards. However, Bergé and his men succeeded in placing Lewes bombs on 21 aircraft, a number of vehicles and a fuel dump before withdrawing. They were unwittingly assisted by an RAF aircraft, which happened to bomb the airfield at the same time, thereby causing confusion that the raiders used to good effect.

After successfully completing their task, the groups spent the next two nights travelling, having been forced to lie up during the day. Bergé's group was within a few miles of the beach and was due to RV with the submarine on the following night. While Bergé and the three other Frenchmen hid in a cave, Captain Jellicoe and Lieutenant Costi went off to a nearby village to make contact with a Cretan who would signal the submarine to confirm the pickup. Unfortunately, during their absence, some local people accidentally discovered Bergé and his companions and betrayed them to the Germans. As a result, the four Frenchmen found themselves facing three enemy patrols that heavily outnumbered them. Bergé decided to stand and fight, intending to hold out until he and his men could slip away under cover of darkness. Sadly, however, the Frenchmen ran out of ammunition and had no option other than to surrender. He and his men were taken to Heraklion, where they were tortured before being executed. When Captain Jellicoe and Lieutenant Costi returned to the cave, they discovered their companions' fate. Three days later, accompanied by 20 Cretan refugees, they were taken off the island by the submarine. As a result of the raids, the Germans murdered 50 civilians from the Heraklion area.

Despite the loss of men, overall the raids had been a great accomplishment. In total, 50 aircraft were destroyed by the SAS before Rommel attacked and advanced towards Egypt. As the Germans pushed forward, the SAS continued to mount attacks behind enemy lines. One such raid, on the night of 7 July 1942, led by Major Stirling and Captain Mayne, was a great success. After an overland approach in vehicles, the initial attack on the airfield was carried out by a group of four men under Captain Mayne, while Major Stirling established a roadblock nearby to attack any enemy vehicles. Lewes bombs were placed on a total of 40 aircraft, but because of faulty primers only 20 exploded. A further 14 aircraft were then attacked and destroyed as Stirling's force raced down the runway in three jeeps, guns blazing. Major Stirling and his men then withdrew without loss. There is no doubt that these raids and the destruction of German aircraft severely hampered Rommel's advance, allowing Montgomery to prepare his counteroffensive.

Bigamy was the code name given to an SAS raid in September 1942. Montgomery, who had recently become the new commander of the 8th Army, was planning a big offensive for the end of October to start from the Alamein front. However, he had concerns about Rommel's Afrika Korps still being supplied and strengthened by regular supply convoys arriving at the ports of Tobruk and Benghazi. It became essential to Montgomery's plan that these ports were put out of action and the supply of equipment either stopped or slowed down. He called on Stirling and L Detachment of the LRDG, along with Commando units and the Special Boat Service (SBS) to raid Benghazi and nearby airfields while a combined force of commandoes and infantry launched a simultaneous seaborne strike against Tobruk. Stirling was against the plan from the start and pointed out that it was against the ethos of the Regiment and why it had been established in the first place. However, he was overruled and the raid went ahead. It was a difficult raid from the start, involving travelling around the edge of the Great Sand Desert. Unfortunately, the raid ended in failure when an Italian roadblock discovered the raiding party and Stirling decided to withdraw to Kufra. Due to a lack of cover during the withdrawal, the Luftwaffe was able to destroy 70 of the raiding parties' vehicles. (Those that survived the raid eventually formed into the 1st Special Air Service Regiment.)

The Tobruk raid was similarly disastrous. Allied losses included 300 Royal Marines, 160 troopers and 280 sailors. The anti-aircraft cruiser *Coventry*, the destroyers *Sikh* and *Zulu*, two motor launches, four MTBs and several small amphibious craft were also lost. The Royal Marines suffered 81 deaths and the Navy suffered the loss of another 217, who went down together with their ships. And around 576 of the attacking forces were taken prisoner. In comparison, there were only 15 Italians and one German killed, with 43 Italians and seven Germans wounded. The attacks on the airfields of Barce and Benghazi were a little more successful. Led by Lieutenant Jake Easonsmith, 12 LRDG trucks carrying around 30 men each crossed 750 miles of desert, reaching within 20 miles of Barce as planned. The airfield was well defended but there were holes in its defence. The Regiment exploited those weaknesses and managed to destroy 16 aircraft and damage seven more, as well as a supply truck. During their retreat, however, enemy fighters constantly attacked them and managed to destroy 10 of their vehicles. Stirling was furious about the entire operation, especially the staff officers who he referred to as 'fossilized shit'. Stirling later wrote, 'It was a sharp lesson which confirmed my previous views on the error of attacking strategical targets on a tactical scale.'

During the battle of El Alamein the following November, Stirling, although not officially required to contribute, was determined to assist in General Montgomery's advance to Tripoli. He devised a plan which meant that his men would launch a minimum of two raids a week on the stretch of land between El Agheila and Tripoli, concentrating in particular on the roads being used by the retreating Germans and Italians. At the same time, the Allied landings in the French North African colonies (Operation Torch) resulted in the retreat of Axis forces into Tunisia. Although the SAS had been quite successful during the 8th Army's advance, the Tunisian countryside of scrub-covered hills and cultivated valleys was far less suitable for their operations than Libya's deserts. The population was also more sympathetic to the Axis and, as a result, the SAS operations did not achieve the success that had been expected.

On 28 September 1942, L Detachment was formally renamed the 1st Special Air Service Regiment. At the same time the SBS came under SAS control, as did the 114 men of the Greek Sacred Squadron. Although Stirling was promoted to Lieutenant Colonel, his independence was diminished as 1 SAS now came under the control of the Director of Military Operations. Shortly afterwards, in January 1943, the success of 1 SAS was temporarily interrupted when Stirling was captured. He and his team had been en route to raid Sousse, and during a brief break had taken shelter in a cave. German troops appeared and started searching the area; as a result, Sterling and one of his men were captured. Stirling managed to escape two days later, but was betrayed by Arabs and recaptured by Italian troops.

He spent the rest of the war languishing in Colditz. However, 1 SAS continued to evolve, and at the time of Stirling's capture it totalled 47 officers and 532 other ranks. By this time David Stirling's brother, Lieutenant Colonel William Stirling, with the British First Army, had also formed 2 SAS.

Mayne Takes Over

When the North African campaign came to an end in May 1943, there followed a brief period when the SAS's future was in question. However, the invasion of Sicily meant its skills were in demand once more. With Stirling in Colditz, it fell to 'Paddy' Mayne to take over command. By this time the SAS had acquired considerable waterborne skills, and at the end of the North African campaign 1 SAS was renamed Special Raiding Squadron (SRS), while the SBS came under the command of Jellicoe, now promoted to Major. The SBS was assigned to the Aegean and the Adriatic, while the SRS moved into Sicily and Italy.

The Aegean Sea

The Dodecanese Islands in the Aegean Sea were the scene of operations by the SBS commanded by Jellicoe. German forces occupied a number of islands including Crete, Karpathos, Leros, Kos, Simi, Tilos, Astipalaia and several of the smaller ones. Together, these formed part of a defensive perimeter against Allied operations in the Mediterranean.

The SBS established 40 heavily camouflaged anchorages to serve as bases for operations among the Dodecanese Islands. A schooner, the *Tewfik*, acted as a forward headquarters for the SBS while a fleet of armed caiques, motor launches and other small craft put the men ashore. This small flotilla came under the command of Lieutenant Commander Adrian Seligmann RN, who was employed to ferry the SBS squadrons around the islands. Overall control of raiding operations in the Aegean became the responsibility of Headquarters Raiding Forces, based in Cairo, which was formed in late October 1943 under the command of Colonel (later Brigadier) Douglas Turnbull.

However, the SBS had already seen action in the area. Operation Albumen was carried out on 22 June 1943, when the SBS landed on the south coast of Crete near Cape Kochinoxos. The mission was to destroy enemy aircraft on airfields at Heraklion, Timbaki and Kastelli. These were targeted by patrols led by Lieutenant Kenneth Lamonby, Lieutenant Ronnie Rowe and Lieutenant Anders Lassen respectively. Lamonby found no aircraft but destroyed a large fuel dump, while Rose found his objective deserted.

Lassen's patrol, despite engaging in a firefight with alert sentries, succeeded in destroying four Stuka aircraft, an armoured vehicle and a fuel dump. Despite being betrayed by a Cretan villager, Lassen and one of his men succeeded in evading capture and returned safely to the squadron's base, where he met the rest of his patrol.

Attack on Simi

On 7 October 1943, the Germans attacked the island of Simi, which was at that time occupied by a force of 40 members of M Squadron SBS under Major Ian Lapraik. The German attempt to capture it failed, but on the following day Luftwaffe bombers carried out raids during which 20 Greek civilians and two SBS soldiers were killed. One of the bombs landed on Major Lapraik's headquarters and two men, Guardsman Thomas Bishop and Corporal Sidney Greaves MM, were buried under the rubble. As others fought to rescue them, it became apparent that Private Bishop could not be freed without further debris and rubble falling on Corporal Greaves. The only solution was for Bishop's foot to be amputated, and to this he very bravely and selflessly agreed.

By the light of a candle, lying on his back and working with only the minimum of instruments an SBS medic, Sergeant Porter Darrell, carried out the operation under the guidance of an RAF medical officer, Flight Lieutenant Leslie Ferris, who could not perform the operation himself as he was suffering from an injured wrist. It took 27 hours, as air raids continued, to free Guardsman Bishop. Unfortunately, however, he died soon afterwards from pain and shock. Sadly, his death was in vain, as on being pulled clear, Corporal Greaves was found to be dead. Simi fell to the Axis, but on 20 November 1943, the SBS returned to the island in the form of a raiding party led by another outstanding officer, Lieutenant Bob Bury. He and his troops faced a German and Italian garrison totalling some 100 men.

Having landed, the SBS advanced into the town of Castello and reached the Governor's house. Entering the building, Bury came upon the quarters of a light machine gun detachment whose members were swiftly dispatched when he threw a grenade into their room. Immediately afterwards, Sergeant 'Tanky' Geary, who had been covering the main entrance to the house, killed eight Germans who appeared outside on the quayside by the building, and Bury shot another before detonating a 25-pound explosive charge in the building next door, which demolished it and also part of the Governor's house. Having planted a booby trap in the street, which was set off soon afterwards by the enemy, Bury and his men withdrew.

Lieutenant Bury returned to Simi on the night of 13 July 1944 as a member of a combined force of some 220 men of M Squadron SBS together with the Greek Sacred Squadron. The force landed on the island unobserved by the enemy. At dawn on the following day, the castle on Simi was subjected to heavy fire by machine guns and mortars. Bury's patrol was part of a force which attacked enemy positions in a monastery, eventually forcing their occupants along a promontory at one end of the island, where they were subsequently persuaded to surrender.

In late October that year, Bury was given the task of carrying out a boat reconnaissance along the coastline of the island of

Spetsia. Approaching a bay occupied by royalist partisans who were expecting an attack by communist ELAS guerrillas, his boat was fired on. The partisans had mistaken Bury's boat for the ELAS unit and their fire hit the helmsman. Recognizing that the vessel was not under fire from German weapons, Lieutenant Bury leaped up to take over the tiller and steered the vessel nearer to the shore in an attempt to land, while at the same time trying to make his identity known to the partisans. In doing so, however, he was fatally wounded and died shortly afterwards. His men and the partisans buried him on Spetsia the following day.

The SRS in Italy

While the SBS was in action in the Aegean, the SRS involved itself in the Italian campaign, starting with an assault on a coastal battery at Cape Murro di Porco, south of Syracuse in Sicily, on 12 July 1943. It was taken easily, and the SRS was immediately given the job of seizing the town of Augusta, which was achieved with minimal casualties. In September the SRS was ordered to capture the port of Bagnara in order to cut German communications and ease the advance of Montgomery's ground forces from Reggio, and its next job was to capture Termoli, which was achieved on 3 October. The Germans launched a heavy counter-attack two days later. The SRS took heavy casualties, but with reinforcements from 2 SAS (the first time the two regiments had fought side by side), together they succeeded in holding the town. Termoli was to be the last operation carried out by the SRS: in December the unit was shipped to Scotland for reorganization.

Commanded by Bill Stirling, 2 SAS had been more involved in the Italian campaign. The unit had taken part in a series of submarine-delivered reconnaissances of Mediterranean islands in May 1943, and during the invasion of Sicily took part in two operations: Narcissus and Chestnut.

On 10 July 1943, 40 men from A Squadron carried out Narcissus. They landed from the *Royal Scotsman* vessel on the south-east coast of Sicily to assault a lighthouse, where it was suspected that enemy artillery pieces were being stored. On reaching the lighthouse, they found it to be deserted and so returned to the ship, which was lying offshore, having achieved their objective without any loss of life.

Operation Chestnut was designed to support Operation Husky, the Allied invasion of Sicily on 9 July 1943. The mission became a memorable example of good planning and logistical support, emphasizing how essential these are for successful military operations. The original plan was to land two parties of 2 SAS by submarine in northern Sicily to destroy enemy communications. Captain Pinckney led the 'Pink' Party, and it had the task of severing roads and telephone lines along the north-east coast of the island. In addition, it was ordered to destroy the Catania-Messina railway line. By contrast, 'Brig' Party, under the leadership of Captain Bridgeman-Evans, was detailed to attack hostile convoys and the enemy headquarters near Enna.

However, on 17 June, the 15th Army Group postponed the operation until the day before the main Allied invasion of Sicily, which was expected to take place on 11 July. On 20 June the SAS operation was cancelled altogether, but was then resurrected on 6 July, and on the night of July 12 the two parties landed by parachute.

Almost immediately, both encountered serious difficulties. The majority of 'Pink' Party's equipment and radios were damaged on landing, and the men were scattered over a wide area. 'Brig' Party was dropped too close to urban areas, which unintentionally alerted the enemy.

Bridgeman-Evans was captured but later managed to escape. On 13 July a night-time reinforcement drop was planned, but the damaged radios meant that the aircraft were unable to contact either party, and consequently no men were dropped. No further forces were committed to the operation. On the ground, neither party achieved anything worthwhile. The only positive result of Operation Chestnut was that most of the SAS soldiers successfully returned to Allied lines. This was 2 SAS's first parachute drop and the poor preparation resulted in a badly executed drop with many of the troops being widely dispersed. The official report on the operation stated: 'The value of damage and disorganization inflicted on the enemy was not proportionate to the number of men, amount of equipment and planes used. It provided valuable experience for future operations and pointed out the pitfalls which are inevitable in any operation which is the first of its kind.'

On 7 September 1943, two seven-man teams from 2 SAS were dropped into the Spezia/Genoa area of north-west Italy, led by Captain Pinckney and Captain Dudgeon, respectively. Their task was to sever the railway lines transporting German reinforcements and supplies to the front. Splitting into two smaller groups, the SAS succeeded in derailing several trains and blowing up large sections of track. Nevertheless, they did encounter some misfortune. The poor weather conditions and unhealthy diet caused several of the men to fall ill; in addition, the teams lost one of their commanding officers, Captain Dudgeon, who was captured and shot by the Germans. Due to their ill health, the return to Allied lines was extremely fragmented: some men returned after operating for 54 days, others after 73 days, while Sergeant 'Tanky' Challen spent seven months behind enemy lines, including a stay in an enemy hospital.

Despite these problems, this operation is a classic example of a Second World War SAS mission, demonstrating how small groups of men could inflict severe damage on the enemy while remaining at large behind the lines for long periods.

Disaster – Operation Jonquil

Operation Jonquil, the next raid, proved to be one of the most disastrous SAS missions in the Second World War. The idea was sound enough: send just over 60 members of both the SAS and 8th Army Airborne to round up large numbers of Allied prisoners of war who were wandering around the Italian countryside after Italy's surrender. Operation Begonia was to be the airborne element, while Operation Jonquil was to be the amphibious landing of the operation. The airborne element began on 2 October and the seaborne landings took place between 4 and 6 October. The seaborne plan involved four parties from B Squadron, 2 SAS, landing between Ancona and Pescara on Italy's Adriatic coast to act as guides for the POWs. However, there were failures with the planning. It was difficult to find identifiable places to land and the weather wasn't good, making navigation difficult. Fishing vessels were assembled as transport, but a German attack at Termoli on 5 October meant they had to be moved back to Barn (the Germans had also impounded a number of fishing vessels). For their part, the POWs made it to the beaches, but due to lack of communication they arrived to find no boats, or otherwise the boats arrived and there were no prisoners. Ironically, the bad planning probably saved the mission and many lives, as the Germans were well aware of the mission right down to the fine details, including landing zones and objectives. Although hundreds of POWs were eventually rescued, the SAS only managed to claim 50 of them. This was mainly due to a lack of radio communication, which proved a problem throughout the war. Although many see the operation as a failure, this raid did divert German troops away from the main fighting to guard their lines, weakening their resistance. The SAS returned to the area, this time to attack the railway line between Ancona and Giulianova. In November, led by Major Roy Farran, a small force of 16 men split into four patrols and embarked in an Italian motor torpedo boat (MTB) commanded by a Royal Navy officer. Despite the presence of an enemy U-boat charging its batteries on the surface, Farran and his men disembarked from the MTB in pitch darkness at the mouth of the river Tronto, some 35 miles north of Pescara, and paddled ashore in rubber boats. The four-man patrols, commanded respectively by Major Farran, Captain Grant Hibbert, Sergeant Rawes and Sergeant Seddon, marched until dawn before lying up for the rest of the day. On the following evening, a reconnaissance of the railway line, which lay about 500 yards away, was carried out. During the night, three of the patrols reached a predetermined RV, but there was no sign of Sergeant Rawes and his men. Major Farran decided to postpone the attack because of the appalling weather and the three patrols dispersed once more.

On the following night, Sergeant Rawes and his men succeeded in making the RV, and Major Farran went ahead with the attack. Three of the patrols laid charges on the line, blowing it in at least 16 places. Meanwhile, Sergeant Seddon's patrol laid Hawkins mines on roads, destroying seven telegraph poles. Sergeant Rawes's patrol also destroyed three enemy trucks that were unlucky enough to arrive on the scene.

Having completed their tasks, the patrols set out on a long exfiltration, walking some 70 miles towards the coast, where they would be picked up by the MTB. The poor weather and difficult terrain hindered their progress and, furthermore, one of the members of Major Farran's patrol was suffering from a severe attack of malaria. They were forced to hide during the day and could move only by night. A lack of food also obliged them to seek food and shelter from the local people. The slow going meant Farran's patrol had to march during daylight hours if it was to make the RV with the MTB. On arriving at the appointed beach, Farran signalled out to sea with his torch, but there was no sign of the torpedo boat. By dawn, he had no choice but to disperse and move inland once more. Fortunately, on the following night the MTB appeared and Farran and his men were taken off. Two of their number, Sergeant Seddon and a member of his patrol, were missing, however, and it is assumed they were captured and executed. Nevertheless, as all tasks had been completed, the operation had been successful.

Three more missions were mounted during November and December 1943, once again to cut the railway lines. Operation Maple, on 7 January 1944 involved an attack on the railway lines radiating from Terni and Orvieto. Most of the targets were destroyed, but all the parties were captured while making for the pickup.

Railway bridges between Pesaro and Fano were attacked in Operation Baobab, which took place on 30 January 1944. All the men returned safely. Operation Pomegranate was to be 2 SAS's final mission in Italy. Six men were dropped by Dakota to raid San Egidio airfield to aid the Anzio landings. The party split when challenged by a German sentry, leaving two officers to carry out the attack. Only seven aircraft were destroyed, and the surviving officer, Lieutenant Hughes, was captured. Hughes was treated for his injuries in a German military hospital. Befriended by two German officers, Hughes managed to have his status changed from political prisoner to prisoner of war; they advised him to escape rather than be shot as a saboteur. Hughes's escape confirmed rumours that the Germans were executing captured Allied parachutists and raiding parties under Hitler's infamous 'Commando Order'.

By March 1944, most of the SAS units had returned to Britain. From its small beginnings only a few short years previously, the Regiment now totalled some 2,500 men. Not everyone was happy with this growth, and many of the original desert veterans saw the SAS turning into a regular army unit. Bill Stirling, commanding 2 SAS, pushed the point hard, claiming that the men were better used in their original role of small party raiders. This conviction led to his resignation, and Lieutenant-Colonel Brian Franks was assigned to replace him.

The SRS was reformed into the SAS Brigade under the command of Brigadier R.W. McLeod. The Brigade comprised 1 SAS under 'Paddy' Mayne, now also a Lieutenant-Colonel, 2 SAS under Franks, 3 and 4 SAS (French) and 5 SAS (Belgian); F Squadron of 'Phantom' (GHQ Reconnaissance Regiment) also came under McLeod's command.

Phantom

Founded by Major-General Gerald Hopkinson – later killed while commanding the 1st Airborne Division in Italy – Phantom was a remarkable unit. It began secret operations in France as early as 1940. However, its existence was not revealed until the end of hostilities in Europe in May 1945.

Made up of 150 officers and 1,250 other ranks, their job throughout the war was to gather and swiftly pass back vital information. Known officially as GHQ Liaison Regiment, it adopted the nickname of 'Phantom' and achieved excellent results by working directly with the front-line troops, keeping Army Group and Base headquarters informed, almost minute by minute, of all that was happening, and of the positions of troops actually on the ground. Messages were sent from under the noses of the enemy by means of very small wireless sets invented specially for the purpose by Captain Peter Astbury. During the fighting on the Western Front prior to the fall of France, Phantom, then commanded by Lieutenant-Colonel McIntosh, sent more than 70,000 of these messages from the battle areas to the headquarters of the 12th and 21st Army Groups.

When France fell, men serving through Phantom were among those evacuated back to England via Dunkirk and other Channel ports, and sections were deployed around the coast at locations where a German invasion was thought most likely, so news of any attempted German landing could be speedily passed on. Their headquarters were in very innocent-looking surroundings in St James's Park, London. Here was the base for the wireless sets on which Phantom worked, passing information to GHQ. The headquarters in St James's Park also contained several lofts for the carrier pigeons that supplemented the Regiment's wireless.

Towards the end of 1940, one of the Regiment's squadrons left Britain for the battlefront in Greece and, while almost all were captured, they continued to transmit messages to the end. Phantom suffered yet more casualties when they adopted a commando role, sending a squadron to join the raid on Dieppe. In November 1942, two squadrons went with the 1st Army to North Africa and operated throughout the campaign, finally joining up with the 8th Army. There, they listened in to the wireless talk of the German tanks, gleaning every scrap of information that would be of interest, and from the chaos of battle formulating a clear picture, reporting positions, casualties and strengths. In early 1944, F Squadron of Phantom, commanded by Major the Hon. J. J. 'Jakie' Astor, was assigned the role of providing rear link radio communications for the squadrons of 1st and 2nd SAS regiments (1 and 2 SAS) deployed in France from D-Day onwards; its patrol operators communicated with the squadron base located at the headquarters of the SAS Brigade.

With a strength of six officers and 102 other ranks, F Squadron was organized as a headquarters and four patrols. Two patrols, under Captain Moore and Captain Sadoine, were attached to 1 SAS and two, under Captain Hislop and Captain Johnsen, to 2 SAS. Each patrol comprised an officer and four other ranks. The two French units in the SAS Brigade, 3rd and 4th French Parachute Battalions, and the Belgian Independent Parachute Company, possessed their own signals units, but F Squadron provided training for them in the use of the newly developed lightweight radio sets. All F Squadron personnel were parachute-trained and, during the first half of 1944, underwent training with the rest of the SAS Brigade in Scotland prior to deployment on operations with 1 and 2 SAS in June.

Some Phantom members were parachuted into France before D-Day, while others went in with the assault troops (it was they who sent back the first news of the Normandy landings). By July the entire Regiment was in France, deployed with the British, Canadian and American armies. This was the result of an inquiry by General Eisenhower who, in the early stages of the assault on Normandy, visited the British 2nd Army headquarters, then located near Portsmouth, and was considerably impressed by the complete intelligence picture of operations. He asked how it was done. The answer was 'Phantom patrol'. It was explained to him how the organization flashed back to England the positions of brigades and battalions in the beachhead battles. General Eisenhower immediately ordered Phantom units to work with the American formations. Likewise,

General Crerar's 1st Canadian Army secured a substantial proportion of its intelligence from Phantom, and General Patton, commanding the US 3rd Army, acknowledged the value of its assistance. During the attempted German breakout in the Ardennes that winter, hour by hour, the Panzers every move was reported by Phantom, distinguished only by a small letter 'P' on the right shoulder.

Towards the end of the war, it was Phantom who made known the first details of the German concentration camps and prisoner-of-war camps and, in one last, spectacular coup, it coordinated the link-up between the Russians and the American 1st Army, as always, transmitting the news faithfully back to GHQ.

The SAS and D-Day

Though he had gone, Bill Stirling's pleading eventually bore fruit in the planning for Operation Overlord. The SAS Brigade had originally been assigned to drop behind enemy lines and prevent any German reinforcements reaching the Normandy beachhead. This was later changed, and instead the SAS was used to consolidate the various resistance groups scattered around France, Belgium, Holland and Italy. Acting on their own initiative, they were to organize the resistance movements into fighting forces to attack the Germans at each and every opportunity.

Many of the SAS were parachuted in prior to D-Day, but reinforcements continued to be infiltrated up until November 1944. Much of this work was done using the American-made Douglas DC3, known in RAF service as the Dakota, a twin-engined transport aircraft with a maximum speed of nearly 200 mph and an 800-mile operational range. The Dakota had a crew of three and could carry 46 seated troops or 20 parachutists. A total of 780 sorties were flown, dropping men, jeeps and equipment, and only six aircraft were lost.

Operation Houndsworth

This mission involved A Squadron, 1 SAS, under the command of Major Bill Fraser. His orders were to establish a base in the densely wooded country to the west of Dijon, disrupt German communications, cut railway lines and assist local resistance (Maquis) units. They established a base in the Morvan mountains (between Dijon and Nevers) and operated largely from there. The advance party, including Johnny Cooper and Reg Seekings, was dropped by parachute on the night of 5 June, D-Day minus one. The weather was foul and the drop took place in zero visibility, as a result of which Cooper hit a stone wall on landing and knocked himself unconscious. However, the party managed to assemble and release carrier pigeons carrying intelligence reports (though they never reached England).

After making contact with the local Maquis, a landing strip was made ready to receive more supplies and reinforcements. Bill Fraser was the first to arrive, along with two 'sticks' of parachutists led by Captains Wiseman and Alec Muirhead. The Houndsworth unit eventually numbered 18 officers and 126 other ranks, with nine jeeps. Over the next three months, the SAS force repeatedly cut the railway lines around Dijon. Of course, such a force, combined with varying numbers of Maquis, did not go unnoticed, and enemy forces soon moved into the area to deal with them. The opposition consisted of Russians in the service of the Germans, together with the despised Milice, a Vichy-supported French national police force that was armed by the Germans and acted in concert with the Gestapo.

The major enemy garrison was at Château Chinon, and in early July the German-led Russians began a campaign of intimidation in the local villages, taking hostages and burning property. In one incident, they took a number of Maquis sympathizers from Montsauche and set off towards Château Chinon, where their prisoners would face almost certain torture and execution. Alec Muirhead's troop and members of the Maquis set an ambush for them, but the site was far from perfect, having forest on one side and open country on the other.

Johnny Cooper, one of those who took part in the ambush, recalls: 'The first three-tonner, crammed with enemy soldiers, drew level with a woodpile and over came two plastic bombs. One hit the bonnet and the other the rear of the vehicle, causing pandemonium among the occupants. Many were killed by fire from the Maquis as they fled across the road towards the open fields. Our Brens opened up with devastating effect and many of the Russians retreated back to the ditch, which was in Reg's sights. It was a massacre. Three trucks were set on fire, the hostages were released unharmed from two civilian cars, but the German light vehicle bringing up the rear managed to turn round and make off. In retaliation for this attack the Germans executed 13 hostages from the village of Montsauche, after which they burned the place to the ground.'

Major Ian Fenwick, commanding D Squadron, 1 SAS, had decided to disperse his force for added security. He sent Lieutenant Leslie Bateman with a patrol to link up with a large group of several hundred Maquis at Thimory. These were under the command of a colourful Frenchman called 'Captain Albert', who was preparing for an attack on Orleans. Shortly after Bateman's patrol arrived at the Maquis base, a large enemy force equipped with armoured vehicles and flame-throwers, attacked the camp. The resistance fighters scattered and the SAS patrol, which was travelling in civilian cars, came under heavy fire as it made its escape. The vehicle carrying Lieutenant Bateman, Corporal Wilson, Lance Corporal Essex and a shot-down US Army Air Force officer, who had been sheltering with the Maquis, was hit. Bateman was wounded but succeeded in leaving the vehicle and reached the cover of the woods, though the American was killed as he attempted to crawl under the vehicle. Corporal Wilson received a head wound and was initially knocked unconscious. On coming round inside the vehicle, however, he drew his Colt .45 pistol and opened fire on four Germans as they approached, killing or wounding three of them. He was subsequently taken prisoner and, after interrogation, was sent to a hospital in Orleans – from which he was released by American forces, which arrived in the city two days later.

Lieutenant Bateman, meanwhile, had met two of his patrol who had also been wounded in the ambush. The three men remained in hiding until they linked up with the Maquis and eventually made their way to an area in the forest where their commanding officer, Lieutenant Colonel Mayne, was waiting. Bateman remained with the Maquis, while his men accompanied Mayne to meet C Squadron at Le Mans.

Undeterred, the SAS decided to attack a German synthetic petrol plant using a mortar section of A Squadron, 1 SAS. The target was well-guarded and protected against air attack by strong anti-aircraft defences. Led by Muirhead, the SAS approached their target without incident and set up their three-inch mortars in dead ground. At 01:30 hours, in bright moonlight, they opened fire on the plant, discharging a total of 40 high-explosive and incendiary bombs in rapid succession. Within seconds, the fuel storage tanks and plant buildings were ablaze and continued to burn for three days. The mortar section was able to withdraw unhindered as the enemy, mistakenly thinking it was an air raid, had retreated to underground shelters.

Houndsworth continued its operations. In one spectacular incident, another plant manufacturing synthetic petrol, near Autun, was destroyed by a mortar attack in early August. Despite being hunted continually by the Germans, they were able to avoid capture or have their mission compromised thanks to good intelligence from the French SAS. The Germans eventually discovered the location of the SAS bases and attacked in force on 20 August. However, and once again thanks to good intelligence from the French SAS, they were ready for the assault and fought off the German forces. The German forces were eventually forced to divert their forces eastward. By the beginning of September, A Squadron, having continued to hit the enemy at every opportunity in conjunction with Maquis units, was exhausted, and the decision was taken to replace it with

C Squadron: the latter arrived on 6 September. Houndsworth had been a great success: 22 railway lines had been cut, 200 Germans killed or wounded and 30 bombing targets reported. They also destroyed much of the German communications.

SAS forces had suffered only 18 casualties.

Operation Bulbasket

From 6 June to 7 August 1944, Operation Bulbasket was carried out by a troop of B Squadron, 1 SAS, commanded by Captain John Tonkin and 3 Patrol of F Squadron, Phantom, under Captain R. J. Sadoine. At 01:37 hours on D-Day, Tonkin and one of his officers, Lieutenant Crisp, were dropped blind into the area ahead of the rest of the troop and shortly afterwards made contact with 'Samuel', a local Special Operations Executive (SOE) agent who advised them that the area was too dangerous and that they should move to a safer location. Tonkin's primary mission was to reconnoitre the area of the Vienne and determine whether it was suitable for use as an SAS base. In addition, he was also to gauge the strength of enemy forces and investigate the organization and strength of the Maquis in the area.

On the following night, an advance party of nine men, led by Lieutenant Tom Stephens, was dropped successfully to link up with Tonkin and Crisp. The rest of the troop and Phantom patrol were dropped on the night of 11 June. One aircraft succeeded in locating the dropping zone (DZ), dropping 12 men and a number of equipment containers. A second aircraft, having spotted the lights of an enemy division on a main road close to the DZ, turned away and dropped eight members of the troop and Phantom patrol some 30 miles away.

The rest of the troop had been dropped in four small groups tasked with attacking railway targets in the area before making their way to RV with the rest of the troop. Lieutenant Morris and his patrol dropped near the main railway linking Poitiers and Tours and successfully cut the line, as did Sergeant Holmes and his men. Similarly, Lieutenant Weaver's patrol succeeded in derailing a train on the line between Bordeaux and Saumur. However, the fourth patrol, under Corporal Kinnevane, suffered misfortune when it was dropped well away from its intended DZ, landing instead in the small town of Airvault. One man was captured and two others lost their weapons and equipment while making good their escape. Despite the loss of one of their number, all four patrols succeeded in rejoining the rest of the troop.

Meanwhile, the rest of the troop was active. The railway line between Limoges and Poitiers was cut on 12 occasions, a train destroyed, another derailed and roads in the area mined. In addition, information on rail targets for air attack was transmitted back to England, and this resulted in 11 fuel trains and 35 locomotives being destroyed. All this activity inevitably generated considerable activity by enemy forces in the area, and Tonkin was forced to move his base on a number of occasions, which was difficult due to his force's lack of mobility. Furthermore, the Phantom patrol had still not joined him, and thus his rear link communications with the SAS base in England were hampered. Nevertheless, he succeeded in submitting a request that four armed jeeps be dropped to him, and this was done on the night of 17 June.

During the following weeks, Tonkin's troop mounted repeated raids on the local rail network, despite increased enemy activity in the area. On 25 June, he moved his force to a new base in the forest near the small town of Verrières. A week later, on the morning of 3 July, a large enemy force attacked the base; because of lax security and other lapses on the part of the SAS, it was almost a total surprise. During the ensuing action, 30 members of the troop, together with a shot-down American airman, were captured and subsequently taken to Poitiers. On the night of 6 July, they were transported in trucks to the forest near Saint Sauvan, where they were executed by firing squad, once again under the terms of Hitler's Commando Order of October 1942. They were buried nearby.

Captain Tonkin and some 14 of his men, three of whom had been away from the base in a jeep at the time of the attack, escaped and linked up with Captain Sadoine's Phantom patrol. They subsequently carried out a small number of attacks on rail targets, but having lost three of the jeeps (destroyed by Captain Tonkin before he escaped), they were limited in their mobility. During the first week of August, Tonkin and his men were relieved by the 3rd French Parachute Battalion, and together with the Phantom patrol were subsequently evacuated by air to England.

Free French soldiers had served and fought in the SAS since January 1942. By 1944, although under British command, it should not be forgotten that almost half of the SAS Brigade consisted of French soldiers. Their actions, especially in Europe, were among the most daring in SAS history. On 6 June 1944, 160 men of 4 French Parachute Battalion (4 SAS), with four jeeps, landed by parachute in the Vannes area of Brittany. Here, they established the 'Dingson' base, contacting and organizing the local resistance in order to interrupt the movements of enemy forces. By 18 June, the leader of the SAS party, Commandant Bourgoin, had three fully equipped battalions made up of resistance fighters and a company of gendarmes. Unfortunately, however, these men had little or no military training and were quickly dispersed when the Germans attacked the base later that day. Around 40 SAS men managed to escape with no loss of life and a new base was quickly established near Pontivy, codenamed Grog. The French had better success during Operation Dickens when, between 16 July and 7 October 1944, 65 members of 3 French Parachute Battalion (3 SAS) parachuted into the Nantes/Saumur area of western France. Their mission was to organize the local resistance, disrupt rail communications and gather intelligence about German activity. The mission was a total success, costing the Germans 500 troops and 200 vehicles, with the complete destruction of the railway network.

Desert Fox Out of Action

Operation Gaff involved a plan to kill one of Germany's greatest Generals: Field Marshal Erwin Rommel. It was decided that kidnapping him was far too difficult so eliminating him was the only way. Rommel was one of the greatest thorns in the Allies's side, previously in the Desert and now in France, where he fought back against the Allies as they progressed through France, causing serious casualties. On 25 July 1944, six members of the SAS, led by Jack William Raymond Lee, were parachuted into France. The plan was to attack Rommel at his HQ in the village of La Roche-Guyon. Unbeknown to the raiding party, Rommel had been badly injured in a car crash on 17 July and was in a hospital too far away to consider at attack. Abandoning the mission, the raiding party made their way back to Allied lines, attacking German patrols and destroying German communications as and when they could. They finally reached safety on 12 August. Rommel took his own life on 14 October 1944 after being implicated in the plot to kill Hitler.

Keeping Up the Pressure

Operation Derry was conducted between 5 and 18 August 1944. With 89 men of 3 French Parachute Battalion (3 SAS), led by Commandant Conan, the group was dropped by parachute into the Finistère area of Brittany. The plan was to suppress the German advance on Brest and prevent the destruction of the viaducts at Morlaix and Plougastel. The mission was successful on both counts and enormous damage and injury was inflicted on the enemy.

Towards the middle of August, Operation Kipling was undertaken. This mission was designed to aid the Allied airborne landings that were due to take place in the so-called Orleans Gap. The SAS party – 107 men of C Squadron, 1 SAS, with 46 jeeps – began its work on 13 August, when an advance party under Captain Derrick Harrison dropped into the area west of Auxerre. Landing successfully and establishing a base, the SAS was then informed that the airborne landings had been cancelled: a change in tactics was therefore required.

At this time the situation was very fluid, with the Allies making deep penetrations into German areas. Patton's US 3rd Army was nearing Reims, while other Allied units were pushing north following the Anvil landings. The Kipling party therefore took advantage of the confusion among the Germans to launch a series of daring attacks. Harrison himself attacked the village of Les Ormes, and ran straight into Waffen SS troops who were in the process of executing suspected Maquis. In a savage firefight, Harrison's two jeeps set the Germans' vehicles on fire, though they were then forced to retire and Harrison was obliged to leave his own damaged jeep behind. For this exploit, he won the Military Cross.

Because of erratic supply drops, the Kipling party suffered fuel shortages, but nevertheless they still managed to mount a number of successful patrols. Some of the latter joined the French First Army and took part in the surrender of Autun's 3,000-strong German garrison. By 26 September, Kipling was over and the SAS soldiers were at Cosne enjoying a well-earned rest.

The Germans became highly frustrated at having the enemy snapping at their heels, and reprisals were swift and savage. The first of many such incidents of revenge happened during Operation Loyton. Lieutenant-Colonel Franks was to lead some 91 men of 2 SAS; their mission, to strike at enemy installations and cooperate with the local Maquis (which was problematic at the best of times). They would be situated in the mountainous Vosges area of eastern France. The advance party, together with a Phantom patrol and a Jedburgh team, was dropped on the evening of 12 August 1944, with subsequent drops due to take place over the following days. Jedburgh teams were three-man units set up to train French resistance fighters and were, at least nominally, composed of a British, a French and an American member, though this ideal composition was often not possible. Unfortunately, the

Germans had placed large numbers of troops on the crests of the Vosges and the east bank of the river Moselle: the SAS party thus parachuted into an ambush. To make matters worse, the Gestapo was also in the area, at Nancy and Strasbourg, and both locations had anti-partisan units. The SAS men had to contend with large numbers of enemy troops and traitors within the Maquis. There were also a number of reprisals against local villages in response to SAS successes. The entire male population of Moussey, for example, was rounded up and packed off to concentration camps: of the 210 men between the ages of 16 and 60 who were taken, only 70 returned. Bedevilled by a lack of supplies and erratic resupply drops, Franks brought the operation to an end on 9 October, by which time two SAS soldiers had been killed and 31 captured (all of whom were shot by the Gestapo).

Another SAS operation was undertaken around Doubs in eastern France, between 27 August and 22 September 1944. Operation Abel, under the command of Captain Sicand, comprised 82 soldiers of 3 French Parachute Battalion (3 SAS). One company successfully carried out several blocking actions and hit-and-run raids in a combined effort with Maquis units, troops of the advancing French First Army and the US Seventh Army. The aim was to capture a strategic pass between the Vosges and Jura Mountains known as the Belfort Gap. In this and other operations carried out by 3 SAS between 16 July and 7 October, the battalion lost 96 men, either killed, wounded or captured. However, it accounted for 2,340 Germans killed, a further 2,976 wounded and 1,090 taken prisoner, in addition to causing the enemy enormous material damage.

Meanwhile, men of 5 SAS, the Belgians, were dropped in the areas of Le Mans and Chartres to commence operations Chaucer, Shakespeare and Bunyan. Operation Chaucer was conducted between 28 July and 15 August 1944 by two patrols operating north-west of Le Mans, with the aim of harassing the retreating Germans. The first party was commanded by Lieutenant Ghys and landed on 28 July: the second, commanded by Captain Hazel, on 9 August. Unfortunately, however, the drop was executed too late and the groups were forced to pursue the enemy on foot, managing only to catch the rear of the retreating German forces.

On 16 August, Major Blondeel and 40 men, together with some jeeps, were parachuted into the Ardennes in Operation Noah. Shortly thereafter Operation Benson began, on 28 August, when a second Belgian patrol was dropped north-east of Paris with the task of reporting on enemy dispositions and movements. The operation was highly successful, not least because, as well as sending back a large amount of other information, the patrol captured a copy of the German Order of Battle for formations deployed along the river Seine. The speed of the Allied advance north to the Seine, however, meant that this operation was somewhat short-lived.

On 2 September, patrols of the Independent Parachute Company were dropped into Belgium in Operation Brutus, their task being to link up with the Belgian Resistance. Three days later, on 5 September, a small force of men from the company was inadvertently dropped into Germany as reinforcements for Operation Berbang, thus becoming the first SAS troops to enter the country.

Bucket Force

The SBS was also busy during September 1944. The Germans were withdrawing from southern Greece and the Peloponnese in order to meet the threat from the Red Army as it advanced through Bulgaria, Romania and Poland. At the same time, the decision was taken by the British War Cabinet that every effort was to be made to liberate Greece at the earliest opportunity and prevent the communists there taking power. It was recognized that any liberating force would need air support, which would in turn require airfields from which to operate.

An ad hoc force, code named Bucket Force and commanded by Lieutenant Colonel the Earl Jellicoe, was rapidly assembled for the task. Bucket Force comprised L Squadron SBS under Major Ian Patterson; two companies of the 2nd Battalion, Highland Light Infantry; 2908 Squadron Royal Air Force Regiment; a patrol of the LRDG; a section of 40 Commando, Royal Marines; a Royal Navy Combined Operations Pilotage Party; and a number of RAF ground staff.

The first element of Bucket Force to land in Greece was an SBS patrol, led by Captain Charles Bimrose and dropped in the hills to the south of Araxos airfield. Bimrose reported that the airfield was clear of the enemy but that the port of Patras to the east was still held by the Germans. On the morning of 23 September, the rest of L Squadron was dropped on the airfield and shortly afterwards Major Patterson dispatched patrols to the port of Katakolon to the south to reconnoitre it for use by the seaborne element of Bucket Force. On the following day, Lieutenant-Colonel Jellicoe and his headquarters staff flew in by Dakota and landed at Araxos.

Advancing eastwards towards Corinth, resistance was first encountered at the town of Patras, occupied by a German garrison and a battalion of Greek fascists. After negotiations with Major Patterson, the Greeks decided that discretion was the better part of valour and disappeared. A combination of the SBS armed jeeps and the RAF Regiment squadron's armoured cars produced sufficiently heavy firepower to influence the German garrison to withdraw by ferry.

During the following week, Bucket Force succeeded in reaching Corinth. Heading north thereafter, SBS patrols encountered a force of some 700 Germans who were fighting a determined rearguard action. Shortly afterwards they reached Megara, 40 miles west of Athens, where they secured an airfield to be used for the arrival of reinforcements in the form of the 2nd Independent Parachute Brigade Group. On 12 October, the SBS was relieved by C Company, 4th Parachute Battalion, plus supporting elements, who were dropped in very high winds on the airfield. On 14 October, the 5th Parachute Battalion was also dropped on Megara, and three days later the SBS and 2nd

Independent Parachute Brigade entered Athens, shortly after the withdrawal of the last German troops from the city.

In early 1945, the SAS Brigade, commanded by Brigadier Mike Calvert, was given the task by the 1st Canadian Army of undertaking Operation Amherst, which involved landing SAS units behind enemy lines in north-east Holland. Their job was to harass German forces and prevent them from forming a defensive line against the advance of 2nd Canadian Corps. This action prevented the demolition of 18 bridges over the canals; where bridges had already been blown, the Brigade reconnoitred alternative routes for 2nd Canadian Corps, secured Steejnwijk airfield for the RAF, reported back on enemy movements and dispositions, provided guides for leading ground force units and lent support to Dutch Resistance operations in the area.

Operation Amherst

This mission was a joint Free French and British SAS assault on Dutch canals, bridges and airfields, led by the legendary Brigadier Mike Calvert. Their task was to capture key German positions and defend them from any counter-attacks. The operation was carried out by a total of 700 of all ranks from 3rd and 4th French Parachute Battalions, which had by then been redesignated the 2ème and 3ème Regiments de Chasseurs Parachutists (2 RCP and 3 RCP). On the night of 7–8 April 1945, a total of 50 patrols were dropped in bad weather by Stirling bombers of 38 Group RAF. The majority were dropped over the province of Drenthe, where they captured bridges and ambushed retreating German patrols. A subsequent drop of armed jeeps an hour later had to be cancelled because cloud was obscuring the lights marking the dropping zone.

Another group, led by Captain Pierre Sicaud, was dropped south-east of Friesland. Sicaud was injured during the landings but continued, with the help of the Dutch resistance, to attack German formations and positions. One of these locations was an important bridge near the town of Appelscha, which seriously curtailed German movement in the area. The Germans did what they could to push them off the bridge and serious fighting continued for five days.

On 8 April, further troops were dropped in and landed near the village of Haulerwijk, around six miles from Appelscha. They were quickly discovered and a small battle developed between the SAS and the defending Germans. One French SAS trooper was killed and others were captured, while several managed to make their way to Appelscha to reinforce Captain Sicaud. The Germans counter-attacked, killing a number of the defending SAS troopers and civilians and destroying a good part of the town. However, the SAS (French) stood their ground and with great tenacity and bravery beat off the German attack. Eventually, the SAS force was relieved by the advancing Canadian troops of the 8th Reconnaissance Regiment.

The French parachutists carried out all their tasks with skill and aggression, on several occasions attacking enemy-held villages with only small arms. During the following seven days, assisted by the Dutch Resistance, they succeeded in tying down enemy units, intercepting their movements and preventing them from forming any cohesive defence until the arrival of the forward elements of 2nd Canadian Corps, which thereafter continued its advance to the North Sea. Casualties suffered by both French battalions were 29 killed, 35 wounded and 29 missing. Enemy losses totalled 270 killed, 220 wounded, 187 captured and 29 vehicles destroyed.

Operation Cold Comfort

Later to be renamed Zombie, this operation was aimed at blocking the railway line leading to the Brenner Pass in northern Italy with a landslide. A successful attack would mean the Germans would be unable to send their troops south through the Alps. A 13-strong party from 3 Squadron, 2 SAS, was dropped by parachute on 17 February 1945, just to the north of Verona. Unfortunately, the party was widely dispersed on landing and resupply was impossible on account of the abysmal weather. An additional complication was the hostility of the local inhabitants, who had Germanic origins. As a result, the SAS party was forced into hiding, and the group's two commanding officers, Captain Littlejohn and Corporal Crowley, were captured and subsequently executed under Hitler's Commando Order. By the end of March, the mission was declared a failure and the remainder of the party were evacuated from Italy.

Operation Archway

Carried out by a composite force, Operation Archway comprised elements of A Squadron and D Squadron, 1 SAS, under the command of Major Harry Poat, and A Squadron, 2 SAS, commanded by Major Peter Power. Later in the operation, A Squadron, 2 SAS, would be joined by another two SAS squadrons under Major Grant Hibbert. The entire force, commanded by Lieutenant-Colonel Brian Franks, the CO of 2 SAS, was christened 'Frankforce' and numbered 430 of all ranks. It was mounted in 75 armed jeeps, some carrying three-inch mortars, and a number of 15-cwt and three-ton trucks transported the administrative 'tail'. The 1 SAS element was divided into three large troops commanded respectively by Major Bill Fraser, Major Alec Muirhead and Major John Tonkin. A Squadron, 2 SAS, was organized in two troops under the command of Captain Mackie and Captain Miller.

'Frankforce' departed from England on 18 March 1945, and having landed at Ostend, made its way to a concentration area west of the Rhine to prepare for operations after the main assault crossing of the river, code named Varsity, which would be carried out by the 2nd British and 9th US armies. On 25 March, its two squadrons crossed the Rhine in Buffalo tracked amphibious vehicles and thereafter pushed forward through the area held by the 6th Airborne Division to take up its main role of reconnaissance. Thereafter it operated under the command of the 6th Airborne Division, the 11th Armoured Division and the 15th (Scottish) Division.

Confronted by a variety of enemy units, including Fallschirmjäger of the German 1st Parachute Army, Hitler Youth and Volksstürm home defence units, 'Frankforce' experienced hard fighting during the advance into Germany. On 8 April, a section of one of the 1 SAS troops commanded by Captain Johnny Cooper, while reconnoitring an area of woodland in advance of an armoured car squadron of the Inns of Court Regiment, was ambushed by enemy troops, supported by three armoured vehicles. Three men were killed and five wounded, the latter including Lieutenant Ian Wellsted.

A week later, on 14–15 April, 1 SAS elements of 'Frankforce' reportedly arrived at Belsen concentration camp, where they found some 50,000 to 60,000 inmates living in conditions so appalling as to be beyond description; 'reportedly' is used here because the official documentation on the operation makes no mention of the visit. Four days later, several patrols were deployed in support of the Field Security Police, who were hunting down known Nazi war criminals, and carried out a number of arrests.

Occupation

Subsequently, 'Frankforce' rejoined the advance through Germany. At the crossing of the river Elbe at the end of April, it was joined by Major Grant Hibbert's squadron of 2 SAS, which had earlier been deployed on Operation Keystone, involving the capture of bridges north of Arnhem, and which had subsequently been cancelled. Thereafter, it continued its advance through Germany, heading through Schleswig-Holstein and eventually reaching Kiel on the Baltic coast. Shortly afterwards, it was withdrawn to Belgium and on 10 May departed for

England. Its losses during Operation Archway had been light: seven killed and 22 wounded.

Back in Italy, 2 SAS was harassing the Germans. The village of Albinea in Italy's Po Valley was the location of the head-quarters of the German 51st Corps, which was quartered in two houses, called Villa Calvi and Villa Rossi, and whose staff numbered some 300 personnel. After an overnight march down from the Appennine Mountains on 24 March, an attack was carried out on the following night by elements of 3 Squadron, 2 SAS, under the command of Major Roy Farran, supported by a force of 170 Italian and Russian partisans, the latter being escapees from German prison camps. Two groups, each of SAS and 20 partisans, attacked the villas, while the remainder of the partisans formed a screen to the south of the objective to block any enemy reinforcements approaching the area. There was fierce fighting at both houses and enemy casualties were heavy, including a number of staff officers killed; among their number was the headquarters' Chief of Staff, Oberst Lemelson. It later transpired that the Corps commander, General-Leutnant Hauk, was away from his headquarters at the time. The SAS suffered three men killed – Lieutenant Riccomini, Sergeant Guscott and Corporal Bolden; and two wounded – Corporal Layburn and Parachutist Mulvey. The partisans suffered five wounded and six captured. Also wounded was Major Michael Lees, an SOE liaison officer working with the partisans who had attached himself to the SAS. Nevertheless, Farrans's force succeeded in withdrawing and, having avoided German forces searching the valley plain, made its way back to its base in the mountains.

War Is Over

As the war began to wind down, the SAS Brigade began to dis-integrate. The French contingent, 2 and 3 RCP, were reabsorbed into the French Army in July. The Belgian company had been expanded early in 1945 and was redesignated the Belgian SAS

Regiment, subsequently serving in Denmark and Germany in a counter-intelligence role, but later in the year was handed over to the Belgian Army and redesignated the 1st Regiment Parachutist-SAS. It was based initially at Westmalle but subsequently, from April 1946 onwards, at Poulseur, with a training school located at Schaffen. Members of the regiment saw service during the Korean War as part of the Corps Volontaires Corea (CVC), which saw a considerable amount of action until its withdrawal in 1954.

The British element found they were doing the oddest of jobs, such as Operation Apostle, a mission to disarm the 300,000 German soldiers remaining in Norway at the end of the war. HQ SAS Brigade, 1 and 2 SAS, all under the command of Brigadier Mike Calvert, undertook this task. The two regiments were shipped from Ostend to Tilbury, and in England they were issued with new jeeps, clothing and equipment.

An advance party made up of representatives from both regiments and a detachment from brigade staff arrived at Stavanger on 12 May 1945, and by the end of the month a total of 760 troops, 17 motorcycles, 68 trailers and 150 jeeps were in the country. The SAS Brigade was based at Bergen to administer the operation. The four months the SAS soldiers spent in Norway were hardly taxing, and most of the men regarded the time as a sort of holiday. The Germans gave them no trouble, the locals were largely friendly (although there were clashes with Quislings – Norwegian collaborators) and the weather was warm. The SAS returned to England at the end of August. An amusing footnote to the operation is the so-called 'Battle of Bergen'. The young ladies of the town were quite fond of the daring British soldiers in their midst, a fact resented by many young Norwegian males in the town and members of the local police force. This culminated in a large-scale brawl in the town's centre, which the SAS won hands down. The 'victory' resulted in British diplomats in Norway urgently requesting the War Office to evacuate the SAS to England.

Some SAS work remained unfinished, the majority of which was tracking down Germans wanted for war crimes. However, it was clear that the Allied governments of Britain and the United States were not keen on searching for the large numbers of Nazis still at large. Faced with a renewed threat from the Soviets, the Allies preferred to recruit their former Nazi enemies rather than to prosecute them for war crimes. The SAS had more backbone, however, and set up an organization to bring as many Nazis as possible to trial.

Final Operations

Major Eric 'Bill' Barkworth was the Intelligence Officer of 2 SAS. In May 1945 he was dispatched by his Commanding Officer, Lieutenant-Colonel Brian Franks, with a small party of 2 SAS to investigate reports of the discovery of the bodies of British troops in Germany. Barkworth's group, designated the SAS War Crimes Investigation Team, identified some of the bodies as those of members of 2 SAS deployed on Operation Loyton in August 1944. Captured by the Germans, they had been taken to a concentration camp at Rotenfels, in Germany, summarily executed and buried. Another mass grave was uncovered at Gaggenau near Baden-Baden: it contained the bodies of 28 captured SAS men who had been tortured and murdered by the Gestapo. Barkworth and his men continued their investigations, travelling to Moussey, in the Vosges Mountains of north-eastern France, where they uncovered the remains of more men of 2 SAS. Despite the disbandment of the SAS in 1946, the group continued investigating the deaths of men from both SAS regiments whose fates were unknown until 1949. Several men identified as being responsible for the atrocities were tried by military courts sitting at Wuppertal and were hanged – though some stories from the period suggest that some of those Nazi officers captured failed to make it to court, with the SAS men preferring a slightly more direct and appropriate form of retribution.

3

1950s

JUNGLE TRAINING AND DESERT OPS

I N 1942, WITH the fall of Singapore to the armies of Imperial Japan, the British suffered their biggest military disaster. General Percival's surrender condemned thousands of British and Commonwealth troops to three years of brutal incarceration.

More importantly, the sight of white soldiers from the previously invincible British Empire being brought to their knees by a smaller Asiatic army made many imperial colonies raise an eyebrow. This meant work for the British in general, and the SAS in particular.

Despite their bitter hatred of the Japanese, the British still refused to arm the local Chinese population, preferring to keep the defence of the small island exclusively in the hands of its predominantly white defenders. The British had always had trouble trusting the oriental inhabitants of their Empire. With the help of the local population – mostly members of the Chinese Communist Party of Malaya, who had been in existence since the 1930s – a few diehard officers, such as the remarkable Freddie Spencer Chapman, stayed on and began organizing resistance against the Japanese. Weapons and equipment were supplied by Force 136, a department of the Special Operation

Executive headed and run by men such as the SAS Regimental Adjutant Major C.E. (Dare) Newell OBE. With the desperation that war brings, it wasn't considered what the outcome of arming, training and equipping so many communists might be after the war was won. So blind were the British authorities to the threat, that after the war they not only awarded the communist leader Chin Peng an OBE in the Victory Honours list, but also invited him to London to take part in the celebrations.

In truth, as soon as the Japanese had been defeated in 1945, the communists greased and then buried their weapons. By now there were at least 4,000 British and captured Japanese weapons at their disposal, together with tons of ammunition and equipment. In three short years they had grown from a small, ineffective political party to a well-equipped, well-trained and highly motivated force. Inspired by Chinese leader Chairman Mao and his defeat of the western-backed Nationalist Chinese Army during a protracted guerrilla war, the Malayan Communists returned, inspired by the 1948 communist convention in Calcutta. Chin Peng quickly realized that the ongoing campaign of urban disruption through strikes and riots was gaining them little – and it was probably costing them much popular support. Armed rebellion seemed to be the only answer. Taking advantage of the dissatisfaction felt by the half million or so Chinese squatters, living in squalid conditions close to the jungle edges, the guerrillas changed their name from the Malayan People's Anti-Japanese Army (MPAJA), to become the self-styled M.P.A.B.A. – Malayan People's Anti-British Army. Following the doctrine of the Chinese master tactician, Sun-Zu – 'Kill one, frighten a thousand' – they began their campaign. Their plan was a simple one. From secure bases concealed deep inside the Malayan jungle, they were going to strike out and, through a campaign of murder, intimidation and economic disruption, instil fear and terror into the local population and – more importantly – their imperial masters. During the Second World War, they eliminated in excess of ten thousand so-called informers and collaborators.

With this in mind, thousands of wartime guerrillas dug up their weapons and equipment and returned to the jungle in 10 'regiments', only one of which was not entirely made up of Chinese veterans. The odd one out was made up of Malays as the communists attempted to claim that they were fighting a war of liberation against the British for everyone, not just for the communist cause. In reality, the Malays took little part in the fighting. The communist regiments were also given support in the field by the Min Yuen, a clandestine group of Chinese civilians who supplied the armed wing with food, intelligence and money. They proved to be very effective.

Red Menace

Between April and June 1948 the communist offensive began. Using time-honoured methods of terrorism, any individual person of prominence, such as Chinese managers and officials, would be hunted down and murdered, using methods that were as public and painful as possible (these were adopted to good effect by the Viet Cong and North Koreans). After invoking terror in the local Chinese and Malay population, it was soon the turn of the Europeans to suffer at the hands of the CT (Communist Terrorists). During the early morning of 16 June 1948, three Chinese youths cycled into the Elphil Estate in Perak and shot dead British planter Arthur Walker. A short distance away Mr Ian Christian and his manager Mr J. Alison were bound to chairs and murdered in front their workforce. A State of Emergency was declared the same day.

The war escalated quickly from urban terrorism to full-blown jungle battles. At the beginning of the emergency, the 6th Gurkha Battalion took on the brunt of the fighting, but it was poorly equipped and several men were found to be suffering from tuberculosis. The Gurkhas quickly received reinforcement from the Devon, Inniskilling and Seaforth battalions in Singapore, as well as two further battalions of Gurkhas. Despite their efforts, they achieved little except discovering how organized and well equipped the CT were. The guerrillas seemed to be able to attack and murder at will with very little practical retaliation from the British Forces. The regular army was neither equipped nor trained to tackle the kind of campaign it was now being asked to sustain. The Malayan jungle provided a guerrilla's paradise. That had been proven during the Second World War and many of the CT were experienced campaigners.

Malaya was a federation of states ruled by hereditary sultans who governed as constitutional monarchs while their British advisers prepared the country for independence. It was made up of a mixed population of aboriginal tribesmen, Chinese, Tamil Indians, Malays and just over 12,000 Europeans, mostly rubber planters, civil servants and managers. About 500 miles long, the Malayan peninsula is four-fifths jungle.

Trees climb to over 200 feet in height, blocking out the light and turning day into permanent dusk. In parts, visibility is so limited that entire patrols could pass next to each other without knowing. Deep, evil-smelling swamps combined with the extreme heat, humidity, and a score of different insects and reptiles that are able to bite, suck your blood, infect or poison you, turned the jungle into a highly specialized theatre of war.

Initially, the army cobbled together a group of veterans from force 136 together with a few volunteers from the regular army and 47 Dyak trackers from the Iban tribes, brought in especially from Borneo. This unlikely combination of fighters became known as the Ferret Force. Although effective in discovering and destroying several CT camps, it was a drop in the ocean. After losing several officers to other units, the Force was finally disbanded.

Despite all their efforts, the British seemed powerless to combat the CT or stop their campaign. By March 1950, 863 civilians, 323 police officers and 154 soldiers had been murdered. Despite their advances, the CT didn't act with complete impunity suffering 1,138 dead, 645 captured and 359 who surrendered. Despite these losses, however, the CT showed no sign of reducing their campaign.

General Sir John Harding, Commander-in-Chief of Far East Land Forces, had to come up with a solution quickly or risk losing the peninsula itself with all the implications that went with it. In 1950, he sent for Brigadier 'Mad Mike' Calvert. Calvert was a legend. If Stirling was the founder of the SAS, then Calvert can certainly lay claim to being the modern father of the Regiment. Calvert was a hard, tough, unorthodox man, with a sharp mind who was famous for his idealism, chivalry and leadership. Calvert had always taken an active interest in guerrilla warfare. In 1940, he had written a paper on the subject entitled, 'The Operations of Small Forces behind the Enemy Lines', when a German invasion of England was considered imminent. Calvert also worked with Ian Fleming's brother Peter to organize a guerrilla defence force in Great Britain. A Cambridge double blue (one for boxing), he gave up his commission to see some action, and later he became a founder member of the Commandos, serving for three years behind Japanese lines in Burma with Wingate's Chindits and becoming an expert in jungle warfare. Finally, in 1944 he took command of the SAS Brigade from Rod McLeod and led it for the rest of the war. Bored and cooling his heels in Hong Kong, Calvert jumped at the chance of becoming operational once more.

Events Unfold

Harding, together with Lieutenant General Sir Harold Briggs, had several meetings with Calvert. Harding eventually instructed Calvert to prepare a report on the emergency and come up with serious counter-terrorist proposals. Over the next six months, Calvert travelled over a thousand miles and interviewed hundreds of people, both civilian and military. Calvert even joined military units patrolling the jungles, being ambushed at least twice. Although Calvert's work was important and set the base for all future plans, it was the controversial Briggs plan that was to set the pattern for the eventual destruction of the CT in Malaya.

Briggs, also a veteran of the Burma campaign, had been coaxed out of retirement to act as Director of Operations in Malaya.

The essence of the Briggs plan was to deny the CT food by cutting them off from their sources, supplies and intelligence. To achieve this plan, Briggs proposed moving the Chinese squatters into protected new villages. This was no mean achievement as it entailed relocating some 600,000 people from 410 'villages' over a period of two years. Calvert's contribution was to establish a force that could attack and disrupt CT lines of communication, attack their bases and curtail their patrols. However, his force, which became known as the Malayan Scouts, would have to remain in the jungle for weeks and sometimes months on end. The patrols would have to live in, and live off of, the jungle, something never achieved before by British troops. Calvert began to search for likely recruits throughout the Far East. One of his main problems was time. Under pressure from Whitehall for quick results, he had no time to spare with involved recruitment techniques or a prolonged training schedule.

As a result, he eventually recruited a mixed bag of some one hundred men to form A Squadron. Some were useful former members of SOE, SAS, Force 136 and the Ferret Force. Others, on the other hand, were just bored with their lives and looking for some action. One group surprisingly consisted of 10 deserters from the French Foreign Legion who had jumped ship en route to Indo-China. Calvert then went in search of high quality officers and NCOs. For these, he was more successful recruiting from a group of wartime reservists now forming part of the Territorial Army unit, 21 SAS (part of which had been recruited for operations in Korea, but they never materialized). Commanded by Major Anthony Greville-Bell, it boasted such luminaries as Alastair McGregor and Bob Bennett – one of David Stirling's 'Originals'. These highly experienced men arrived in Malaya in January 1951 and formed B Squadron. After a short trip to Rhodesia, Calvert recruited a further 100 men from over 1,000 volunteers. These men formed C Squadron and, after a similar visit to Hong Kong, he brought back Chinese interpreters and counter-guerrillas, who had also previously served in Burma, to form the core of his Intelligence staff.

Their original camp was established at Kota Tinggi near Johore (later Calvert also established an operation headquarters at Ipoh), where training was done under the watchful eye of Major John Woodhouse. Woodhouse, who would go on to command the Regiment, was a former Dorset Regimental Officer with little interest in the formalities of army life, but he was a stickler where battle discipline was concerned and was undoubtedly one of the best squadron commanders the Regiment ever had. Stirling himself agreed that Woodhouse was as important as himself to the founding of the SAS. Prior to Woodhouse's influence, training was at best ad hoc, with no specialist instructors and most of it done on the hoof. It wasn't long before Woodhouse saw the limitations and long-term problems this was going to cause, and he established a new tough selection course before retuning to Malaya to command 22 SAS. For the time being, however, his men had to learn quickly and mainly through patrol experience. The jungle wasn't the easiest landscape to fight a campaign, and the men not only had to cope with an active enemy but also the jungle itself. Johnny Cooper, another of Stirling's Originals, gives one of the best descriptions of conditions during a patrol in his memoirs:

'Apart from the enemy, leeches were our main adversary. They would fall off leaves and latch on to one's softest areas, around the neck, behind the ears, under the armpits, and on a long patrol they would even find their way to one's private parts. You couldn't feel them, but as they slowly sucked blood they enlarged into horrible black swollen lumps. If you were a smoker, it was easy to get rid of them – just a touch with a burning cigarette and they would fall off.'

Operationally, Calvert's idea was to send 14-man patrols with a powerful radio, assisted by Chinese interpreters and police officers into the jungle to establish front-line bases. From these bases, four-man patrols were sent out to explore the jungle, plot CT lines of communication and set up effective ambushes. To achieve their objectives, these patrols would have to learn to live in the jungle for weeks at a time. Army thinking at the time was based on the concept that a patrol could not survive in jungle conditions for more than seven days. However, with the introduction of helicopters used for the first time during the Malayan campaign and flown by Royal Navy pilots, these periods were being gradually extended. One patrol led by Lieutenant Michael Sinclair Hill remained in the jungle for 103 days, a record and a remarkable achievement.

These patrols also made contact with local tribes. Calvert realized how important having these tribes on his side was to the eventual success of the operation and began a campaign of 'heart and minds'. To this end, primitive but effective clinics were established from where drugs such as penicillin were dispensed, curing local tribesmen and their families of a variety of diseases, including the contagious tropical skin disease known as yaws. Although there are no official casualty figures for the CT during this period, Calvert's casualties numbered four: one police officer, a Chinese auxiliary, an SAS soldier killed while staying with a local tribe and a second man killed during a fierce firefight with the CT.

In late 1951, Calvert was finally invalided home, suffering from malaria, dysentery, hookworm and 12 years of hard soldiering. Although questions always remained about the behaviour of the Malayan Scouts, especially A Squadron, Calvert was as loyal to his unit as ever. There can be little doubt that many A Squadron men were totally unsuitable for Special Forces, and equally their methods could be unorthodox. However, Calvert considered that most acts of so-called indiscipline, which included drunkenness, fighting and reckless discharging of firearms at base camp, were no more than soldiers letting off steam after long periods in the claustrophobic jungle conditions. He also blamed newly arrived reservist officers who were, he considered, 'a bit soft'. John Woodhouse, one of Calvert's most gifted officers, probably summed up the general feeling. He wrote:

'Numerous widely publicized, sensational and mainly true stories circulated for years, and very nearly led to the disbandment of the unit. But if Calvert must accept much of the blame he deserves credit, too, for his far-sighted perception of the broad strategy and tactics of counter-insurgency, which I learned mainly from him... Another cause of the bad start in Malaya was the woeful inadequacy of the administrative and "Q" staff. Malaya Command should have known that a strong staff was essential, but they failed to appoint one, and Mike Calvert did not insist on replacements. Blame us by all means for our failings, but learn from them, too. Most of us had our hearts in the job and if we had not made a start perhaps no one else would have done so.'

Whatever was said about Calvert and his techniques later, he had the satisfaction of knowing he had resurrected the SAS into an effective and necessary fighting unit.

Reorganization

Calvert's replacement was Lieutenant-Colonel John (Tod) Sloane, an orthodox infantryman who had been second-in-command of the Argyll and Sutherland Highlanders in Korea. Having no Special Forces or jungle warfare backgrounds, he recruited the help of both John Woodhouse and Dare Newell (who became the Regimental Adjutant) to assist him in reorganizing the Regiment. Sloane was a keen disciplinarian who was insistent in bringing a new order and discipline to the Regiment. Weapons would now have to be clean, all administrative matters affecting soldiers' welfare brought up-to-date and many of the Regiment's 'bad boys' returned to their parent regiments, or any other regiment that would take them. It was estimated that half of those recruited in Malaya were disposed of in this way. Although it sounds like a drastic measure, the men left behind were of the highest calibre, as indeed were the new recruits that began to come through from the UK, having undergone a proper selection process and training. The SAS was also pulled out of deep penetration operations into the jungle until a period of further training could take place. The

SAS now had four squadrons in Malaya: A, B, C and D. Sloane immediately removed the Regiment from the jungle, insisting that it required specialist training if it was going to be effective. In essence this involved not seeing the jungle as your enemy but, like the desert during the Second World War, as your friend. To this end, the training had to be hard and effective if the SAS was going to be able to achieve its objectives.

In February 1952, three of the SAS squadrons took part in Operation Helsby. Thanks largely to the success of Gibbs's plan in keeping food from the CT, they were forced to start growing their own. In order to do this, they had cleared large areas of jungle. These areas were easily and quickly spotted from the air, giving the government forces an opportunity to attack the communist camps. One such location was situated in the Balum Valley, close to the Thai border, where just over 100 communist guerrillas were subsisting off the land while using the base to strike out at a variety of targets. Operation Helsby was designed to destroy the base and flush the CT into the open, where they could be destroyed. A Squadron and C Squadron, together with a detachment of Royal Marine Commandos, a few Gurkhas and local police, approached the valley on foot, while just over 50 members of B Squadron were dropped in by parachute (the first time the SAS had parachuted into an operation since 1945). Although later the Regiment perfected the art of jungle stealth, on this occasion the operation was a total failure. The sound of hundreds of men pushing their way through the jungle warned the CT in good time and they had long gone.

To get to your target quickly and silently, parachuting seemed to be the answer. Dropping into Europe is one thing but dropping into the dense foliage of the Malayan jungle is another. That, combined with the fact that most of B Squadron hadn't dropped since the Second World War meant there were no training facilities and no instructors (although all this was later sorted out). Safe jumping zones are rare in the jungle, and even these are fraught with danger, namely high trees and sharp bamboo that shatters easily, causing serious injury to descending and vulnerable troops. To try to make parachuting in jungle conditions safer, 'tree jumping' was introduced. The idea was simple enough: each trooper was issued with a 100-foot coil of rope. After a parachute snagged on a tree, each man first lowered his pack and then himself on to the ground safely using the rope. Although it proved effective and there were few injuries on Operation Helsby, future experiments proved less successful. Major John Salmon, second-in-command of 22 SAS, who admitted to feeling terrified during his parachute jumps, explains the feelings and experiences he had when jumping:

'Next thing you know, you are floating through the air and it's one of the most wonderful feelings in the world; then you see the trees coming. You are coming down beautifully, steering for the middle of the trees. The hot air makes you swing violently, as if a giant had caught hold of you. You let the air spill out of the chute and look for a good, healthy tree. Sometimes you make that spot; often you don't. It's hard to tell until you're a few feet away. When you hit a tree, you don't know whether you'll stay there or not. Often the branch snaps, you hurtle down, smashing into branches on the way, until you finally come to a halt. If it holds you, then you know you're safe.'

Later, with several deaths and numerous injuries during training (including the new Commanding Officer (CO) Lieutenant-Colonel Oliver Brooke, who had just taken over from Slone), and the introduction of the helicopter for dropping troops and equipment into specific areas (which was used by the army for the first time in Malaya), the method was eventually abandoned.

With the effects of the Briggs plan being keenly felt by the CT, they moved deeper into the jungle, and the SAS went after them. Armed now with the new Patchett carbine and shotguns, they led jungle operations in both Pahang and Kelanton, parachuting or being dropped in by helicopter. While the regular units continued to attack the CTs, the SAS began to contact local aboriginal tribes. Landing in groups of 15 and staying with the local tribesman for up to 13 weeks, they turned the villages into armed camps as well as building landing strips and medical centres to treat the locals. It was also often the job of a single trooper to convince local tribes to assist the government forces and adopt a policy of self-defence.

The policy of 'hearts and minds' came from the new and highly resourceful Military High Commissioner, General Sir Gerald Templar. In answer to a question about the number of men he had on the ground to fight the communists, Templar replied 'The answer lies not in pouring more soldiers into the jungle, but rests in the hearts and minds of the Malayan people.' With these few well-chosen words, Templar summed up the SAS philosophy that has remained with it to this day. It was never SAS numbers that made a difference, but the originality of its ideas. This had also been Calvert's dream when he established the Malayan Scouts.

Major Operations

Between 1952 and 1958 the SAS was involved in numerous operations, two of the most noted being Operation Hive and Operation Termite. The first of these operations, Hive, was in essence a continuation of the Gibbs denial policy and was carried out in late 1952, in the state of Negri Sembilan. During the eight-week operation, together with the Gurkhas and Fijian units, it patrolled large areas of Serembon and disrupted the CT's lines of communication, denied them food, kept them away from the local population and forced them to fall back on their own supply dumps. Working deep inside the Malayan jungle, the hope was to kill upwards of 100 guerrillas known to be operating in the area. The eventual tally was only 16 killed, not many it would seem, but in the context of the overall campaign, where the SAS killed just over 100 communists in nine years, it wasn't a bad tally.

The problem with Hive, like in so many other operations that the SAS was involved in, was its strategic misuse. It was quickly understood that the Regiment was better employed in gathering intelligence and in shaping the opinions of the local population. Although the men weren't 'medal chasers' and won few awards, their role was significant and it was largely due to their presence that casualties among British soldiers fell dramatically. The SAS 'hearts and minds' campaigns were proving more successful than anyone could have hoped for. However, although Operation Hive wasn't all they had hoped it would be, the SAS once again learned valuable lessons.

During Operation Sword in January 1954, the SAS suffered three dead as a result of parachuting into the jungle in Kedah. However, during its next major operation, Operation Termite, which was to last from July to November 1954 and was designed to wrest control of a large area of country, including the central mountain spine from the CT as well as establish relations with the local tribes, all three operational squadrons dropped into Perak. Despite continuing to try and perfect tree jumping, they succeeded with only four injuries, largely due to unstable thermals throwing troopers all over the sky. The operation had begun with heavy jungle bombing to clear areas for the later airborne assault. Jungle bombing, like tree jumping, however, was a controversial tactic. The bombing was indiscriminate and killed and injured as many friendly aborigines as it did CTs. It was considered to be, especially by the Regiment, counter-productive and a 'damn nuisance'. Again, like tree jumping, it was a mistake that wasn't to be repeated in Borneo. Despite using two squadrons of the SAS plus an additional four infantry battalions, total casualties among the CT were only 15: a small return for such a large and dangerous operation. It was estimated at the time that it took 1,800 man-hours of patrolling to kill one CT. The SAS quickly discovered that the CT wasn't its biggest enemy, the jungle was. Soldiers had to learn to live within this hostile environment quickly, making the jungle their friend not their enemy. Interestingly, despite all the problems, the historian Gregory Blaxland points out that Termite was a success not so much for the number of the CTs killed, but in the conversion of the aborigines to the SAS cause. It was a classic example of the power of the 'hearts and minds' campaign.

The years 1955 to 1956 were highly significant to both the campaign in Malaya, and to the long-term development of the Regiment. John Woodhouse returned to the Regiment after years of heading up training in the UK, as a squadron commander, under the command of the new CO, Lieutenant-Colonel George Lea. A large man in every sense, Lea was another in a long line of tough commanding officers. He quickly disposed of any officer that he considered was not up to the mark and returned each to his parent regiment. He also recruited a number of top quality officers, including Captain Peter de la Billière (who later went on to command the Regiment) as well as promoting many of those he inherited. C, Rhodesian Squadron – commanded by another hard man, Peter Walls (who went on to command all Rhodesian forces after UDI) – was returned to Africa (although it retained its SAS identity).

Although effective, C Squadron were susceptible for some reason to the various jungle diseases, as well as having problems relating to the dark-skinned aborigines, which wasn't good for the 'heart and minds' campaigns. To replace them, D Squadron was raised locally and commanded by the legendary Johnny Cooper (one of Stirling's Originals), who established his own training programme. During this period, the Regiment's time was largely taken up building jungle forts and building relationships with local aboriginal tribes. Once the fort was finished, it was handed over to the Malayan police and regular army detachments. This fort building really marked the start of the SAS's involvement with Templar's 'hearts and minds' initiative. The men of the Regiment learned the native language and ate their food.

Typical of operations at this time was D Squadron's first patrol in October 1953. Accompanied by a number of Iban trackers, the patrol set off to establish Fort Brooke. Cooper, followed by his patrol, pushed into the jungle in Pahang. Following the Sungei Brok River, they slashed their way through the dense foliage until they reached their destination. Establishing a small clearing, they radioed in for a location check. They then cleared an area of jungle big enough for a helicopter to land and to build a bridge across the river. Once all this had been established, they began to patrol, seeking out the local aborigines and searching for CT camps. One CT gang was successfully broken up, but in another contact two squadron troopers were killed in an ambush. The patrol stayed out for 122 days, during which time 50 per cent of the original complement had to be evacuated due to disease, fatigue and jungle fever. Finally, on 7 February 1954, the remaining 40 men of D Squadron, exhausted, emaciated and with their uniforms in tatters emerged from the jungle to be replaced by a police detachment. It was a remarkable achievement.

Change of Command

John Woodhouse, returning from England, took over command of D Squadron and Johnny Cooper was promoted to Major and took over command of B (Big Time Bravo) Squadron. During the summer of 1955, a squadron was raised in New Zealand. Commanded by Major Frank Rennie, the squadron was put through a tough recruitment and training programme before being sent to Malaya during the latter half of the year. Its total strength was about 140 men, a third of whom were Maoris. They worked well with the local tribes and were first-class trackers. Their presence in the Regiment also encouraged a number of the equally tough Fijian soldiers serving in Malaya to apply for selection, and several were recruited. During the same period, a squadron recruited from the Parachute Regiment (Parachute Regiment Squadron), commanded by Major Dudley Coventry, further reinforced the SAS.

By the latter half of 1956, 560 soldiers comprising five squadrons each with four troops of 16 men, plus headquarters personnel and attached specialists, were operating within the jungles of Malaya. As a result, the number of people murdered by the CT fell further to about six a month: an impressive result by anybody's standards. The campaign then moved to more strongly focus on search and destroy. It was estimated that approximately 2,000 CT were still operating from their increasingly remote bases, deep inside the jungle, from where they launched a number of attacks. To deal with this final phase of the campaign, 22 SAS were to gain considerable prominence.

Not that the Regiment was in the jungle all the time. After a lengthy tour of duty patrolling in the jungle, the troopers would find themselves with three months' pay in their pockets and two weeks to spend it. Life followed a pattern. Two months in the jungle, two wild weeks spending and enjoying life with all the things that Malaya had to offer a tired, stressed and frustrated soldier, followed by two weeks of retraining and then back out into the jungle. During training, new skills were being continually practised: parachute jumping, small boat training, demolitions, attacks on RAF stations and jungle knowledge. Training was continual and vital and formed the basis for the modern-day SAS.

By the end of 1955 the CT were in retreat. Their leadership had fled. The reward policy made many surrender. The army and police were taking a steady toll of those who refused to surrender, and with the success of the 'hearts and minds' campaign, the aborigines were no longer scared of the CT and stopped supplying them with food and shelter. It was now that Lea had a radical rethink about the role of the SAS in Malaya. Lea started to put individual squadrons into a jungle base and leave them there for several months so they could thoroughly familiarize themselves with the terrain, the local tribes, and, using the skills they had learned as trackers, ambush and pick off CTs in ones and twos as they moved through what use to be safe routes. These tactics began to play on the morale of the CTs. There were no large-scale battles, no set-piece actions, just slow, deliberate and patient picking off the enemy. There was great inter-squadron rivalry over how many CTs each could kill. This rivalry became know as the 'kill to contract' ratio. A good example of this involved the legendary Johnny Cooper, this time as commander of B Squadron.

An intelligence report had been received that the communists were running a radio station from the jungle a little south of the Thai border. It was causing problems and Cooper was ordered to destroy it. It wasn't a short or easy trip. First, his team had to travel by canoe from Kota Bahru – famous for the Japanese landings in 1941. The squadron then had to cross the Akik Ring range of mountains on foot before descending into the oddly named 'Valley of no Return', where it was believed the transmitter was being operated. It took Cooper and his troop eight hard days marching before they reached the crest of the mountain. Here, Cooper split his company into four troops before descending. It was 'Punchy' McNeil's troop that discovered the transmitter, as is often the case in the jungle, quite by accident. Punchy discovered what appeared to be a water wheel suspended over a fast-flowing stream. This makeshift but effective contraption was turning a dynamo powering the radio. Launching an attack, the CTs were forced into the jungle and the transmitter destroyed. The CT were chased but escaped over the Thai border. Cooper wanted to follow and finish the job, but permission was refused. During the same patrol, they managed to track down and kill two further terrorists as well as discover a previously unheard of aboriginal tribe. Often when meeting these tribes for the first time, the troopers would be subject to incidents they could not have imagined in their wildest dreams. Pete Scholey remembers coming across one such tribe in Borneo. One of the women was breast-feeding a monkey, when Pete enquired why he was told in quite a matter-of-fact way that it was being fattened up for the kill. It was to be their meal that night.

While Johnny Cooper was making history in the jungle, the Parachute Regiment Squadron was busy making its own headlines. After shooting dead a female terrorist in the Ipoh region, it was discovered that she was carrying a six-month-old child. The squadron 'captured' and cared for the child as one of their own.

Without doubt, one of the greatest characters to serve with the SAS in any capacity was Sergeant Bob Turnbull of D Squadron, a former gunner from Middlesbrough. He became close to an

Iban tracker called Anak Kayan and achieved an eye for a spoor as accurate as Kayan himself. He became one of the finest trackers in the Regiment and was as good as any of the Iban that had taught him their skills. On one occasion, he led a three-man patrol in pursuit of a CT unit whose tracks he had picked up. His patrol followed these tracks for several days through some of the toughest regions in Malaya. Finally, Turnbull heard voices behind a clump of bushes. He moved forward slowly, locating the enemy sentry, and then sat down to wait. After a short while and due to the heavy rain, the sentry moved back into camp. Turnbull followed, silently. When the rest of the patrol was in position, they opened fire and killed all four of the CT inside the camp. Turnbull's weapon of choice was the pump-action shotgun, with which he killed the infamous bandit Ah Tuck – a senior member of the communist leadership. The two men discovered each other by accident. Ah Tuck was reputed to always carry a cocked and ready-to-fire Sten gun. Despite this, Turnbull was too quick for him and fired three times. People who witnessed the incident said the shots were fired so quickly that it sounded like one long shot rather than three individual ones.

By 1956–57, the campaign in Malaya was all but won and it began to wind down. The Regiment had played a significant part in the battle for the jungle and it had not gone unnoticed. In April 1956, Brigadier Fitzroy Maclean who was then serving as Under-Secretary of State for War, visited the Regiment. One of the first men recruited by David Stirling in 1941, Maclean had taken part in several of the Regiment's early raids, and he had parachuted into the former Yugoslavia as head of a mission sent by Churchill to organize Tito's resistance. He was the ideal choice to congratulate the Regiment on its efforts.

In 1957, the Parachute Regiment Squadron returned to England, where its parent regiment needed it. The Regiment was sorry to see it go because it had done a good job, made many friends and had played an important role. The next to go were the New Zealanders. They had accounted for 15 of the enemy during their two-year stint. The CO George Lea was sent home at about the same time. He was awarded a well-earned DSO, the first such decoration the Regiment had been awarded since the Second World War. His citation read as follows:

'He personally directed the operations of his men, was parachuted with them into thick jungle, descended by rope from a helicopter aircraft and shared every hazard, danger and discomfort inherent in jungle operations against a ruthless and fanatical enemy.'

More Change

Lea's replacement was Lieutenant-Colonel Anthony Deane-Drummond, a first-class officer and an excellent choice. The Regiment's last action during the Malayan campaign was Operation Sweep, which commenced in February 1958. The plan was to surround and destroy a band of CTs led by a terrorist leader called Ah Hoi, who was nick named the 'Baby Killer'. He had once slit open the belly of a pregnant woman because her husband was a suspected police informer. Hoi was known to be holed up in the Telok Anson swamp, a miserable insect-infested place 18 by 10 miles on the Tengi River to the north-west of Kuala Lumpur. D Squadron, under the command of the larger-than-life Major Harry Thompson, a Royal Highland Fusilier, had been selected for the task. He decided to parachute into the area, a risky business in the jungle, but wanted the element of surprise. Unfortunately, Trooper Jerry Mulcahy, one of the 37 troopers that dropped from the RAF Blackburn Beverley, got caught in a tree before dropping to the ground and breaking his back. A helicopter had to be sent in to evacuate him. The patrol's first job was therefore to make a clearing so the helicopter could land. Due to the swampy nature of the terrain, that was impossible and the helicopter had to hover just above the ground while the stretcher was forced on board. Although helicopters are versatile and effective – especially in the jungle – they are also noisy. Harry Thompson's element of surprise had gone.

Thompson knew he had to move quickly. Following the course of the river, he divided his force into two groups to track the terrorist passage through the swamps. In doing so, the SAS found itself coping with some of the worst conditions ever experienced in Malaya. The weather was appalling and it rained almost continually. The troopers were up to their necks in brown, leech-infested swamp water and had to cut their way through acres of sword grass. Mosquitoes continually attacked them, biting their way through their clothes, and their boots rotted off, so several men had to walk barefoot. Peter de la Billière's troop followed the CTs trail for 10 days keeping in touch by radio. They came across several CT camps littered with the shells of turtles eaten by the terrorists. The other troop, led by Sergeant Sandilands, tried to cut them off. Several rubber dinghies were dropped in by air, and Sandilands used these to move his troop by night along the river, desperately trying to sniff out the communists' campfires. Later, one of these patrols made first contact with the enemy. Several CTs were cooking a meal close to the riverbank. Unfortunately, before they came into range, the terrorists spotted the patrol and deserted their position, leaving their equipment behind. Later, an aborigine reported seeing a man and a women standing by the river. Suspecting an ambush, Sandilands took Corporal Finn with him when he went in search of the couple. The aborigine hadn't been lying and Sandilands quickly located the couple. Creeping up behind them Sandilands killed the man, but Finn missed the women, who disappeared back into the jungle. The patrol set of in hot pursuit. The woman's trail was easy to follow and the patrol found what was left of two CT camps. While Thompson was pushing on into the interior and calling up his reserves, the army and police were surrounding the swamp. After nine weeks the net began to tighten around the terrorists. Although working in two distinct groups, they were difficult to pin down. The big breakthrough came when one of the group, a women named Ah Niet, walked out of the swamp and told the authorities that her group were almost out of food and needed help. At first she tried to impose conditions for their surrender. She wanted £3,500 for each of her group and amnesty for those already in prison. The British knew she was in no position to negotiate and refused her demands. Finally, she agreed to bring the terrorists out that night. True to her word, five terrorists walked out of the jungle and surrendered to Harry Thompson, including Ah Hoi, the infamous 'Baby Killer'. Brian Connell witnessed the surrender: 'He was still arrogant, still ranting that the reds would win in the end.' He was eventually given the choice of prison or exile to China. He finally chose prison, but he was packed off to China anyway. After the initial surrender, Ah Niet walked back into the jungle to persuade several more of her former comrades to surrender, which they did 48 hours later. Although a few diehard CTs kept up the fight and the SAS kept patrolling in Johore in cooperation with the security forces, that was the end of any serious campaigning.

By the time the Malayan campaign ended, the SAS was a different animal to that which had been established in 1941. It had also justified its existence in a post-war world. Several outstanding officers had already served with the Regiment, including men like John Woodhouse, Peter de la Billière, Tony Jeapes, John Watts and Mike Wingate-Gray. The Regiment had also produced first-class NCOs who were the backbone of any regiment. By the end of the Malayan campaign, the only man left serving with the Regiment who had also been with them during the Second World War was Johnny Cooper. Many new lessons had been learned and new tactics practised; some were excellent, such as the 'hearts and minds' campaign, and some (the tree jumping) were disastrous. A number of officers and men wondered what would become of the Regiment after the campaign in Malaya finished. Training continued apace while they waited. The campaign had lasted longer than the Second World War. It had seen the re-establishment of the SAS as a far different animal to that of the 1939–45 conflict. The worth of the Regiment, however, had been established and, as Britain withdrew from the British Empire and a dozen small campaigns threatened, the SAS would be needed more than ever.

Oman and the Jebel Akhdar

In 1950, Sultan Said bin Taimur ruled Oman. The country was desperately poor. Those who disagreed with his policies or angered him would find their wells filled and their families banished. His one staunch ally was Britain, who had signed a treaty with the Sultan of Muscat back in 1789. This extended commercial rights to the East India Company in exchange for protection from the Royal Navy. The latter's presence in the area did much to stabilize the coastal trade, from which the sea-faring Omanis prospered. The agreement held and was passed down through the years from Sultan to Sultan and then, in 1950, oil was discovered. This would turn this huge desert peninsula into one of the richest regions in the world. Most of this oil would have to pass through the Strait of Hormuz, in northern Oman, thus making it of particular interest to the British.

However, in 1952, neighbouring Saudi Arabia invaded parts of Abu Dhabi and Muscat, both of which were rich in oilfields. The Sultan of Oman turned to the British who, at first, negotiated with the Saudis. Nevertheless, it soon became apparent that a Saudi-backed rebellion had started in Oman. By 1957, the situation had developed into open rebellion. The Imam of Oman, Ghalib bin Ali, and his brother, Talib, established a theocratic state and sought to overthrow the Sultan of Oman, Said bin Taimur. The rebels were well entrenched in the mountainous plateau of Jebel Akhdar in the north of the country. Ghalib bin Ali and his brother mustered little more than 100 followers, but they had the backing of Sheikh Suleiman bin Himyar, a powerful tribal chief who had disagreed with the Sultan. The area controlled by Sheikh Suleiman bin Himyar and his tribe was a huge mountainous plateau in northern Oman known as Jebel Akhdar.

There were no roads around the mountain, and access to the scattered mountain villages was only possible on foot. Donkeys made up the local transportation, and even these were restricted to a few pathways. This made the area easy to defend, especially against assault. No foreigner had conquered the Jebel since the Persians in the tenth century. While the British had sent a detachment of Life Guards, equipped with Ferret armoured cars, they could do little more than surround the Jebel. In turn, they soon became a target themselves as the rebels' mined the tracks along which the armoured cars would travel. Equally, the Sultan's local army was no match for the rebels, and after several attempts to gain access to the Jebel they withdrew to a safe distance. In desperation, the Sultan requested more assistance from Britain, which responded by ordering units of the SAS to be sent from Malaya to Oman.

The first mission of D Squadron, on 24 November, was to establish a base on a mountain that overlooked the stronghold of Aquabat al Dhafar in the north-west. It was to be done in two parts, with 16 and 17 Troops attempting an assault from the north while 18 and 19 Troops made their way up from the south. On the afternoon of the 25 November, 18 and 19 Troops went to ground as an exchange of fire took place, it was still daylight and the rebels trapped them near the bottom of the Jebel. Sadly, during the firefight, Corporal Duke Swindells, was hit in the chest by a sniper and killed. Swindells was from the Middlesex Regiment and holder of the Military Medal. He was buried in a secret location in a landlocked bay close to the shoreline. His death served to highlight the exposure of moving in daylight and thereafter most patrols were carried out in darkness to avoid the danger of rebel snipers.

The northern SAS units, comprising 16 and 17 Troops, made better headway and managed to reach the top of the plateau unopposed. This in part was due to a local guide who had shown them a route known as the Persian Steps. This ancient route to the summit was well protected by sangers (stone circular defences) but the SAS had found them unmanned by the rebels. They had stashed most of their equipment at a small village and made the climb in darkness.

Once at the top, the officer in command, Captain Roderic 'Red Rory' Walker, decided to consolidate his position. He ordered 17 Troop to descend the 6,500-foot track to where they had left their equipment, while 16 Troop held the plateau. It took 17 Troop a full 24 hours to descend to the village where their stores had been dumped and then remake their way up the Persian Steps. While no rebels were encountered by 16 Troop, it did intercept a small group of tribesmen who were moving by night. So grateful were the tribesmen at not being shot by the SAS that they offered to work for them, transporting water, supplies and ammunition. Once 17 Troop had returned, they reversed roles and 16 Troop descended to collect their equipment, however, this time they had four donkeys to help them. Firmly established on the Jebel, the SAS sent out patrols to locate the enemy, although they tried to avoid contact where possible.

From there on the SAS would either send out night patrols or man strategic Observation Posts (OPs). The latter normally consisted of six SAS soldiers, all heavily armed and capable of defending themselves even against much greater odds. For their part, the rebels resorted to ineffectual long-range sniping with the occasional machine gun or mortar attacks on the SAS positions. For the present, the situation was allowed to settle down, but it was plain that one under-strength squadron couldn't shake the rebels from their stronghold.

On the 1 January 1959, progress was made when the Commanding Officer of 22 SAS Regiment, Lieutenant-Colonel Tony Deane-Drummond, arrived in Muscat. On 10 January, A Squadron, commanded by Major Johnny Cooper, also arrived in Muscat, having flown from Malaya. Upon arriving at the SAS headquarters in Tanuf, A Squadron set about climbing the Persian Steps in order to relieve D Squadron. Captain de la Billière, who guided them to the sangars on Cassino and briefed Cooper on the current situation, met them at the top. Once this was done, D Squadron then redeployed to the Tanuf Slab area and mounted operations in the area to the south of Sabrina.

Two weeks later the combined squadrons mounted a full attack on the Jebel. The SAS devised a deception plan in order to draw most of the rebels away from the commanding positions. Part one was to create an elaborate deception by planning an attack on a plateau stronghold known as Sabrina. Part two was to casually let the donkey handlers know of their plans. The SAS had known from the start that the local donkey handlers were passing vital information to the rebels. The handlers got their briefing from Deane-Drummond, who told them that a diversion was to be made up the Wadi Kamah, but the real assault was to be launched from Tanuf, and the donkey trains would be going up that way.

On the evening of 25 January, A Squadron moved forward for an assault on the northern slopes of Sabrina. At 03:00 hours, they received the order to commence their assault. Three troops climbed, all using different routes, while the fourth provided covering fire with machine guns. They reached the summit just before dawn, at which time a fierce firefight developed. The fighting was hard with many accounts of hand-to-hand combat but, in the end, the SAS was victorious. Then to continue the deception, three of the troops descended to waiting trucks, leaving only 4 Troop to defend Sabrina.

D Squadron, in order to convince the rebels that the main attack would come from the west, also launched a diversionary attack. Once the fighting was over, they too left 1 Troop in position while the rest made their way back to SAS headquarters in Tanuf. By evening on the second day, six SAS Troops were making their way by road to the village of Kamah, ready to begin the real attack.

Hauling ammunition and water in laden rucksacks weighing in excess of 100 pounds, A Squadron and D Squadron made their final push to the summit of Jebel Akhdar. The route the SAS had chosen was one the rebels would not expect. Climbing was difficult at best, but the heavy loads made it almost impossible. Nevertheless, the SAS did the impossible. It cost the SAS three lives, but it had taken the impregnable Jebel Akhdar.

Colonel Deane-Drummond was awarded a DSO for his planning of the operation, while Military Crosses went to Rory Walker, Tony Jeapes (then a Lieutenant with A Squadron), Johnny Watts and Peter de la Billière.

4

1960s

FROM THE JUNGLE
TO THE DESERT

I N 1960, 22 SAS was still barracked at Merebrook Camp at Malvern in Worcestershire: it was the Regiment's first permanent camp since the SAS had been reformed. However, later that same year it moved to the old Royal Artillery Barracks in Hereford, known as Bradbury Lines. The buildings, known as 'spiders', were constructed of wood and had been erected during the Second World War. The whole camp was second-rate and in dire need of repair, but it served the Regiment well.

The change of address also heralded a change in SAS training – the development of a modern method of fighting known as close-quarter battle (CQB). It had two forms: armed and unarmed. Armed CQB covered a wide range of pistol and submachine gun techniques, while SAS unarmed combat perfected fast and deadly methods of killing. These include learning about the defensive and offensive parts of the body, and how best to use them or protect them.

The early 1960s also saw many new recruits enter the SAS, among them several Fijians. The relationship between Fiji's fighting men and the Regiment had started in September 1952 when D Company of the 1st Fijian Infantry took part in a joint operation with two SAS squadrons called Operation Hive (see page 73). A few years later, a number of Fijians joined the British Army, some making their way into the SAS. They achieved great standing with their peers; two in particular, Corporal Labalaba and Trooper Savesaki, are remembered for their outstanding courage during the battle of Mirbat.

In addition to recruiting new blood and evolving new and unique training techniques, the Regiment also took delivery of new equipment. In the early 1960s, the first specialist Land Rover aimed at meeting the specific requirements of the SAS was developed. The Regiment decided to paint its new vehicles pink after learning that an old aircraft shot down during the Second World War had been found in the desert and the wind-blown sand had burnished it pink.

The 'Pinky' or 'Pink Panther' was a cab-less, door-less, long wheelbase vehicle that held a crew of three, including the driver, a front-seat passenger and rear gunner. This latter crewman occupied a small seat fitted between two long-range fuel tanks, which were self-sealing if ruptured by enemy fire, and from which a centre-pivoted General-Purpose Machine Gun (GPMG) could be fired. The drop-down tailgate was used for storing the crew's bergens and other necessary equipment, and the vehicle was fitted with sand channels, which hooked on both sides of the main body, as well as two rifle boots, fixed for easy access over the front wheel arches. The vehicle was fitted with four banks of three smoke dischargers: two on the front bumper and two on the rear superstructure. Other additional items included spotlights, astro-navigation equipment and vehicle camouflage nets. The original Pink Panthers suffered many problems, not least the underpowered engine and weak half-shafts, which had a tendency to break in the most isolated patch of desert. However, they survived until the mid-1980s, when the new Land Rover 110 replaced them.

On the political front, Britain faced two areas of possible confrontation: Aden and Borneo. Aden had been under British rule since 1839. By 1963, it had joined the British-governed Federation of South Arabia (FSA), originally set up in 1959 as an amalgamation of several small states, emirates and sultanates. Aden joined the FSA on the stipulation that Britain would maintain a presence there after full independence, scheduled for 1968 or before.

However, the Soviet Union had thrown its weight behind unrest in neighbouring Yemen, leading to the overthrow of the ruling Imam in a military coup instigated by Colonel Abdullah Sallal on 26 September 1962. Sallal, who also had the backing of President Nasser of Egypt, declared the Yemen an Arab Republic. Yemen claimed territory in the lands held by the FSA and supported two resistance groups in the Aden Protectorate: the National Liberation Front (NLF) and the Front for the Liberation of Occupied South Yemen (FLOSY). The deposed ruler, Imam Mohammed al-Badr, escaped and raised an opposition army, based in the Aden Protectorate, secretly aided by the British and French governments.

As their man on the spot, the British chose an SAS officer called Johnny Cooper, an outstanding soldier who had joined the original SAS as a trooper. In 1959, while commanding A Squadron in Malaya (see page 67), he had been badly injured tree jumping into the jungle: withdrawn from Malaya, he was transferred to Oman, where he took up a position as second-in-command of the Omani Muscat Regiment. In June 1963, an eight-man party consisting of French and SAS troops and led by Cooper made an RV with royalist forces near Sana. The group included three members of 22 SAS – Sergeant Dorman, Corporal Chigley and Trooper Richardson – who trained the royalist tribesmen, arranged for them to be supplied with weapons by air and gathered intelligence, which confirmed Sallal's reliance on Egyptian aid.

After three months the group was ordered to leave the country, but Cooper returned to assimilate more intelligence and to arrange further airdrops to the royalists. He continued to work alone in this way for a further 11 months, although prior to the airdrops he was joined by two SAS men, Cyril Weavers and David Ailey. Cooper spent a total of three years in North Yemen, gathering information on Egyptian forces and training royalist soldiers. The nine airdrops were carried out by the Israeli Air Force – a fact entirely unbeknown to the Arab guerrillas. In 1963, in response to calls for assistance, Britain intervened with military aid. Cooper's solitary mission in Yemen was finally completed in 1966.

Borneo

Around the same time, but thousands of miles away, trouble was once more brewing in the Malayan archipelago. Initially, the focus of the problem was the Sultanate of Brunei, a former British Protectorate tucked away in the north-west corner of the island of Borneo and sandwiched between the Malaysian states of Sarawak and Sabah.

Malaysia was seeking to bring together Singapore, Sabah, Sarawak, the Sultanate of Brunei and itself under the banner of the Federation of Malaya – an idea fully supported by Britain. However, the Indonesian President, Sukarno, vehemently opposed the move, as it threatened his own designs on the rest of Borneo. In 1962, a small anti-Malaysian element rebelled in Brunei, with the backing of Malaysia. It was led by Sheikh Azahari, who planned to become Prime Minister of Brunei, Sarawak and Sabah, an area he wanted to unite and call North Kalimantan. The revolt did not last long – it was crushed within eight days by British troops brought in from Singapore.

However, by the following year the situation in Borneo had deteriorated again, with well-trained Indonesian insurgents infiltrating over the border from the Kalimantan region. In response, Britain raised a force of Malaysian, Commonwealth and British troops, including the SAS, to deal with the situation. Unfortunately, the force was only a small one and the border stretched for 700 miles. Not only did they face a threat from the Indonesians, but also from an internal terrorist element, the Clandestine Communist Organization (CCO), made up mainly of Chinese settlers from Sarawak.

The British commander in Borneo, Major-General Walter Walker, initially wanted the SAS to parachute into the jungle, as they had in Malaya, and recapture any helicopter landing areas that had fallen into rebel hands. The CO of 22 SAS at the time, Lieutenant-Colonel John Woodhouse, remembering the high casualty rate from tree jumping in Malaya, persuaded Walker that the SAS would be better suited to patrolling the border instead.

At the time, A Squadron consisted of only 70 men, a small number to patrol such a long stretch of border, especially in such hostile jungle conditions. However, by operating in 21 patrols of two or three men and staying in the jungle for long periods of time, they were able to provide early warning of any Indonesian military or communist incursions. As well as patrolling the border, the SAS took on another very important task – that of winning the 'hearts and minds' of the native people. By gaining an understanding of their lifestyle and language, by living with them and dispensing medical aid when necessary, the SAS gained important allies in intelligence gathering. The local people, who still crossed the border freely into Kalimantan to trade their goods, often brought back valuable information on Indonesian troop movements.

The SAS also recruited some of the local people as Border Scouts. Their role was primarily one of gathering intelligence, as they proved unsuited to a conventional combat role. In September 1963, a Scout post at Long Jawi, 28 miles from the border, was all but wiped out by a substantial group of well-equipped Indonesians. As a result, Walker restricted the Scouts to intelligence-gathering only. It was in this capacity that they really proved their worth to the SAS, frequently complementing individual SAS patrols by facilitating communication between the forces and the native inhabitants.

From 1964 onwards, the SAS recruited and trained a number of local people into what was to become the Cross-Border Scouts. This force consisted of 40 specially selected Iban Dyaks, who took part in raids across the border into Kalimantan. The British believed the Ibans would be highly skilled at moving quietly and efficiently through the jungle and, in the event that a mission was unsuccessful, the Ibans would be the most likely to escape alive. Under the supervision of Major John Edwards of A Squadron, 22 SAS, training began in the summer of 1964. The Scouts' first mission was in August, following which they were employed along the border, especially in western Sarawak and around Bemban.

Claret Operations

In mid-1964, the Malaysian and British governments approved a request by the Director of Borneo Operations, Major-General Walker, for permission to conduct cross-border operations during the Indonesia-Malaysia confrontation in order to pre-empt anticipated or suspected Indonesian attacks. Initially, the maximum distance from the border for these operations was limited to three miles, but later the same year it was increased to 11 miles for a small number of specific operations. These operations, code named Claret, were conducted between July 1964 and July 1966 from East Malaysia (Sarawak and Sabah), crossing the border into Kalimantan, the Indonesian part of the island of Borneo. The plan was to close the Indonesian forces down, who were being directed from their base at Kalimantan, and stop them having a free hand to attack where they wanted to and when. To stop any escalation in what was essentially a local conflict, while at the same time stopping the Indonesian's claiming 'Imperial aggression', Claret operations remained top secret and no publicity was allowed. Any casualties caused by enemy actions were publicly reported as being from East Malaysia.

One of the main tactics used by the SAS during this conflict was ambush, and it proved highly successful. The operations varied in size from four-man Special Forces reconnaissance patrols to infantry fighting patrols in company strength. All operations that involved crossing the border were considered to be of 'plausible deniability' in order to avoid accusations of violating a sovereign state. The operation was a great success for both British and Commonwealth forces, achieving almost all of its objectives.

The troops involved comprised A Squadron and D Squadron, 22 SAS and the Guards Independent Parachute Company – the latter assigned due to a manpower crisis in the SAS. It was decided that the Guards Independent Parachute Company would be trained in SAS jungle tactics. Initially used for border surveillance, in September 1965, the Company, under Major L. G. S. Head, was allowed to carry out cross-border operations. It achieved excellent results, in one instance ambushing 40 Indonesian soldiers, killing nine and wounding many others. In 1965, several members who had served with the SAS in Borneo were chosen to form the backbone of G Squadron SAS. Other units used during Claret operations were the Gurkha Independent Parachute Company, 1 Squadron and 2 Squadron of the Australian SAS Regiment, and detachments of the 1st Ranger Squadron, NZSAS. In addition, 1 and 2 Special Boat Sections, Royal Marines, carried out small-scale raids on coastal targets on either flank.

The Australian Special Air Service Regiment (SASR) was formed on 4 September 1964 with 15 officers and 209 other ranks. Initially, it comprised a headquarters consisting of three officers and 37 other ranks, and two Sabre squadrons (designated 1 and 2, respectively), each of which comprised six officers and 86 other ranks. Each squadron consisted of a headquarters and three troops, each of the latter numbering twenty-one, including all ranks. In December 1964, a headquarters squadron was added to the Regiment's establishment and the strength of each squadron was increased by one troop. Shortly afterwards, authorization was given for the raising of two further squadrons, to be formed by December 1965 and June 1966, respectively. During the period from February 1965 to July 1966, 1, 2 and 3 squadrons saw action in Borneo, where they came under the command of 22 SAS. SASR also participated in cross-border Claret operations.

Typically, these operations consisted of interdiction of tracks, rivers and other routes being used by Indonesian troops, who were mainly well-trained regulars of the Indonesian National Army, the Tentera Nasional Indonesia (TNI). These included para-commandos of the Resemeu Para Kommando Angaton Daret (RPKAD) and marine commandos of the Korps Kommando Operasi (KKO). More than 22,000 TNI troops were deployed in the border areas, supported by large numbers of volunteer irregular forces.

The conduct of Claret operations was governed by a set of regulations laid down by Major-General Walker and known as the 'Golden Rules'. These stipulated that all operations had to be authorized by the Director of Borneo Operations personally and that every operation had to be meticulously planned, rehearsed and carried out with maximum security. They were only permitted to use tried and tested troops, and under no circumstances were troops to be captured, dead or alive, by the enemy. All operations were to be carried out with the aim of deterring and thwarting aggression by the Indonesians. Furthermore, the depth of penetration from the border was to be strictly controlled, and it was emphasized that air support could not be given except in instances of extreme emergency. Artillery and mortar support was, however, available on call with 5.5-inch guns, 4-inch pack howitzers or 3-inch mortars being lifted forward, singly or in pairs, by helicopter to bases on the border in support of specific operations.

During the winter of 1964–65, patrols by B Squadron were concentrated in the Pueh range of hills of western Sarawak, a favourite route for CCO agents on their way to Lundu, where a number of communist cells were located.

Captain Robin Letts

Perhaps Captain Robert Letts was not everyone's idea of an SAS hero, being self-effacing, shy, short-sighted and a great lover of books and music, but he nevertheless showed great initiative and bravery during the Borneo confrontation. In April 1965, he was put in charge of a patrol detailed with collecting intelligence on Indonesian communication routes across the border. The rest of his patrol consisted of Corporal 'Taff' Springles – the signaller, medic and soldier with the most experience – Trooper Brown and Trooper Hogg.

Members of B Squadron had already mapped out the area in question, mostly consisting of swamp, making navigation easier for Letts and his men. Nevertheless, the going was slow, as they were trying to keep their movements quiet. After six days of living in mud and water, the sound of an outboard motor drew them to a 12-foot-wide stream, one of the main tributaries of the swamp, draining into the river Sentimo. Finding an area of dry land about 40 yards back from the stream, Letts and Hogg took off their bergens and left them with the other two men, intending to do a little reconnaissance. To lessen the likelihood of their tracks being spotted by the enemy, they took to the stream, walking and sometimes swimming along it. A short distance downstream they saw a domestic water buffalo and heard voices, a sign that there was a village not far away. Letts realized that their progress through the river had been just a bit too easy: none of the usual debris of underwater logs or vegetation had blocked their way at any point. This could only mean that the waterway was regularly cleared to allow water traffic through. This realization meant that the men had to get out of the stream – and fast. At any moment a boat could come along and they would be sitting ducks.

Rejoining Springles and Brown, they soon found an observation point that was ideal for monitoring traffic on the waterway. It was set on a loop in the stream with clear visibility 60 yards to the left and 30 yards to the right. Late that afternoon their patience was rewarded when two boats, both containing two armed soldiers, paddled past them heading downstream.

Leaving Hogg at the observation point, Letts and the others returned to the lying-up point (LUP) to signal base and ask permission to engage the enemy if the chance was repeated. While they were gone, two more boats unexpectedly appeared. Hogg, who was standing up, still watching after the first two boats, was caught unawares, his head exposed. He feared for his life, thinking that he had been seen, but luckily the two boats, with their unobservant occupants, passed by without incident.

By morning, there had still been no word back from base giving the patrol approval to attack the enemy. Letts decided the opportunity was too great to pass up and that they would act anyway. The stream was obviously more important than it had previously appeared, and probably served as a main supply route for men and equipment to the enemy's forward base at Achan. The village Letts and Hogg had discovered earlier possibly served as a staging point, which meant that any attack would bring swift retaliation.

A plan was drawn up and, at dawn, Letts positioned his men at various positions around the loop. Manoeuvring in the stream at this point seemed to be difficult for the boatmen and required all their concentration, leaving them less alert to the possibility of attack. The layout of the loop also meant that once a boat had passed a certain point it was no longer visible to those following behind, thus creating the perfect conditions for an ambush. With Letts at the apex of the loop, Brown to his left and Springles to his right, the men were ready to take on any boat, no matter from which direction it came. However, as most of the water traffic seemed to be coming from their left, Letts positioned Hogg along that side, too, to give warning of any problems. Letts also worked out an escape route; if his assumption about the village was correct, they would need to get out of the area as quickly as possible.

At 20:15 a boat came into view, but this time it carried three armed soldiers instead of two. The extra man sat in the stern, acting as sentry, alert to any dangers ahead. The next boat was the same: two armed men sitting in the front paddling and another, cradling a weapon, in the rear. This new development upped the stakes.

The first boat passed by Brown, as planned, but the second one managed to crash into the bank right next to him. Luckily,

Above: The SAS used LRDG trucks for transport from late 1941 until early 1942. However, Lieutenant-Colonel David Stirling believed that the SAS should have its own form of transportation, and in July 1941 this materialized in the form of the Willys jeep.

Below: David Stirling talking to Patrol Commander Lieutenant McDonald prior to leaving for a raid.

Above: Many people believe the SAS was entirely British, but this is not so. Here Major General Surtees inspects members of the Belgian SAS.

Below: Major Anders Lassen, one of four SAS soldiers to win the Victoria Cross. Lassen, a Dane, joined the British Army at the beginning of the Second World War. He was killed in 1945, during fighting around Lake Comacchio.

Above: Troops guiding in a helicopter landing in a jungle clearing at Ula Langat, near Kuala Lumpur, November 1957.

Right: An SAS soldier fully kitted for jungle operation. The record for a continuous jungle stay was 103 days.

Below: 'Hearts and minds', a policy originally conceived by General Sir Gerald Templar, the Military High Commissioner in Malaya. Its purpose was to gain local support, thereby obtaining the upper hand in defeating the communist terrorists. It was so successful that the Regiment adopted it in subsequent counter-insurgency campaigns.

Top and Centre: SAS troops in the jungle, including Peter Scholey, around the time of the 1966 Koemba Ambush.

Above: Donald "Lofty" Large (right) (1930–2006), was part of the SAS unit involved in the Koemba Ambush.

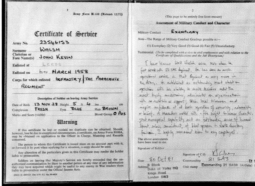

Top left: A very rare photograph of Colin "Paddy" Millikin.

Top right: Peter Scholey (1938–2016) was a 20-year SAS veteran, known as "The Joker".

Above and Right: Kevin Walsh (1938–1986); Walsh's certificate of service, and medals.

Row 1, l to r: Pete "Snapper" Winner ([left] with Firquat tribesmen), Talaiasi "Laba" Labalaba (KIA).
Row 2, l to r: Austin "Fuzz" Hussey, Mike Kealy, Sekonaia "Tak" Takavesi.
Row 3, l to r: Roger Cole, Thomas Tobin (Died of wounds), Bob Bennett.

Above: The movements of a troop on patrol in the Oman desert are traced by Lance Sergeant Ian Smith and Sergeant Peter Harding.

Below: Bob Bennett's medals (left to right): Military Medal, General Service with four clasps, Regular Army. They were sold for £110,00 at auction in 2018.

Above: The 81mm mortar was the mainstay of the SAS defences throughout the war in Oman. This picture illustrates a typical mortar pit which was the first thing to be constructed in any SAS firm base.

Below: A typical BATT patrol in Oman during the early 1970s. Living conditions were little more than a hole in the ground, and conflict with the enemy a daily accordance. The soldier, third from left, suffered terrible injuries from a landmine. He never fully recovered from his injuries and died some years later in Hereford.

the crew was too busy trying to rectify the situation to notice him. As the boat struggled to regain its course, a third boat came into view. As with the others, it also carried three armed soldiers. Eventually, the first boat reached Springles' position and Letts gave the signal to attack. He took aim at his first target – the armed sentry in the second boat – but was surprised when one of the paddlers grabbed his gun with amazing speed and lined Letts up in his sights. At this close range, Letts really had no chance to get out of the way or to change his aim to the man in the bows. It looked as though he was about to be killed when Springles fired at the Indonesian and killed him.

All the patrol members opened up on the boats in a furious hail of fire. During the firefight, the crews of two of the boats managed to flip them over, throwing themselves into the water. Later, it was surmised that this was part of an anti-ambush drill, as some of them soon re-emerged on the bank with their weapons at the ready.

Seeing the boats go over, Letts fired into the water, hoping to hit some of their occupants. At the same time, the only man remaining alive in the second boat managed to take aim at Letts. The Captain realized his predicament, almost too late, and jumped to one side before turning his weapon on the man and firing. The Indonesian fell forward into the boat. For a split second, Letts looked away to see how Brown was coping with his boat, when the man he had just shot seemingly came back from the dead. Although wounded, he raised himself up and took aim at Letts again. Letts reacted quickly and shot him twice. This time the wounds were definitely fatal.

Distracted, Letts had failed to notice that he had become a target for another of the Indonesian soldiers. One of the men from the overturned boat had finally managed to reach the near bank and had immediately taken aim at Letts. Once more, Springles saved his life, shooting the man dead. Instantly, another soldier emerged from the water and made a grab for the dead man's weapon. Of course, he never had a chance and was killed alongside his companion.

Brown had dealt with the occupants of his boat relatively easily, and they all lay dead. A fourth boat now came into view but, as the occupants realized what was happening, they quickly reached the bank and pulled their boat backwards, out of sight. Hogg fired off a few rounds, but the enemy was already gone. The firefight was over; the whole thing had taken only four minutes.

Dead Indonesians littered the water, the bank and the boats. Only one managed to escape the ferocity of the patrol's onslaught.

Letts gave the order to retreat and the patrol made haste to their LUP, picked up their bergens and headed back in the direction of the border. With the Indonesians now alerted to their presence, they knew they had little time before search parties were sent out. The hunters had now become the hunted, and Letts decided that they would have far more chance if they relied on speed rather than concealment. Their extreme fitness served them well, and they managed to cover a great deal of ground before the enemy mortared the ambush position. Apart from speed, the other advantage Letts and his men had was that the Indonesians had no idea how big a force they were up against and, seeing the damage done, probably over-estimated the numbers they were facing. They would therefore have expected a larger force that would be moving more slowly through the jungle, giving Letts' patrol a much-needed head start.

The patrol covered most of the six miles back to the border by the time dusk fell. Springles set up his radio and contacted base to tell them of their success. Before he could do so, he was told that permission had been granted for them to attack the enemy. Luckily for them, the *fait accompli* had worked out well, especially as, in the heat of the moment, they had forgotten that they had still been waiting for that permission to be given. In the morning they continued, and cautiously made their way back over the border. They called for an extraction and were winched out by helicopter through a break in the forest canopy. The helicopter arrived far quicker than usual, much to their surprise, and they had to forego a tasty dinner cooked by Hogg.

Hogg's bad luck didn't end there: while being winched up by the helicopter a jungle vine became tangled around his neck, and he was almost strangled in mid-air and mid-rescue.

Nevertheless, the whole operation had been a complete success, and a few months later Letts was awarded the Military Cross for his part. Shortly afterwards, he joined the Australian SAS so that he could take part in the Vietnam War.

Captain Malcolm McGillivray

After a short break, D Squadron returned to Borneo in May 1965. This time it was commanded by Major Peter de la Billière, who set up a new regimental headquarters in Kuching, the capital of Sarawak. The fading Colonial house had rusting wrought-iron gates bedecked with barbed wire, and was known as the Pea Green House or PGH. D Squadron continued the cross-border raids with the aid of the Gurkhas, but the enemy often proved elusive. The patrols established likely ambush sites and potential helicopter landing zones. They made notes of all the likely places the Indonesians would try to infiltrate, and charted a previously unexplored region known as 'The Gap'. All intelligence collected was relayed back to SAS headquarters on high-frequency radios, where it could be acted upon immediately.

In July 1965, 2 Troop, commanded by Captain Malcolm McGillivray, was given the task of searching Mount Kalimantan for Indonesian units and destroying them. McGillivray had come into the ranks of the SAS via the Black Watch. At first his superiors had not wanted to let him join the SAS, but he managed to persuade them otherwise. First, he completed SAS selection, without permission from his commanding officer to do so. Then, when his regiment persisted in its reluctance, he showed his displeasure by eating nothing but porridge, day after day. Finally, his fellow officers could stand his obstinate protest no more and agreed to let him go. His qualities soon served him well in the SAS.

His team consisted of 10 SAS soldiers, including Corporal Roberts and troopers Franks, Henry, Bilbao, Condie, Callan and Shipley, as well as 21 Scouts recruited from local tribes. Air reconnaissance photographs showed that there were a number of huts high up on the mountain, situated in a clearing. Regarding this as a good target, McGillivray had a full-size replica of the huts built and made his team practise an assault on them again and again until he was convinced they had it right.

Preparation complete, McGillivray and his men set out on 9 July 1965, crossing the river Bemban and trekking up through the foothills. This first part of the journey took five days. On the sixth day, McGillivray split the men into six patrols to search the area for any signs of enemy occupation. At first, the intelligence on which they had been working seemed to be right on target, as a patrol of Scouts returned with the news that they had found bootprints and could smell cooking. After a long conversation, made more difficult by the language barrier, McGillivray finally worked out where the enemy force was likely to be found. He gathered his team together again and they set off. Unfortunately, by the time they reached the place where the Scouts had found the camp, there was no sign of it; every evidence of human occupation, if there had been any, had been removed. Either the enemy was very clever or else all their intelligence had been wrong and the Scouts had imagined what they saw and the aromas. McGillivray looked about him at the landmarks he had memorized from the photographs and other intelligence, and found that they matched what he saw in the surrounding landscape. This was definitely the place, but minus the camp.

No matter how hard they searched, the camp could not be found. However, they were near to a track that was obviously used by the CCO as a supply route to Batu Hitam. At least they should be able to mount an ambush on any Indonesian troops who came their way. After a spot of reconnaissance, McGillivray decided the best ambush point was at a gully just north-west of the river, spanned by a large log. On the north side, where they were, the ground levelled out to provide a broad, flat space, good enough to fire across from the safety of cover. Anyone trapped on the log when the shooting began didn't stand much of a chance.

McGillivray usually worked with his signaller, 'Rover' Slater. Together, they argued every decision, and although it seemed sometimes that they were always at odds with each other, in fact they managed to work as a team in some strange, antagonistic way: no idea went unchallenged and no possibility was left unexplored.

McGillivray took Slater and two others with him to keep watch on this point. A group of locals appeared, carrying heavy bundles, and crossed over the gully using the log. Convinced now that this was definitely the place for the ambush, McGillivray sent the two other men back to round up the rest of the team while he stayed at the point with Slater. Shortly afterwards, a group of about 11 armed enemy soldiers came into view. However, at such close range and with such odds, it was deemed unwise to take them on.

The rest of McGillivray's men arrived and deployed initially to the LUP, where he and Slater met up with them. He selected 15 men, including Corporal Roberts, to form the first watch. This group was divided into three separate sections, each with a different responsibility during any attack. The men were all then placed individually in one long line 5–20 yards away from the track. The 'killer' team, consisting of Roberts, Franks, Nibau and three Scouts, was placed alongside the log. The group on the right-hand side, consisting of Condie, Callan, Shipley and three Scouts, was responsible for keeping watch for the enemy's approach and informing the others by pulling a cord, which ran down the line. They were also charged with stopping any escapees and warning of the likelihood of a counter-attack. The left-hand group assumed a similar role to the right.

It was the afternoon by now, and no one expected the enemy to return before dusk, so McGillivray carried on with his preparations. Back at the RV area, he decided he was not happy with the position he had picked and so had the men move the bergens to a new place. As usual, Slater pointed out the downside – that the ambush party would not know where to retreat to and, even if they were told, they still might not be able to find it in all the confusion after a contact. However, McGillivray was not unduly worried; he felt he had plenty of time to change the watch over and ensure all the men were fully aware of the new RV location.

An hour later it began to rain heavily, the storm creating difficult conditions for the watchers. Then, halfway through the afternoon, without warning, the soldiers who had passed through before returned. They were obviously wet and uncomfortable, as they travelled at a very quick pace. Nevertheless, they were spotted by Shipley, sitting out on the right flank, who gave five tugs on the cord. The message was passed down the line in the same fashion until it reached Roberts, who alerted his men just as five of the soldiers stepped on to the log. The 'killer' group took aim and fired, sending the Indonesians tumbling into the gully below. Roberts, thinking that all had been killed, gave the order to stop firing. Bilbao, however, spotted one of them trying to crawl away and let off two more rounds to stop him, as he had been previously instructed.

However, the five soldiers killed on the log were only a part of the group, as the men on the right flank were about to find out. Alerted by the gunfire, a second enemy group disappeared into cover next to the track and let loose with rifle and machine gun fire towards the ambushers. It looked as though they were about to storm the position of the right-flank group. Condie, who was a little further back, called out to them to fall back to his position. Shipley, Callan and their Scouts needed no second urging and retreated. Realizing that the area of ground to the rear provided good cover from the enemy's fire, they ran to it – but in the process completely missed Condie, who had taken it upon himself to move forward to see if they had got away and not been wounded or killed. Once Shipley and Callan reached the dead ground they continued on to the old RV point – standard procedure after a contact – expecting to find others. Of course, due to McGillivray's move, they were the only ones there – a fact which caused them great frustration.

McGillivray was also feeling frustrated by Standard Operating Procedures (SOP). They prohibited him from joining the action, although at such close quarters he could hear it going on. Slater, still at his side, reminded him that the ambush party still knew nothing about the relocation of the rendezvous point. Stirred into action again, McGillivray ordered two of his Scouts to go to the old location and guide anyone they found there to the new one. Guiding them part of the way there himself, the Captain was suddenly confronted by the first of the Scouts coming back from the ambush. Once again, communication proved a bit of problem, but McGillivray was sure they were saying that Roberts was in trouble. SOP or no, McGillivray decided that he couldn't hang back any longer, and made his way to Roberts' position. In fact, he had understood the Scouts wrongly; the Corporal wasn't hurt at all, and was instead profoundly displeased that his commanding officer had risked going against procedure so recklessly.

The thick jungle cover slowed the battle and, although the gunfire continued from the enemy's position, they did not seem as willing to advance as they had been before. The bodies of two Indonesian soldiers lay under a log close to Roberts' position, but as yet they had not been searched for weapons or papers. McGillivray turned to two Scouts standing nearby and asked them to carry out the task, something they seemed to be only too glad to do. McGillivray then went to all of his men's positions to check that they had retreated safely before retiring himself.

At the new RV location, the group gathered together to prepare for the journey out. The Scouts whom McGillivray had sent to search the bodies returned with not only weapons and papers but also their heads. The British men stared, shocked that the tribesmen still took heads as trophies: they thought the practise had stopped long ago. Even the more hardened soldiers there were taken aback by the grisly sight and the apparent jubilation of the tribesmen. But, although revolted by the practice, McGillivray and his men made no attempt to stop it or to dampen the tribesmen's celebration in any way. It seemed an important thing to the

Iban, which appeared to raise their morale. And, as McGillivray and his men readily recognized, if it raised the Iban's morale, such an act was likely to lower the Indonesians' once they found the headless bodies of their comrades in the jungle. Nevertheless, the headhunting incident would be wonderful news for any hostile propagandists if it got out, so it was decided that the whole event needed to be kept quiet. Throughout his years in the Regiment, despite the rumours, McGillivray always denied having witnessed any headhunting.

In August of the same year, working closely with the Gurkhas, the SAS launched a series of cross-border raids that met with varying degrees of success. The search for an elusive foe often ended in frustration. In September, for example, 12 four-man patrols from A Squadron conducted a three-week search for a CCO camp in the area between the headwaters of the Sempayang and Bemban rivers, but nothing was found.

Geordie and Jock

Training for the SAS is rigorous and demanding, but the skills and techniques paid off for two soldiers towards the end of the Borneo campaign. Sergeant Geordie Lillicoe and Trooper Jock Thomson were both members of D Squadron, 22 SAS, and involved in one of the Regiment's cross-border operations.

Geordie Lillicoe, a very experienced jungle soldier, took part in many of these Claret raids, and on 26 February 1966, he led his patrol into the area of an old Indonesian camp situated close to the border. The patrol moved very slowly and with caution, conscious that it was in Indonesian territory. The camp had been found the day before and appeared to have been out of use for some time. A cursory search that evening had been cut short by the gathering dusk; however, what little information had been gleaned was of great interest. There were bamboo beds, known to the SAS as 'bashas'; these have no roofs, the latter being provided by a soldier's poncho. Some rusted tins confirmed the camp's military nature: their labels showed they were Indonesian Army rations.

The patrol, eight in number, had withdrawn for the night to the slopes of Gunong Rawan, where they 'bashered up' for the night and Lillicoe reviewed the orders given him by his squadron commander, Major Roger Woodiwiss, in the light of this unexpected discovery. His main task was to watch the river Sekayan, three miles over the border, which was known to be the enemy's main line of communication. The SAS was operating on Indonesian soil and did not wish its presence to become known. Yet another reason for avoiding contact with the enemy was that this was, in part, a training patrol, planned by Woodiwiss for the benefit of several recruits to D Squadron, whose third tour in Borneo was only just beginning. Lillicoe's problem lay not so much with his orders but in having to visit the same place twice, for that would contravene the SOPs. However, few had learned to master the jungle like Lillicoe, and his prime directive was to gather information.

Next morning, Lillicoe decided the camp was worth a second look, but he chose to split his forces. His reasons for doing so were based on clear military thinking. For one thing, the patrol was large enough to be safely divided; in any case, he planned to leave the four new recruits in the relative safety of the overnight camp, which would also serve as the Emergency Rendezvous (ERV). They would act as a rearguard and protect the patrol's bergens, which Lillicoe decided to leave behind.

Dropping their heavy packs would give them greater mobility, and in a firefight the SAS soldier is better off with just his belt kit and rifle.

They made good time, quickly covering the 1,500 yards from the ERV to the camp. Jock Thomson was the first to reach the outskirts of the camp and stopped there, motioning discreetly for the others to do likewise. They waited, listening to the jungle; all seemed quiet, with nothing to raise their suspicions. Thomson turned his head slowly to query Lillicoe; a perceptible nod told him to continue. Ducking under some bamboo laying across the track, he emerged on the other side. There was a soldier with a light automatic weapon no more than 12 yards away to his right. The patrol had walked directly into a well-prepared Indonesian ambush.

Almost immediately, the Indonesian soldier opened fire, and at this signal several more guns opened up on the SAS patrol. Jock Thomson was hit in the first burst, taking a bullet in his left thigh, which shattered the bone. However, the hit knocked him off the track, and he landed in thick bamboo. Here, Jock found himself confronting yet another Indonesian soldier, so close that he could see the tiger's-head shoulder flash of the man's unit. The soldier was very young and extremely scared; he seemed to be having trouble with his rifle. Jock, who had recovered from the initial shock of his wound, found the Armalite rifle he had dropped and shot the young soldier. He then crawled clear of the immediate danger zone. The sight of bright blood pumping from his thigh made him want to stop, but he knew that if he did not clear the ambush area a second and then a third bullet would find him. Therefore, with the lifeblood flowing from him, he crawled into the thick bush. Although not out of immediate danger, Jock felt it was safe enough to dress his wound and stop the bleeding. The pieces of his shattered femur jarred together as he did so, causing excruciating pain, which he dulled by injecting himself with morphine – in action, every member of the SAS carries two pre-loaded syringes, operated simply by squeezing the flexible container. While he was doing so, the gunfire died down to a few sporadic shots, but even so Jock felt it necessary to keep his senses about him by constantly surveying the situation.

A short distance away, he could see Lillicoe, immobile and covered in blood. As patrol commander, he had been immediately behind Thomson, and the initial bursts of fire had hit them both. As Thomson was thrown to the left of the bamboo clump, Lillicoe leapt to the right, firing to his front as he did so. Almost immediately, he was knocked off his feet. Wounded in both legs and unable to get clear, he was forced to return fire while sitting in the middle of the track. Despite their injuries, both men continued to lay down suppressive fire while the remaining patrol members 'bugged out'. Then, as quickly as it had begun, the firing stopped. Both men sat waiting for a few moments before they began the painful struggle to get away from the immediate killing zone.

Then Thomson saw a figure stand up and move out into the open. It was an Indonesian soldier coming out to check the killing area – a serious error of judgement. Thomson and Lillicoe fired together. Once more, the area fell quiet. This time, the two exchanged words, telling each other of their injuries, and Thomson struggled to his feet and came forward to give Lillicoe covering fire. Seeing Thomson and thinking he could walk, Lillicoe called out to him to fetch the rest of the patrol. Thomson shouted back that he was hit, but would try to make it back up the ridge, where he could RV with the others. After covering several yards, he fired several bursts into the area where the Indonesians had been waiting. This fresh gunfire from an elevated position led the enemy to believe that reinforcements had entered the area, and for a while they withdrew. The remainder of the SAS patrol had decided that the best course of action was to move to the nearest infantry post, which was close by, and lead back a stronger party to search the area. This they did, starting back towards the scene of the contact late the same day.

As soon as he felt it safe to do so, Thomson applied a fresh field dressing to his wound and injected himself with his second morphine syringe. Then, very slowly, he continued crawling towards the ridgeline above him. Darkness fell and gave him some protection; to provide camouflage, he settled down in the mud of a pig-hole to wait out the night.

By morning on the second day, Thomson had managed to cover half the distance back to the infantry camp, firing single shots to attract the attention of any search party. He finally reached the RV, where he was discovered by a Gurkha patrol, which had been sent to look for the wounded men. Extremely weak from loss of blood, he required immediate medical attention.

Geordie Lillicoe had also managed to extract himself and hide in the nearby bamboo. There, he too dressed his wound and gave himself morphine. The left leg felt numb and detached; there was no sensation in it. His right leg he could feel, although it would not support him. Everywhere, there was too much blood. A bullet had entered his left leg a little below the thigh and exited by blowing a huge hole through his backside. The lack of pain was because a major nerve had been severed but, luckily, the main artery was undamaged. Bandaging the entry point was easy, but trying to stem the bleeding from his buttock proved an ordeal. These wounds to his legs made it almost impossible to move, but he was able to conceal himself for the night beneath the trunk of a fallen tree. He had lost a tremendous amount of blood, and after a while lapsed into unconsciousness. It was daylight when he recovered, and he could hear Indonesian soldiers all around him. One of the enemy had climbed a tree about 40 yards away and remained there for about half an hour, in full view, scanning the jungle. By this time, a helicopter was airborne, searching for Lillicoe; he could hear it, but with the enemy so near, he was reluctant to activate his Surface-to-air Rescue Beacons (SARBE). It was only when he was certain he would not be detected that he risked using the survival radio, calling in a helicopter, which managed to winch him out.

Both men survived their ordeal, recovered from their wounds and were fit enough to continue serving in the SAS. Geordie Lillicoe, who was awarded the Military Medal, is one of the longest-serving members of 22 SAS and very much respected for his dedication to training, especially in SAS techniques.

The Koemba Ambush

Although one of the Regiment's greatest actions, the Koemba Ambush largely goes unnoticed, having been overshadowed over the years by many other famous SAS actions. The operation was part of Claret operations and took place in September

1966. Having discovered that Indonesian forces were being supplied by shipping along the river Koemba, it was decided to send a four-man patrol into the jungle to attack these lines of communication and either stop or disrupt it. By now, the SAS had been involved in deniable incursions into Indonesia for some time. Four were men selected for the operation.

Sergeant Donald 'Lofty' Large, a legend within the Regiment, was the patrol commander (the Lofty nickname came from his height, being almost six feet six inches tall). He was serving with the Gloucestershire Regiment during the Korean War when he was wounded in the shoulder and made prisoner of war during the Battle of the Imjin River. He survived a ten-day forced march into captivity, where he remained for two years. While there, it was discovered he had been shot not once but twice, and had a further eighteen pieces of shrapnel in his body. During his time as a prisoner, he also suffered from beriberi and dysentery. Eventually in March 1953 a Chinese doctor attended him and removed a tracer round from his ribcage. He lived with the second round inside him for the rest of his life. He was finally repatriated during a prisoner exchange. By then his weight had dropped by a third and he had limited movement in his left arm. However, in 1957, having worked hard to recover his fitness and injuries, he passed selection for the SAS. He went on to serve in Malaya, Oman and Aden.

Peter (the Joker) Scholey was another SAS legend and much-loved member of the SAS Regiment. He did his National Service with the Royal Artillery and later the Royal Army Service Corps (RASC) during the mid-1950s. He left the army but rejoined almost at once, signing up this time for the Parachute Regiment. In August 1963, Peter passed selection into the SAS in Hereford. He served in Aden, Oman, Malaya, Borneo. Despite being the Regimental comedian, Peter was also a fine and capable soldier. He served with the Regiment for 23 years, helping to establish the counter-terrorist team that was successfully used in the siege of the Iranian Embassy in 1980 during that time.

John Kevin 'the Airborne Wart' Walsh, or Kevin as he preferred to be known, joined the 1st Battalion the Parachute Regiment in Leeds on 13 November 1958. He was first posted to Cyprus and saw action against the Greek Nationalists organization EOKA. After passing selection in October 1965, he went on to serve in Aden, Dhofar, Northern Ireland. He was a tough, resourceful soldier, as anyone that served with him will tell you. Kevin went on to reach the rank of Warrant Officer Second Class and Squadron Sergeant Major, seeing service with both B Squadron and D Squadron. It was part of 18 Troop, D Squadron serving in Borneo that he was to be selected to be part of the troop to take part in the Koemba Ambush.

Colin Maurice 'Paddy' Millikin was probably the most gifted signaller within the ranks of the SAS at the time. If no one else could get a signal, Colin would, which made him first choice with most patrols into the jungle. He was a member of 264 SAS signals and saw action in many theatres. He also completed selection successfully, which not all signallers do; if you're considered a good enough signaller, you are kept on the SAS strength anyway.

As part of 18 Troop, D Squadron SAS, these four men formed a patrol that was to go down in SAS history as probably the most effective of the campaign. It started at the beginning of September 1965 and was detailed to last approximately two weeks. The objective of the patrol was to penetrate deep into enemy territory and attack shipping on the river Koemba, which was supplying the Indonesian forces with arms and equipment. It was a daunting task and involved cutting their way through dense jungle and crossing dangerous swamps, while being careful not to be ambushed themselves. After a long and arduous journey, the patrol finally reached their objective on the bank of the Koemba, the first patrol ever to have reached it. Establishing camp, the patrol began to wait and watch, remaining in position for four days. Peter Scholey, in his book *The Joker: 20 Years Inside the SAS*, takes up the story: 'We didn't have to wait long – the river was obviously a major thoroughfare

– and there was evidently a military camp within a kilometre of us, given the number of transports that chugged past us…'

All this intelligence was collated and relayed to the operations room. Lofty finally decided that they had seen enough and began to plan the bug out. Before he did this, however, he needed to carry out the next part of the mission: to attack and destroy shipping and supplies travelling along the river. After permission was given, Lofty planned the ambush. The attack was to take place an hour before dusk. After waiting some while for a target, a boat finally came into view. Peter Scholey takes up the story once again: 'As we watched, this gleaming 15-metre boat slowly slid past us, flying the Indonesian flag and a number of military pennants…' The patrol waited for Lofty to commence the attack but, much to the others' surprise, he didn't. Kevin Walsh was so frustrated that he was heard to mutter, 'What are we waiting for? The fucking Ark Royal?' What Kevin didn't know was that Lofty had spotted that the boat contained at least one woman and there might have been many more. He refused to fire on civilians. What Lofty didn't realize at the time was that the boat also contained Colonel Leonardus Moerdani, Commander of the Indonesian Special Forces in the area (he was later Commander-in-Chief of the Indonesian Army and Indonesian Minister of Defence and Security). Later, Lofty commented:

'There could have been other women and there could have been children on the boat. And we don't do that sort of target, so…it went. And it was in fact the very man we'd been looking for, for three months: Colonel Moerdani of the Indonesian para-commando unit and he was on the end of my rifle and I let him go – but…you can't blast women and kids.'

As the wait continued, a thunderstorm broke overhead and the area was saturated with a heavy downfall of rain. Their patience paid off as a second and even larger boat came into sight. Peter Scholey described it as being much more functional in appearance with a built-in diesel engine.

As the boat passed the patrol, they could see it was full of soldiers and several 40-gallon tanks of fuel. The patrol opened up with everything they had. Peter Scholey described the event, writing: 'Lofty fired off the first shots, taking out two Indos sitting at the back of the launch...keeping up a steady rate of fire into the passenger area'. At the time the SAS's main weapon was the 7.62mm SLR, which had an impressive stopping power. The fire was both powerful and intense and no return fire was received; it was all over very quickly. As the patrol bugged out, the boat finally exploded. After an adventurous few days the small patrol were picked up by helicopter and returned to base. The following night they were back in the old mansion in Kuching in Sarawak, which was used as the D Squadron headquarters.

The patrol had been an enormous success and would go down in SAS history as a classic example of the Regiment's abilities in jungle warfare. For his service in Borneo, Lofty Large was later mentioned in despatches.

Interestingly, 12 years after the ambush, Colonel Moerdani, who became a politician and was working in London, asked to meet the last two members of the SAS still serving with the Regiment, Peter Scholey and Kevin Walsh. He had been on the first boat that passed the patrol's ambush position and because of the presence of civilians wasn't fired on. The two men were duly dispatched to meet Moerdani. They were introduced to the colonel, who greeted them warmly and congratulated them on a brilliant tactical operation. After chatting cheerfully for some time the last thing the colonel said to them was, 'Thank you for letting me live'. He was luckier than many.

Claret operations ceased on 23 March 1966, just 11 days after the overthrow of Indonesia's President Sukarno by General Suharto. In the main, they had achieved their aim of keeping the Indonesians off balance, although early operations achieved only limited success. Within Indonesia, all publicity about setbacks caused by Claret raids had been suppressed, principally because of the embarrassment to President Sukarno, who had promised his people that Malaysia would be crushed by 1 January 1965.

The campaign in Borneo is an outstanding example of the tenacity, resourcefulness and skill of the individual SAS soldier. It illustrated what a small number of properly trained and well-motivated men can achieve. General Walker himself stated: 'I regard 70 troopers of the SAS as being as valuable to me as 700 infantry in the role of "hearts and minds", border surveillance, early warning, stay-behind and eyes and ears with a sting.'

Aden

The Radfan is a highly mountainous area in the northern district of the Republic of Yemen. When Britain became involved in Aden during the 1960s, her forces suffered many attacks by local tribespeople trained and armed by the Egyptians. In response, the British planned an advance into the Radfan Mountains to defuse the tension with these tribes and to try to discourage them from mining the Dhala road, which was then under construction.

The force set up to re-establish British control in the area was code named Radforce. The main thrust into the mountains would be made by A Squadron of 22 SAS, which had recently arrived in the region and established a base at Thumier, 30 miles from the Yemeni border, with the aim of seizing a rocky feature code named 'Cap Badge' overlooking the dissidents' main stronghold of Danaba.

The operation was set for 29–30 April 1964. The approach to Danaba was to be made by 45 Commando via the Wadi Boran, while at the same time 3 Troop of A Squadron was to take 'Cap Badge'. Once cleared, it was to be used as a drop zone for airborne troops from the Parachute Regiment. Commanded by Captain Robin Edwards, 3 Troop was to be taken some of the way by armoured car, continuing the journey on foot.

Edwards and his men were tough, experienced soldiers, used to fighting in the harsh environments of Borneo and Malaya. Even so, they found progress slow in the rough, rocky terrain.

To make matters worse, Edward's signaller, Trooper Terry Warburton, was suffering from severe stomach cramps, and they had to pause every now and then to allow him to catch up.

At about midnight, Edwards realized that at the rate they were travelling they would not reach their objective before daylight, and he made the decision to halt and seek shelter. Nearby were two old rock-built sangars, and Edwards decided that they should spend the rest of the night and the following day holed up there to allow Warburton time to recover. They radioed the SAS squadron commander, informed him of the situation and then settled down for a long wait. The following morning, a goatherd discovered their position. Fearing he would run off and tell the rebels where they were, they killed him. Unfortunately, the shot was heard in the nearby village of Shab Tem and very soon rebel tribesmen surrounded them. A long-range sniping battle broke out, with the rebels soon becoming bolder, climbing the slopes and coming ever nearer to the sangars. The position was out of reach of the artillery, but Edwards managed to call in air support in the form of Hunter aircraft of both 43 Squadron and 208 Squadron. The aircraft held the rebels off for some time, but eventually they had to return to base, leaving Edwards and his men unprotected. Rescue plans were put forward and considered at the SAS base in Thumier, but in the end it was considered too risky to send in another patrol.

Edwards and his men were now on their own, facing an enemy that outnumbered them by eight to one. Deciding to make a break for it, Warburton sent a signal to say they were moving off. Then the radio went dead. Edwards rushed to his signaller's position to find that he had been killed by a single shot to the head.

Leaving Warburton's body where it had fallen, the patrol moved off, hoping to outmanoeuvre the gunmen. They had not gone far when a savage barrage of fire swept their position. Edwards was hit several times and died instantly. During the escape, two more men were also hit, both in the legs. The position was now desperate. Corporal Paddy Baker took command

and the patrol, moving slowly because of the injured men, managed to clear the immediate danger area.

The tribesmen, now confident of victory, moved forward and found the bodies of Warburton and Edwards. They then set off after the others. Baker, knowing the patrol couldn't hope to outrun its pursuers, set its slowest members, the two wounded soldiers, to wait in ambush. As the first rebels appeared, they ran into the trap and were shot dead. This tactic was repeated a number of times, until the rebels thought it prudent to halt the pursuit. Finally, the remnants of the patrol made it back to the Dhala road, where they were picked up by armoured cars and taken safely back to base. The Edwards patrol was soon to become a major news story. Some days later, a report filtered into Aden that the heads of two English soldiers had been displayed impaled on stakes in the main square of Taiz, a rebel stronghold in Yemen. This was confirmed when a British Army patrol reached the area where Edwards and his men had made their stand and found two headless bodies buried in a shallow grave. The bodies were recovered and reburied with full military honours.

Subsequent SAS operations tended to concentrate on establishing covert Observation Posts (OPs) and gathering intelligence about the enemy. These tasks were carried out by members of A, B and D squadrons, who were rotated from operations in Borneo. As the date for British withdrawal neared, enemy activity intensified and the SAS became increasingly worried about a possible attack on its base at Thumier.

Meanwhile, a different kind of war was being fought in the port of Aden itself. The terrorists of the National Liberation Front were operating within the town and the SAS found themselves caught up in counter-terrorism activity. From their base at Ballycastle House, an old married quarters building close to Aden's airport, which had been assigned to the SAS and served as an accommodation and operations centre, a group of 20 men who could pass themselves off as Arabs were busy infiltrating the Crater and Sheikh Othman districts. These operations were known as 'Keeni-Meeni', which is a Swahili word meaning 'snake in the grass'. These covert operations were dangerous but proved well-suited to the men of the Regiment, especially the Fijians, who were able to pass as Arabs more easily. Some of the techniques learned on 'Keeni-Meeni' operations were later applied to other counter-insurgency work.

Despite the manpower, time, hardship and lives invested in Aden, it was a lost cause. On 26 June 1967, Radfan was handed over to the Federal Regular Army and the British Army pulled out, having gained nothing. However, the SAS had at least developed some new and important skills in the art of counter-insurgency.

The British forces preparing to leave consisted not only of the military units scattered around the city of Aden itself, but outlying stations and individuals. Information came in that a large enemy force was about to attack a large and important RAF base used as a refuelling station for aircraft operating throughout the Middle and Far East, where at this time the British military presence was still vast. As the camp's 200 or so inhabitants made ready for the withdrawal, the SAS carried out reconnaissance in the area. Mobility Troop of the newly formed G Squadron made several long-range patrols, but no sign of an enemy was observed. A trooper from G Squadron Mountain Troop, who was sent to evacuate the airbase, recounts the story:

'Two weeks into the baby-sitting role, at 16:00 one afternoon, a "Flash" signal was received by the base commander. The camp was to be abandoned. All documents were to be destroyed; only personnel would be extracted; the camp was not to be destroyed. For the SAS, it was a period of planning. They had received separate orders to extract several VIPs from three separate locations. This was a very simple task: two locations would be evacuated by chopper and one by Mobility Troop using Land Rovers. There was to be no move before 10:00 next morning, so once the tasks had been assigned and kit made ready, most of the men went to the local Navy, Army, and Air force Institutes (NAAFI). As everyone tucked into free drink, the NAAFI manager auctioned off all the saleable stock; it was either that or leave it behind. Cameras and expensive hi-fi equipment were being sold to the highest bidder, in most cases for nothing more than a few pounds. There was also a farewell party, where most people dressed up in white sheets pretending to be Arabs.'

The next morning the camp was a hive of activity; several aircraft had already arrived and some RAF personnel were already being loaded. On the main parade ground, several bins containing military documents were being destroyed with magnesium bombs. By 10:00 a Wessex helicopter had arrived and an eight-man SAS team took off. A soldier on this extraction takes up the story:

'The two men we were tasked with extracting worked with the Foreign Office (FO). They were stationed in a town 30 miles to the north of the base. Upon arrival, the town seemed fairly quiet, but in this remote region a helicopter was a bit of a novelty. We were dropped off on the roof and, leaving two guys to keep an eye on the local crowd, made our way down into the courtyard. The two FO guys must have been there for a long time, and by the amount of gin stored in the cellar had intended to stay there a lot longer. Although they had received a message telling them about the withdrawal, they had done no packing or preparation. They fussed around like two old queens, but getting nowhere. After about an hour, the two SAS guys on the roof reported that the locals were getting restless, and that a crowd was gathering. In the end we just grabbed the two FO guys and dragged them to the roof. They did not seem too worried about leaving the documents behind: they were too depressed about leaving their gin.

'Eventually, all the VIPs were rounded up and taken safely to the base, from where they were airlifted to Aden. By 15:00 that afternoon, less than 24 hours after the bug-out order had been received, the camp lay empty – well, the SAS were still there. We had to wait about two hours until an aircraft came back to pick us up. During this time, I explored the deserted camp. The accommodation barracks had been left neat and tidy: rows of metal beds, with the blankets stacked to regulation requirements. The small hospital was the same, the surgery well stocked with pharmaceutical drugs and equipment. The mess-hall tables stood in neat lines, the chairs stacked on top. In the kitchen, the floor was still wet where someone had mopped it for the last time. In the NAAFI yard, pallets of beer sat in the afternoon sun, while the shop looked as if a plague of locusts had been through it. The saddest thing about the whole camp was the fire station. Three red tenders stood side by side: one of them had only been delivered a month prior.

'At last our aircraft arrived and we piled in, leaving the Land Rovers behind. As we rolled down the runway, we passed thousands of 50-gallon fuel drums, all full. We had wanted to destroy them, but the base commander decided against it. Then, as the aircraft made one last circle, we could see several hundred local Arabs racing for the rich pickings that the British had abandoned. I often think about the fire tenders and wonder what happened to them.

'The SAS moved back to Aden and prepared to leave along with the rest of the British Army. However, once the withdrawal had been announced, things got really bad, and the rebels started attacking any British personnel they could find. In the summer of 1967, the town of Crater (named because it sat in the base of an extinct volcano) went ballistic. The rebellious locals killed almost every white man, woman and child that could be found; rumours of terrible atrocities quickly spread. At the time, I was sitting in Ballycastle House, near Khormaksar airport, which served as the SAS operational headquarters. I was sleeping in my room when the order came to move. Like the rest of the troop, I grabbed my belt kit, shouldered my rucksack and grabbed the L42 sniper rifle from the corner of the room. A helicopter was waiting on the pad, and outside the office a small group had assembled where the OC was making his selection. Taking one look at the L42 sniper rifle in my hand, he said, "You on the chopper; all Crater is hostile."

'Minutes later, five others and myself were flying over Jebel Shamsan, a high mountain that looked down over the town of Crater. As the noise of the chopper faded away, Jock Logan, who was senior, put everyone in the picture. It would seem that the rebels really were slaughtering all the whites, and our task was to shoot anyone or anything roaming the streets with a weapon. That included the local town police, who had sided with the rebels. The patrol, which consisted of six members, all troopers, then made its way into a good defensive position overlooking the town. Three of us were armed with sniper rifles and, as things turned out, this was the ideal weapon for the situation, as most targets ranged from 330–650 yards.

'Over the years, most SAS soldiers become used to death, but in those days I was a novice, and totally unprepared for what I saw. The bodies of butchered men, women and children, had been laid out neatly in the street, deliberately allowing any traffic to run over them.

'The patrol settled down and started selecting targets. At one stage several dissidents climbed a short way up the hill and raised a rebel flag. Jock was on his feet, running down the slope, and ripped the flag down. Thereafter the firing started, but some 10 minutes into the exchange of fire, nothing moved on the streets. Next day, Lieutenant-Colonel Mitchell (Mad Mitch), against the advice of the High Commissioner, bravely led the boys of the Argyll and Sutherland Highlanders into Crater and retook the town. Rumour has it that the local police had cleaned up the bodies and placed them all in tea chests before handing them back to the British – but this was never confirmed.'

Once the British withdrawal had been completed, in late 1967, Aden came under the control of the communist-backed People's Democratic Republic of Yemen. It was this regime that backed the overthrow of the Sultan of its neighbour Oman, a conflict in which the SAS also found itself involved.

There was conflict closer to home, too – in fact, within the SAS's own doors. The formation of G Squadron in 1965 had caused ructions in the Regiment. Members of the Guards Independent Parachute Company were drafted in to form the skeleton framework, but this did not go down well with the older-established squadrons, as these new officers and men did not have to go through the ordeal of SAS selection. To make matters worse, the original G Squadron members had a Brigade of Guards blue-red-blue flash behind their winged dagger badge. From early 1966, all ranks entering G Squadron had to complete SAS selection just like any other volunteers, but the animosity continued until the blue-red-blue flash was removed and soldiers other than those from the Guards Brigade began to fill the ranks of G Squadron.

Out of Uniform – CRW

After Aden, the SAS moved back to Britain and for the next few years had no real active role. During this time, much emphasis was put on training and brushing up on individual skills. New departments started to spring up within the Regiment: one such cell was Counter-Revolutionary Warfare (CRW). At first it consisted of little more than one officer and a couple of men sitting in an office at the back of the cookhouse. Their brief was to study the growing terrorist threat and come up with ways of combating the problem. However, CRW continued to grow and soon became the hub of all anti-terrorist training, techniques and methods. All types of surveillance were practised: vehicle, foot and observation methods. Good camera skills were learned by the SAS, as were the means of developing and printing the film; even infrared photography was taught for night work. BG (bodyguard) courses were organized. Round-the-clock VIP protection drills were learned, and men were sent on police high-speed driving courses. It was a time of change, and the number of SAS men turning up for work in civilian clothes increased dramatically.

The SAS came to prominence again when, on 17 September 1967, a dramatic mid-air rescue made the headlines. Sergeant Michael Reeves was an SAS free-fall parachute instructor watching over students at a civilian club to which he belonged – a non-military weekend activity common for SAS free fallers.

The students were still at the stage of jumping using a static line, which clips on to a rail in the aircraft and opens the canopy automatically a few seconds after the jumper's exit. Normally, the static line breaks safely away from the parachute pack: this time, one of the students exited the aircraft but remained attached, dangling at the end of his static line.

Reeves, who was still in the aircraft, ordered the pilot to increase his height (they had previously been at 2,500 feet), and to circle back over the drop zone. While he did so, Reeves – who had on his own free-fall parachute – climbed out of the aircraft and down the line. When he reached the student, he seized the man in a vice-like grip with his legs before cutting through the static line. As both men fell away free, Reeves activated the student's reserve parachute. Satisfied that the student would land safely, he then fell away, getting to a safe distance before operating his own canopy and floating down to safety.

Another highlight of this quiet period was a visit to Hereford by Prince Charles in 1968. His sister, Princess Anne, followed him a few days later, and she enjoyed herself tremendously at a reception in the Sergeants' Mess. Meanwhile in 1969, Trooper Tom McLean made his famous single-handed row across the Atlantic. A most amazing character, he took up the challenge for a bet, used only Army rations and simply rowed his heart out. After 72 days at sea, he hit the coast of Ireland near Blacksod in County Mayo. He repeated the feat in 1982, but this time established another record by crossing the ocean in the smallest vessel, the *Giltspur*, at only 10 feet long.

For the rest of the SAS, however, the enforced inactivity caused many of its members to leave and search for new excitements elsewhere. It was a trying time; however, the departures soon came to a stop once the Oman War got under way.

5

1970s

OMAN TO
NORTHERN IRELAND

T HE ARRIVAL OF 1970 saw little or no change to the inactivity
the Regiment had endured in the late 1960s. The period
of relative peace which had reigned since the end of the
troubles in Aden (1964–67) had not benefitted the Regiment
much. Despite the extensive training activities embarked upon
by the SAS squadrons, many of the younger members had
started to leave, tempted to become highly paid bodyguards or
by more active security jobs. Around this time, Colonel Johnny
Watts took command of the Regiment and struggled to locate
employment for his men. He found it in Oman. It was also a war
the SAS desperately needed. Unfortunately, the minor exodus of
personnel had by now taken many of the best NCOs, although
some of them did return once the Oman War was under way.

The war in Oman (1970–76) stands out as the classic
SAS operation. It was tailor-made to test the basic regimental skills that set the SAS apart from the rest. Both militarily
and politically, the war had far-reaching effects on the whole
of the Middle East. Moreover, the success of the SAS and the
Sultan of Oman's forces helped stabilize the attitudes of many
neighbouring countries, pushing back the tide of communism

which had threatened to engulf the rich oilfields on which the West depends. It offered a challenge that the Regiment eagerly accepted, and it turned out to be a classic counter-insurgency campaign of modern times.

The size of the Omani conflict was small, yet it combined all the elements of modern warfare. Navy, air force and army were all combined with one goal: to win. It cannot be said that the SAS won this war on its own, as much of the fighting was done by the Sultan of Oman's own forces. However, one thing the SAS undeniably did was to bond together the firqat, the Dhofari irregulars. These firqat and the SAS went on to become the leading elements in most battles in the early days. It was the trust between the Dhofaris and the SAS that won the Dhofar war.

The SAS had served in Oman before, during the Jebel Akhdar campaign (1958–59), and now it was back. In the 1970s, the war took place in the south, on a huge mountain massif known as the Jebel Dhofar (the repressive regime of Sultan Said bin Taimur had goaded the Dhofaris into rebellion). It was a strange refuge for wild tribes and 'freedom fighters'. In summer it is a place of great beauty, where lush green grass blows in the cooling winds and trees give homes to birds and other small animals. The problem was the People's Front for the Liberation of the Occupied Arabian Gulf (PFLOAG), known to the men of the SAS as *adoo* (Arabic for 'enemy'), which occupied most of the Dhofar region with the exception of the coastal towns of Salalah, Taqa and Mirbat. The rebels roamed free over the Jebel Dhofar, eating further into the beleaguered areas around Salalah. The base used by the Royal Air Force just north of Salalah was itself virtually under siege, and without outside intervention the Sultan's small defence force was on the way to defeat.

Although not a military man, the old Sultan had decided to send his only son Qaboos to the Royal Military Academy at Sandhurst, where he was commissioned into a British regiment. His stay in England was far from wasted, for with the encouragement of his friends he had observed the workings of various councils and committees, and in general had familiarized himself with the intricacies of a modern state. His return home had not been a joyous one, though; the young Sultan could see the plight of his country and argued for change. His father's answer had been to further restrict his son's movements and accuse him of becoming a 'Westerner'. However, the young Qaboos bided his time. His chance came on 23 July 1970, when a palace coup took place. Aided by the young Sheikh Baraik bin Hamood, Qaboos deposed his father in a bloodless takeover. Within weeks, men of the SAS had been sent to Oman to provide the new ruler with advice and assistance.

Call to Northern Oman

For some time Colonel 'Johnny' Watts, the commander of 22 SAS, and his second-in-command, Major Peter de la Billière, had been making preparations behind the scenes, and men of the Regiment had undertaken several secret reconnaissances. For the average SAS soldier who was getting on with yet more training, the Oman War came as a bit of a shock, but it was also a welcome break from base routine. For the SAS, the first action started in the northern Omani peninsula, at the very entrance to the Strait of Hormuz. British intelligence had warned of a large arms shipment due to arrive at a small village on the Omani peninsula; this was to be accompanied by a group of Iraqis.

Barry Davies, a long-serving member of the SAS, recalls the event.

'I was walking across the square from the direction of the "Kremlin" (the SAS Operations, Planning and Intelligence cell at Hereford) when a voice called out to me, and I turned to see a colleague running in my direction. Like me, he was dressed in a suit, as many of us were due to attend the marriage of a Squadron member in a few hours' time. "Get your kit; we're going." He didn't stop, but ran on past.

'"Where to?" I shouted at his receding back.

'"Middle East" was all I heard before I, too, broke into a run, heading directly for the accommodation *basha* (a Malaysian word for a jungle home, used by the SAS to describe any form of shelter). There were a few guys still getting dressed for the wedding, but the bulk had already left for a few beers before the ceremony started. The sudden appearance of the squadron commander soon made me realize that this was not a drill. Quickly, he informed those present of the latest situation. It would seem that some Intelligence guy who had been lying low in a village off the Musandan Peninsula had picked up information on a huge arms shipment due to arrive at the tiny coastal village of Jumla. This arms shipment was to be accompanied by a group of Iraqis with communist persuasions. According to British Intelligence, this was translated as the main communist head shed moving into the area to take advantage of the turmoil within Oman. However, the SAS was going to snatch them and nip the whole thing in the bud.

'A few hours later, with most of the squadron still dressed in suits, we made our way to RAF Brize Norton. A day later, after a short stop in Cyprus, we landed at the British airbase in Sharjah. Without leaving the confines of the airport, we loaded our bergens and weapons on to several three-ton trucks and were driven out into the desert. To all intents and purposes this was done for security; in reality, the whole squadron was dumped in the middle of nowhere – yes, still dressed in our suits! Like all good SAS men, we dived into our bergens and changed into combat gear. A few of us then used the spartan scrub to put up some bashas for shelter before making the inevitable brew of tea. We waited.

'Later that evening, several choppers came in and we were ferried over to a campsite on the eastern coast. This was done for several reasons. First, the area was similar to the one we would attack, although it was minus a village. Second, a Royal Navy minesweeper, complete with several Rigid Raiders manned by the SBS, was due to arrive off our coastal campsite.

'The plan called for the SAS to be inserted by the SBS on to the small beaches both north and south of Jumla. This would be done during the hours of darkness and would allow enough time for us to scale the high, rocky peaks that towered out of the sea and surrounded the entire village. By dawn, with the SAS in place to stop any enemy running away, a combined force from local Arab states would assault the village and capture both the Iraqis and the equipment. On the surface, a sound plan: not only would it protect the Strait of Hormuz, through which half the world's oil passes, but it would stop a major catastrophe in the area. But the reality was rather different.

'The night before we left our training area to board the mine-sweeper, a priority signal arrived. By the light of our campfire, Major Alastair Morrison read it to us. We listened with dread to his solemn words. It would seem that the Intelligence guy, whom we assumed was still in the village and still passing back vital information, had seen a ship docking at the small village port. He reported that heavy machine guns and mortars had been unloaded, together with several large boxes of mines. It was suspected that the enemy had received wind of our assault and planned to oppose it. The final words of the message were chilling: "Expect to take up to 50 per cent casualties." Silence fell on the not-so-happy group. Why do they have to tell you things like that the night before a mission?

'As if being blown to smithereens on the beach wasn't enough, the whole plan was delayed for 24 hours, but only after we had gone out to sea. The reason was bad weather. When the time came to leave the minesweeper and load our seasick bodies into the Rigid Raiders, I would have happily taken on the enemy single-handed rather than stay a second longer on that ship. However, as we approached the beach in pitch dark-ness all thoughts of seasickness diminished, and I concentrated on looking through the night scope. There was nothing to see other than a few faint lights coming from the village. We hit the beach at full speed and I was actually thrown from the Raider in what looked like a spectacular, headlong dive. Somehow, I landed with a perfect para-roll and came up on my feet. Several of the guys said the dive looked real gung-ho (I wanted to kill the stupid SBS boat handler!)

'Instantly we started to climb. It was steep and hard going, but Mountain Troop led the way, choosing the easiest route. An hour before dawn we were in position, looking over the village to the open sea beyond, our only casualty a broken finger. I should mention at this stage that some bright spark had come up with the idea of giving every SAS man at least six *shemaghs* (Arab headdresses) of various colours and design. The thinking behind this was simple. The assaulting Arab force was made up of several different local forces, all with a different-coloured shemagh. To avoid any possibility that we might be mistaken for the enemy, as the different units approached our positions we were to change headdress to comply with theirs. In reality, 40 SAS soldiers were all converted into Tommy Cooper looka-likes, as we frequently dived into our bergens looking for the correct shemagh.

'The light rapidly improved and suddenly, about a mile out to sea, we spotted the landing force. It was heading at top speed for the beach. I have to say that from our position, high above the village, it looked impressive. The landing craft hit the beach and several shots rang out. This is it – here we go. Then slowly the villagers started coming out of their homes to greet the soldiers (visitors were rare in this remote area); tea and coffee were distributed and everything seemed very amiable. Then one of the white officers got tough: "OK. Where are the Iraqi rebels? We know they're here in Jumla."

'If they're in Jumla, why are you here in Gumla?' came the surprised reply. Yes, we'd invaded the wrong village! All that hype and planning gone to pot. There were no more than half a dozen villages along this hostile coastline, but Intelligence had picked the wrong one. By the time the head shed had confirmed the fact, and sent us racing across the mountaintop, it was far too late. The rebels had long gone, and so had most of their equipment.

'We were all pulled back to the British base at Sharjah, where we sat around while a new plan was hatched. Apparently, according to intelligence, the enemy had taken refuge in a stronghold called the Wadi Rawdah. Even my best effort at explaining to anyone what that place looked like would not do it justice. It was a mighty bowl within the jebel structure. The sheer rocky walls towered up to 1,000 feet even at the lowest point. On the seaward side there occurred a natural, narrow split in the rock structure, which allowed for entry and exit. The whole valley was the lost haven to a strange tribe called the Bani Shihoo. Reportedly a vicious people who had rarely seen a white man, their main weapon, apart from the odd rifle, was a vicious-looking axe. Like most rumours, it was false: they turned out to be a friendly bunch.

'The operation restarted with a parachute night drop carried out by two free-fall troops. I think I'm right in saying it was to be the first operational free-fall drop the SAS Regiment had ever undertaken. The rest of us would go in by chopper as soon as the boys had secured a landing position. I had time to go to the local base NAAFI for a drink, but just before I left I gave Paul "Rip" Reddy, one of the free fallers, a hand with his kit. He was fairly new to the squadron, but was a great guy with a real sense of humour. He joked about the amount of kit he was carrying on the drop.

'The aircraft took off around 03:00, and an hour later the men jumped from a height of 11,000 feet. "Rip" Reddy was killed. Of all the deaths in the Regiment, this one stunned me. To this day, I can recall wishing him luck before I went off for a beer. He was so young, fit and full of life, but that would sum up most men who have died in the SAS.

'Before the news broke, the rest of the squadron had been trucked to a campsite closer to the wadi. Most of us were still sleeping when the Boss (Captain Morrison) came running round, shaking us awake and telling us to grab our kit and get on the chopper. He never said that "Rip" was dead, but the speed of our move said something was up. This was also the first time I had seen a loadmaster sitting in the door of a chopper manning a fixed GPMG.

'Arriving from the air, the sight of the Wadi Rawdah takes your breath away. But we had more pressing things on our minds than taking in the spectacular view. As the chopper touched down we all jumped clear, fanning out in a defensive arc. That's when I saw two of Free-fall Troop bring a body bag forward and place it on the chopper. As we started to relax, one of the guys told us what had happened. The drop had gone well, but the valley floor was dark and they had used beacon lights and SARBEs to locate each other. Once they were all on the ground, it became apparent that "Rip" Reddy was missing and a search was organized. They found him halfway up a gravel slope. His parachute had operated a fraction too late. This was established from the fact that his chute was fully deployed and he had been in the upright position on contact with the ground.

'We stayed in the area for about two months, using Sharjah as a base. I was pulled off to do psychological operations, an interesting task which gave me a good insight into the northern part of Oman. One of my tasks was to visit the small towns and villages prior to the arrival of the new Sultan. I would dispense a radio to most adults (a new Omani broadcasting service was being set up) and give T-shirts and flags to the kids. One of my visits took me back to the Wadi Rhawdah, where I came face to face with the Bani Shihoo. They were a strange community. They built small houses out of rocks which had been fashioned into uniform blocks, and many had a pitched roof. Due to the lack of water and the rock structure of the wadi, they had carved out huge cisterns to collect rainwater in. Their survival in this inhospitable area (I could see little sign of vegetation, and no animals) is a lesson to the human race in man's ability to adapt.

'Eventually, we went back to England, but only for a short while.'

Southern Oman

After the abortive raid in the north, the war in Oman continued, but this time in the south. After the first initial reconnaissances by Colonel Watts and Major de la Billière, it was decided to occupy the southern coastal towns. An SAS headquarters was established at Um al Gwarif, on the outskirts of Salalah, the southern capital, and just a short distance from the RAF base. Salalah and the air base took several long-range attacks, but an outer ring of firebases called 'hedgehogs' defended them. They were situated in a defensive arc between the Jebel Dhofar and the air base, and were manned by the RAF Regiment. They were well equipped with mortars and Green Archer (radar which detected and backtracked enemy artillery fire to locate the guns), and this ensured that the adoo could not bring their heavy weapons in too close. The more distant towns of Taqa and Mirbat, which were manned by the SAS, were open to the full brunt of the adoo. In the days before the war was taken on to the Jebel Dhofar, these locations came under constant attack: hardly a night would go by without Taqa or Mirbat coming under fire.

Life for the SAS training teams, before taking the war up on to the Jebel Dhofar, was confined to village life and preparing the firqat. Taqa, a small coastal village midway between Salalah and Mirbat, was the base and tribal home of the Firqat Kalid bin Walid. This firqat eventually mustered more than 80 men. They were also fearsome fighters. During the old Sultan's frugal regime, many young men had left the village and travelled widely within the Arab world. Fortunately, for the SAS, some had taken training with the Trucial Oman Scouts and had a very good knowledge of British military tactics. It was common to see the section commanders give the same hand signals that could be seen on the training areas of the Brecon Beacons.

The SAS normally lived in the village with the firqat, and in the case of Taqa occupied a two-storey building overlooking the village square. Daily life for the SAS evolved into a number of days training the firqat and a number of days defending the village. In addition, the SAS would do night penetration patrols and lay unmanned demolition ambushes.

The village was a collection of mud huts that seemed to have stood outside time for a thousand years. Some 660 feet to the south was the sea, and to the north was the Jebel Dhofar. The bulk of the village sheltered under a small escarpment about 50 feet high, on top of which stood an old Beau Geste-type fort. A troop of Baluchistani soldiers occupied the fort, which in turn was surrounded by a razor-wire fence in a half-moon shape. To the left of the fort was a mortar pit, with an artillery piece situated to the right. During the day, two mortar-trained SAS men would sit waiting patiently for the first distant 'plop'. This first indication of an adoo attack would normally bring the customary first two mortar rounds down the tube in reply. It was a kind of game. By day, the attack would normally be from a big gun fired from the tree-lined escarpment that lined the Jebel Aram and looked out over Taqa. The gun was so well hidden that the BAC Strikemaster light attack aircraft of the Sultan of Oman's Air Force could not locate it. The SAS, too, could do little to alleviate the situation. On one occasion, for example, several shells landed in the village, killing one woman and wounding several others. Nevertheless, the adoo did not always have matters their own way. Outranged by the gun, the mortar had its range boosted by pouring 2 inches of petrol down the barrel. This increased the distance dramatically. However, it is not a practice to be recommended as, firstly, the extra range is not constant and, secondly, a careful eye needs to be kept on the bottom of the tube and base plate for the moment cracks start to appear. Nevertheless, the boosted mortar gave the adoo something to think about!

Most of the attacks came at night, when a stand-off battle of some 6,555 feet would be exchanged. These normally lasted for about 10 minutes, initiated by the adoo mortars backed up with small arms. During the monsoon season, the adoo made several daring close-range attacks, managing to get within spitting distance of the wire perimeter before being repelled. There is some evidence to suggest that these close-in attacks were in preparation for the assault on Mirbat that came later.

On one occasion at Taqa, the men in the mortar pit heard noises inside the wire compound and quickly asked the fort to have a quick look with the night-sight. As the mortar pit was isolated from the fort, the ground to the front and the open side had been festooned with razor wire about 3 feet above the ground as a means of stopping any sudden rush by the enemy. The fort reported seeing nothing, and things settled down for a few minutes, until a sudden fall of stones could be heard just a few feet away. Two grenades were quickly thrown in that direction and the fort, from its elevated position, laid down several protective bursts of heavy fire across the pit. At this stage the two mortar men, who normally slept in the pit, made a run for the back door of the fort. Nothing else was heard, but the next day a hole was found in the wire and a dead donkey lay 66 feet away with boxes of Soviet-made ammunition scattered around its body. The position of the mortar pit was comparable to that of the gun pit at Mirbat – the prime target during that engagement.

Operation Jaguar

The firqat were to endure the most of the adoo assault when the SAS and Omani forces finally attacked the Jebel. As it turned out, some firqat were better than others. The firqat from Taqa, the Kalid bin Walid, was superb. Some members had been adoo, but after being alienated by the hard-line ideology of the PFLOAG and having seen the work and determination of the new Sultan, they returned to play a vital part in building their country.

Once the firqat were ready, the time came to attack the adoo in their own back yard, and plans were accordingly made to assault the Jebel Dhofar. Operation Jaguar was launched to establish a firm base on the Jebel Dhofar, and it began in

October 1971. During the Ramadan period, which is normally a time of fasting, the senior Qadi (religious leader) had given dispensation to all Arabs fighting.

This was the start of the war in earnest, with almost two full squadrons of SAS, together with their firqat, spearheading the operation. Additionally, several companies of the Sultan of Oman's Armed Forces (SOAF) and various support units also took part. Johnny Watts, a brilliant commander who above all had the respect of his men, led the whole force. Watts had a quick, decisive mind, yet he would not commit the SAS without committing himself. He was no stranger to the battlefront and often could be seen running forward with one gun group or another carrying boxes of ammunition, shouting orders as he did so.

Getting the men on to the Jebel Dhofar was not easy, even though a diversionary plan had been implemented several weeks earlier (heavy patrolling had been initiated from Taqa and Mirbat in the direction of the Wadi Darbat, which had always been an adoo stronghold, with the intention of making it seem that a full-scale attack was imminent). Helicopter hours were limited, and although some could be used in the initial lift on to the Jebel Dhofar, most would be required to ferry ammunition, water and rations in the early days of the operation. The helicopters were needed to sustain the effort until an airstrip could be built and secured on the Jebel Dhofar, so that the helicopter effort could be replaced and expanded as Short Skyvan fixed-wing transports took over the supply and reinforcement effort.

Later that morning, Omani aircraft brought in the other SAS squadron. The SAS and firqat from Mirbat and Sudh climbed the Jebel Dhofar from the east, scaling a feature known as the Eagle's Nest, and then worked their way westward during the day, thereby helping to divert the attentions of the adoo. Meanwhile, a full squadron undertook a gruelling march to occupy an old airstrip at a place nicknamed Lympne, after an airfield in Kent. This march still stands out in the minds of the men involved. The route was over very difficult terrain, and the bergen carried by each man contained enough ammunition and water to last for several days. Nevertheless, so severe was the march that upon their arrival even the SAS men were in no state to fight until rested. Luckily, the adoo were occupied elsewhere, and later that morning Omani helicopters and Skyvans started bringing in the other SAS squadron and the Firqat Kalid bin Walid. Colonel Watts decided to move to a more defensible position, so on the morning of the second day the SAS and the firqat that had arrived by helicopter – and were therefore fresher than the units that had marched in – set off for a location known as Jibjat. With the Firqat Kalid bin Walid in the lead, the Mountain Troop of G Squadron topped the small rise around Jibjat and came face-to-face with a large adoo group having breakfast. A firefight developed and the surprised adoo started to pull back in an effort to disperse, but not before a full-frontal attack was jointly carried out by the firqat and SAS, who overran the adoo position and continued to clear the area to the south, whereupon any further advance was stopped by a large wadi.

The firefight was unrelenting until the SAS heavy support teams turned up. Each team consisted of a GPMG and three men: one carried the whole unit (gun plus tripod) while the other two carried ammunition and acted as gun loader and spotter (each man carried up to 1,000 rounds of GPMG link ammunition – a ferociously heavy load). In the early days of the war, these gun groups proved decisive in winning firefights, especially as the supporting Omani Strikemaster aircraft were at first not so quick in reaching the scene.

All through the second day of the offensive, small battles could be heard flaring up at one location or the other. By the third day, Colonel Watts had split his force into three battle groups, two of which were dispatched to clear the Wadi Darbat and a ridgeline known as the Gatn, pronounced 'Cuttin' by everyone.

For several days the adoo fought with everything they had, mistakenly thinking this was nothing more than a short operation by the Omani forces and that in a few days they would give up and leave. It was not to be, though. The Firqat Kalid bin

Walid, many of its men back in their own territory, fought as well as professional soldiers, bounding forward stride for stride with the SAS men. By 9 October, the initiative was clearly on the side of the Omani forces, and the adoo broke up into smaller groups and disappeared into the small bush-covered wadis.

Meanwhile the eastern battle group, which had moved to a location called 'Pork Chop Hill', began to have problems with its firqat. This was not the first time the Firqat A'asifat had posed problems: from the start its men had been reluctant to fight in many areas, and now they wished to observe Ramadan. Therefore, despite the Sultan's urgings and the Qadi's dispensation, the firqat was withdrawn to Jibjat for the month of Ramadan. A few days later, Colonel Watts descended on the firqat's leaders and left them in no doubt as to how he viewed their unprofessional attitude. As both sides eased back a little, a main base was established at a place known as White City. By this time, the choppers were quickly running out of flying hours and desperately needed servicing. Likewise, supplies of ammunition (especially mortar bombs) were dwindling, and water was at a premium. It was suggested by Colonel Watts that an airstrip should be constructed in the middle of White City so that the Skyvans could alleviate the supply situation. As troops began arriving at the location, the men of the firqat were sent to picket the high ground while SAS men set to construct the runway. They worked all night, several times coming under enemy fire, but by dawn the airstrip was ready to receive the first aircraft. Again the battle flared up. Each time a Skyvan landed, the adoo were waiting: mortar bombs began to fall and small-arms fire was employed in an effort to shoot down several of the aircraft. To prevent this, heavily armed dawn patrols were sent out to engage and occupy the enemy while the aircraft unloaded. This period saw some of the heaviest fighting of the war.

Despite the problems with the other firqat, the Firqat Kalid bin Walid in the western group continued to fight hard. News arrived that a large contingent of adoo had been observed in the Wadi Darbat, most of them suffering from the terror of recent battles, so the Firqat Kalid bin Walid set about planning a raid. Aerial bombing and artillery bombardment had little effect and ammunition was in short supply, but eventually a strong patrol was sent against the adoo-occupied village of Shahait. A fierce gun battle erupted which left two adoo dead, but many others escaped before the SAS and firqat could arrive.

From a distance of three miles, an SAS trooper spotted a large group of adoo, and after pinpointing their position on his map, he called in an artillery barrage from gun lines at Taqa. It was an unbelievable sight when the first spotting salvo landed smack in the middle of the adoo, and the trooper could be heard screaming into the radio: 'Fire for effect – fire for effect!'

At first, the conflict was fluid as the three main battle groups started in the east and pushed their way west. Those first weeks were by far the toughest and, as with all things new, it took time for the systems to fall into place and for effective coordination to be established with the supporting arms, such as the Omani artillery, Omani Air Force and, most of all, the firqat. It would be remiss not to stress the importance of the bond between the firqat and the SAS. The firqat had certainly been trained to act as military units but, in reality, they were far from being military units in any real sense of the phrase. Yet they possessed a feeling for their own back yard that the SAS did not have. It was not uncommon for their men to wander into battle with their rifles slung over their shoulders and then, quite suddenly, to drop to the ground and start darting forward. It was a movement the SAS soldiers came to recognize: it meant adoo were near. In battle, they were courageous, always dashing into the fight, even if sometimes their firing became a little erratic. They were also honest, and if for some reason the SAS unit did not do as they requested, they would soon make their point obvious. At the same time, when they were around one was guaranteed a good night's sleep. Studying the firqat gave one some idea as to what the adoo were like (in fact, as mentioned above, many of the adoo who had been captured or surrendered themselves would help swell the ranks of the local firqat).

The adoo were mostly well equipped. It was not uncommon after the battle to find dead or wounded adoo dressed in a better kit than the SAS: khaki shorts and shirt, ammunition belt, water bottle and AK-47 assault rifle, all topped off with a blue beret complete with red star (plus a copy of the *Thoughts of Chairman Mao* in his pocket). Dead adoo were often stripped of their weapons and ammunition before being left by their comrades.

In the first weeks of battle, contacts were very close and in large numbers. Rarely an hour passed without one of the three battle groups coming under fire. It was a matter of advancing to contact, holding the firefight, bringing up gun groups and calling in jets. Winning the firefight is the basis of all victories: hit the enemy with a wall of accurate fire and he will stop. For the SAS, this firepower was supplied by two of the best infantry weapons ever: the 3.2-inch mortar and the GPMG.

During one squadron patrol to clear a wadi of adoo, the commanding officer thought it prudent to protect his one exposed flank. The problem lay with a smaller wadi running parallel to the one the British and Omani force intended to search, for this offered the adoo excellent concealment and an escape route. To solve the problem it was decided that one SAS section, complete with about 10 firqat, would patrol the adjacent wadi. This worked out fine until the men reached a dry waterfall in the wadi bed. Fortuitously, for the SAS party, its men happened to be at the top of the falls while a group of five adoo were coming up in the opposite direction. The adoo were trapped, isolated in what looked like a Roman amphitheatre. The firqat called out for them to lay down their arms as they were surrounded. A burst of automatic fire was the only reply, and so the battle was joined. For the SAS men, it was a turkey shoot as they sat on the top of the falls and poured down fire: M79 grenade launchers, LAW rockets and full-automatic fire from at least 20 other weapons reduced most of the larger rocks in the area of the adoo to rubble. When at last the dust settled and a party went forward to investigate, nothing but a few bits of blood-stained cloth remained. Then it dawned on everyone that they had all missed and that the adoo had legged it. They gave chase, close enough for the blood on the rocks still to be wet, but on this occasion the adoo got away. There are many yet untold stories of the Oman war, the most outstanding being the adoo attack at Mirbat (see page 142).

The war progressed into a steady round of stand-off raids by the adoo. In reply, Omani forces, operating from their established bases, carried out strong patrols and ambushes. However, it soon became obvious that to stop the enemy two things were needed: to sever the adoo line of communications and resupply, and to win the hearts and minds of the Jebel people. The first was a matter of laying mines and establishing a firm defence line in order to monitor the adoo's movements. The second was a task at which the SAS have become masters.

To win over the locals, small aid stations were set up and manned by SAS medics, while SAS Arabists would regularly talk to village leaders, and their problems became the problems of the SAS. Civil aid teams soon moved into the liberated areas. Water was found and drilling teams brought it to the surface. In a land where water has a priority second only to life itself, the expression on a jebali's face when the cool, clear liquid gushes from the ground is one of pure wonder and delight. In addition, communications opened up trade and commerce, and this became clear when at last a metalled road linked the Jebel Dhofar with Salalah.

Operation Taurus

One special operation known only to the SAS and a few others was Operation Taurus. Thousands of goats and cattle were rounded up and purchased by the government for food, at the same time denying the adoo of one of its main sources of food. It was a truly remarkable sight as the animals were rounded up by the firqat and, amid skirmishes with the adoo, herded down the Jebel Dhofar to Salalah, support being provided by Strikemaster jet aircraft.

With the establishment of the airstrips and a good resupply system, more adventurous patrols were undertaken. One such task was in the Jebel Aram.

It was cold and dark as the patrol set off from White City at around 20:00. The patrol consisted of some 15 SAS, 30 firqat and a platoon of Omani soldiers. The weight carried by each man made movement very slow. The bulky rucksacks contained mostly ammunition and water, but in addition, three of the SAS men carried an 81mm mortar between them.

This group made up the tail end of the lead group, and behind them each member of the Omani platoon carried two bombs. This was all the support the party would have until it had reached the Jebel Aram and established a strong base upon it.

At last the men came to a halt, and with it the chance to rest from the merciless weight they carried. The SAS, apart from the mortar crew, and the firqat had gone forward for a recon-naissance. It was estimated that they were about 1,635 feet from their objective. The SAS and firqat had almost reached the old tree that was to serve as their objective (old trees in the desert are almost always used as landmarks). There was barely anything for them to see, and no obvious cover from where the enemy could spring an ambush. Thus they advanced fairly swiftly towards the objective.

Like all firqat, the men were sure-footed in their own back yard, and presently they halted the patrol. Suddenly, one of them dropped down on one knee and pointed, whispering 'adoo' at the same time. The SAS used night scopes to survey the ground ahead. There, at the edge of their night vision, stood the ancient tree. The SAS commander signalled for the remainder of the group to close up and indicated the direction by pointing into the darkness. Then he quietly relayed the information back to the Omani commander. When he had finished, he gave instruc-tions to set up the mortar. As this was done, the men of the Omani platoon dropped off their bombs to the mortars, then spread out in defence, covering the rear. Once everyone was ready, the SAS and firqat moved to the base of the tree.

The cold, damp atmosphere signalled that the coming day was not far away: even as they approached the tree, the sky to the east showed a thin, grey band. Then it happened. From the silence and the darkness came a crashing orchestra of light and sound, turning the desert into daylight, and the weird tapestry of hell unfolded. Everywhere, men could be seen running or diving for whatever scant cover they could find. Almost instantly, the SAS mortar thundered into action, the ground thumping as the bombs hit the pin at the base of the barrel and the propellant ignited. 'The base of the tree,' someone yelled, and blindly everyone fired in that general direction. Abruptly, several 'gimpies' (GPMGs) began their steadfast chattering, with reassuring effect. Suddenly, the commanding officer's voice cut in with clear and concise fire orders. Slowly the firefight died, the silence interrupted only by long-distance sniper fire.

By daylight, the patrol had settled down and set up a defensive position overlooking the Jebel Aram. This included the construction of a mortar pit and the clearing of a helipad for the delivery of ammunition, water and defence stores. That evening, short patrols were sent down into the wadi situated at the back of the Jebel Aram. These small patrols could rely on accurate covering fire from the mortars and GPMGs, all of which had spectacular views of the immediate area.

An SAS soldier present during the conflict takes up the story:

'For a few days we settled in nicely; then it was decided to send out a day-time patrol down into the wadi bed. Things went well until they got "bumped" by the adoo and started to withdraw. The wadi bed was filled with short bushes and trees, making observation difficult for accurate mortar control with our own friendly forces in the area. So it was decided that a reinforced patrol would move further down the hill to give support. It was a big mistake. The adoo had anticipated our move and had cleverly concealed themselves in the long grass. I was part of the reinforcements and, as we rushed forward, they caught us in the open. The first thing I remember was seeing the firqat next to me stop in mid-air. His feet were off the ground and his rifle dropped from his hand. In that split second I watched a plume of bright red blood explode from his back – he fell dead. I saw the adoo. He was lying some 50 feet away, behind a few rocks, his head and weapon the only parts of him exposed. I thought of firing, but running downhill my momentum just seemed to pull me on. I saw the adoo fire and knew instantly that I was hit. Luckily, for me, the burst hit the rocky ground just in front, before smashing up into my legs. I remember vaguely going up and turning over in the air; then I slammed back down on to the hard rock. Reality seemed a long way off as I collapsed. At first the pain wasn't so bad; then it registered, and darkness came and blocked it out. Through dulled senses, the noise of gunfire returned and I remember screaming for my partner, Jock Logan. Painfully I rolled my head to one side and saw the dead firqat close by. His chest was ripped wide open and bloody bubbles popped and oozed as air escaped from his shattered lungs. Suddenly Jock dropped down beside me. Quickly he started to pull the small rocks together to improve the protection around our shallow hole. Jock was breathless and panting like an excited dog. Finishing the meagre shield of rocks, he thrust his 'gimpy' over the top and sent a couple of blasts in the general direction of the adoo. Then he turned back to examine me. "It's your knee, but it's not too serious." He was laughing as he applied the field dressing. "Medevac choppers are on the way." 'Some 20 minutes later I was on the operating table at the Field Surgical Hospital in Salalah. Jock had been right; the damage was light. Most of the bullets had hit the rocky ground first and splintered; the one which had stayed intact had lodged itself deep into my left kneecap. Whatever, two weeks later I was hobbling around the bars of Hereford. To this day I still have the AK-47 bullet head the doctors gave me.'

Despite the casualties, by the end of 1971 the SAS had established a presence on the Jebel Dhofar and had saved the Sultan's regime.

Battle of Mirbat

The war in Oman continued, and at dawn on 19 July 1972, a large rebel force some 250 strong attacked the port of Mirbat on the southern coast of Oman. Similar to the neighbouring town of Taga, Mirbat was protected by an old fort situated to the north-west. A small SAS unit, stationed a short distance away inside the town, operated both the fort and gun. The official report records that the fate of Mirbat and of its occupants during the battle depended wholly on the resolve of the Civil Action Team. But for the action of these nine men, and particularly the leadership of Captain Mike Kealy, the town would undoubtedly have fallen.

Mirbat was the last great attack by the adoo. The rebels of the People's Front for the Liberation of the Occupied Arabian Gulf (PFLOAG) had planned it well: they had been losing ground, and the assault was designed to show the people their continuing power. Only a single stroke of bad luck threw out their calculations, for by coincidence there were two SAS squadrons in Oman at that time due to an end-of-tour handover. This simple fact, combined with the professionalism of the Sultan of Oman's Air Force (SOAF), truly upset the adoo's plans. Had the result been different, the SAS war effort would have suffered a severe setback.

The skill of the adoo's planning and preparation was surpassed only by their security. To mass such a body of men, together with heavy support weapons, and bring them out on to the coastal plain undetected was in itself a major achievement. They arrived under cover of darkness, almost an hour before the first grey skies would filter through the monsoon mist. It was this seasonal cover of low cloud upon which they relied, not just to protect themselves from SOAF aircraft but also to provide a clandestine approach.

At around 05:00 the picket at the top of Jebel Ali, a small hill around 3,300 feet to the north of Mirbat and halfway towards the Jebel Dhofar, was being manned by a section of Dhofar

Gendarmerie (DG). The Jebel Ali is a dominating feature covering the town and the surrounding coastal area. The DG section was the first to be taken out. Surrounding the location to make sure there were no escapees, the adoo attacked; stealthily at first, as they cut the throats of those still asleep, and then, as the alarm was raised, opening up with small arms. The men in the British Army Training Team (BATT) house could hear the exchange of fire. It was soon to be followed by 'thump, thump, thump' as the adoo mortars kicked in. Inside the BATT house, this chorus of explosions gave little cause for alarm, as the enemy often lobbed in a few mortar rounds each morning. The first rounds had been off-target, but by the third salvo, they were shaking off the plaster inside the BATT house.

Quickly the boys ran up the makeshift stairs leading to the roof. Here, a defensive barricade of sandbags had been erected to form two gun pits: one for a GPMG in the north-west corner, and one for a 0.5-inch Browning in the north-east corner. Just in front of the house was a 3.2-inch mortar pit. Captain Kealy, the BATT commander, and his men observed the fire coming from the direction of the Jebel Ali. They also saw several streams of tracer fire lace their way over the house and into the town. Almost at once, several more mortar bombs fell close to the DG fort situated on the northern side of town. In addition, the adoo had opened up with several artillery pieces, and a crushing barrage descended on the town. As the shells exploded, the adoo rose in waves and advanced towards the DG fort.

The BATT house took more incoming rounds but the SAS men, although ready to defend, held their fire. Among them were some of the most experienced soldiers the Regiment had; men who had already seen their share of action. To them, this sounded like nothing more than a stand-off attack, and so the first thing was to assess the situation. From the roof of the BATT house, Captain Kealy could see the firefight raging on top of the Jebel Ali. Turning, he checked to see what damage had been done to the town itself. He then shouted orders for the 81mm mortar to open fire in support of the Jebel Ali, while the rest of the SAS men took up their positions behind the sand-bagged emplacements and waited for targets. The amount of incoming fire worried Kealy, and as a safeguard he ordered his signaller to establish communications with SAS headquarters at Um al Gwarif. Additionally, a big Fijian, Trooper Labalaba, left the house and ran the 1,635 feet to the DG fort, where he manned its old Second World War-vintage 25-pounder artillery piece. By 05:30, it was light enough for Kealy to make out the silhouette of the gun position and the DG fort just to its east.

Despite the ferocity of the attack, at this stage there seemed no reason to think that this was anything more than a strong stand-off attack. However, the duty signaller at Um al Gwarif was informed and told to listen out.

The rest of the guys back at base were happily getting showered and making ready for the ranges. Most of them were from G Squadron. Their signals sergeant, 'Ginge' Reese, passed comment over breakfast about the attack: 'Mirbat are still taking a hammering; it's a bit long for a stand-off.' Five minutes later, 'Duke' Pirie, the B Squadron commander, started to organize a relief force.

At Mirbat, most of the firqat was out on patrol, leaving the town lightly defended, the houses manned by old men, women and children. Only a few firqa members had remained behind and these, together with the group of DG manning the old fort (the Wali's Fort), were the only help the SAS could call on.

Around Mirbat, adoo shellfire continued to increase. Suddenly, a vast amount of small-arms fire started pouring into the town. Through the mist, figures could be seen approaching the perimeter wire from the direction of the Jebel Ali. At first, there was some hesitation as to their identity; it was possible that the firqat had returned. Then the advancing figures opened fire: they were adoo. As battle was joined, both SAS machine gun bunkers opened up, and at the same time the 81mm mortar increased its rate of fire. In the gun pit by the DG fort, the 25-pounder gun sent shell after shell into the massing adoo. The battle flowed back and forth: then a radio message came through on the Tokki (a small commercial walkie-talkie used by the SAS throughout the Oman war) from Labalaba, saying that he had been hit in the chin while operating the 25-pounder gun. A man of such stature is not given to reporting such trivia, and those at the BATT house suspected he was badly injured. Immediately, Captain Kealy sent Labalaba's Fijian countryman, Savesaki, to his aid. The gunners provided supporting fire from the roof of the BATT house as they watched Savesaki run the gauntlet of tracer and exploding shells. Zigzagging, he ran as if on the rugby field going for a try. He finally dived headlong into the gun pit.

Savesaki found Labalaba firing the gun on his own. The big Fijian gave no indication that he was injured. Instead, he pointed to the unopened ammunition boxes, and indicated the desperate need to keep the gun firing. Much of the adoo attack was now directed against the gun itself, and its crew needed more help. For a brief moment, Savesaki left the pit to solicit help from the DG fort a few feet away. As the rounds zipped past his head, he banged on the fort door until at last he was heard. The first man to appear was the Omani gunner, and Savesaki grabbed him. Together, both men raced the short distance back to the gun pit. Savesaki cleared the sandbags, but the Omani gunner fell forward as a bullet ripped out his guts.

It was now light enough to see groups of men near the outer perimeter fence that protected the three open sides of the town. Behind them, wave after wave of adoo could be seen advancing towards Mirbat in support. At that moment several rockets slammed into the DG fort, causing great chunks of masonry to be blown from its ancient walls. The adoo looked calm and seemed disciplined, moving forward in sections of about 10 men. From all around, whistles could be heard driving the adoo on. Suddenly another mighty blast rang out, and the front of the fort exploded in a cloud of dust, totally obliterating it from sight. As vision returned, the SAS on the BATT house roof focused on a new threat. The adoo were at the perimeter wire. Swarms of young men threw themselves headlong on to the barbed, razor-sharp steel: as one died another took his place. Men could be seen all along the wire, but the main break-through seemed to be in front of the fort. At this stage, most of the enemy fire was concentrated on the fort in general, and at the gun pit in particular. Several more heavy explosions were heard, and once more the old fort disappeared in a cloud of dust (it was discovered later that apart from the recoilless guns and mortars, the adoo had a Carl Gustav rocket launcher which had been stolen from British forces in Aden some years earlier).

The adoo were now inside the perimeter and advancing on the fort and the gun position in large numbers. In support of Labalaba and Savesaki, the men at the BATT house brought all their guns to bear. When the adoo still outside the wire started to realize where all the return fire was coming from, they swiftly retaliated.

There is a corroborated story that as the adoo penetrated the wire perimeter in the early stages of the assault, a lone figure could be seen driving them on. He was described as being very tall and extremely well dressed in full Chinese army uniform, with courage to match. In full view of the horrendous firefight surrounding him, he stood proudly urging his men on – until a bullet took him down.

The gun, now levelled directly at the wire, boomed as Labalaba fired point-blank into the charging figures. Both Fijians moved in unison, Savesaki passing the rounds and Labalaba slamming them home, before blasting them into the wall of humanity just a few feet away. Suddenly, Savesaki cried out, 'I'm hit!' and slumped back against the sandbags. Without a loader, the gun fell silent. His shirt soaked with blood, Savesaki propped himself against the sandbags, grabbed his SLR and continued to fire; Labalaba made a quick grab for a small 60mm mortar that lay close by. He almost made it, but then a bullet took him in the neck. The mighty mountain of a man, a true gladiator, fell dead.

Communications with the gun pit had been lost, and Captain Kealy decided that he and an SAS medic, Trooper Tobin, would risk going forward to give assistance. Before they left, Kealy contacted Um al Gwarif, informing them that things were not going too well and that air cover was desperately needed. He also requested a helicopter to evacuate Labalaba. Additionally, he explained that if the firefight continued at its frenetic pace, more ammunition would be required. It is a little-known fact that if an SAS man gets into serious trouble, he requests 'the Beast'. This call alerts the headquarters unit to the seriousness of the situation, and every SAS soldier who can carry a weapon is pressed into service. In the case of Mirbat, the Beast had been put on standby. Most of those mustered were from the newly arrived G Squadron. The men were already dressed and equipped for the range; all that was required was a little extra firepower. It was customary for senior troop leaders to go off to the locations where they would be taking over. While they were doing this, the rest of the squadron would unpack stores and test-fire their weapons on the range. Such was the case on the morning in question. As 'Ginge' Reese spread the news throughout the cookhouse, most of the men stopped eating and ran for the armoury. It took about five minutes for 22 of them, under the command of Captain Alistair Morrison, to get together an impressive array of weapons. Eight GPMGs and several grenade launchers were among the group – the enemy was going to know about it when these men entered the fray. The total ammunition count for the reinforcements was in excess of 25,000 rounds.

In Mirbat, Captain Kealy and Trooper Tobin were working their way forward to the gun pit. As they approached, the firing intensified and both dived for cover. Luckily for them, there was a shallow wadi running in their general direction, and this afforded them a measure of protection. With a final dive, Tobin rolled into the gun pit. Kealy was about to follow but, realizing there was not enough room, and tripping over the body of a dead gendarme, he threw himself headlong into the sandbagged ammunition bay.

Tobin could not believe the mess. Labalaba lay face down and was very still; Savesaki sat propped against the sandbags,

SLR still in hand, and nearby the Omani gunner moaned as
he clutched the wound in his stomach. Assessing the priorities,
Tobin quickly set up a drip on the severely wounded Omani
gunner. Savesaki was badly wounded in the back, but despite the
severe loss of blood he continued to fight, covering the left side of
the fort. The firefight had reached its height, and the adoo made
a real effort to overrun the gun. As Kealy concentrated amid
the mayhem, he saw adoo close by the fort wall. They threw
several grenades, which bounced by the lip of the gun pit before
exploding. An adoo appeared at the side of the gun pit, but Kealy
cut him down. In the pit, Tobin reached over the inert body of
Labalaba and then, realizing there was little he could do, made
to move away. At that moment, a bullet took away half his face.
His whole body stiffened, and then he fell by the side of the big
Fijian, mortally wounded. The gun pit seemed done for. Kealy,
rapidly running out of full magazines, reloaded quickly, keeping
his head below the sandbags. Suddenly there came an almighty
explosion – the SOAF jets had arrived. Kealy called into the
Tokki, managing to make contact with the BATT house: 'Laba's
dead. Tak and Tommy both VSI. Get help.' Back at the BATT
house, they heard the sound of an aircraft and, thinking it was a
casevac (casualty evacuation) helicopter, one of the soldiers went
to check it landed safely. Then he realized it was not a chopper
but a BAC Strikemaster light attack aircraft. The soldier ran
back to the roof and, snatching up his SARBE radio, directed the
pilot with precise information regarding enemy forces. Despite
the monsoon weather, the pilots had dived out of the cloud just
feet above the ground. There before them was the enemy. Their
machine guns roared as the first two jets made pass after pass,
driving the adoo back into a large wadi outside the perimeter
wire. As Kealy silently thanked the pilots, he saw a large 500-
pound bomb unhook itself from one of the Strikemasters and fall
into the wadi where the adoo had taken refuge.

The SOAF pilots did a fantastic job, streaking over the DG
fort and keeping the adoo from any further penetration through
the perimeter. Time after time they dived from the low cloud

to run the gauntlet of ground fire pouring up towards them. Barry Davies was at the airport ready to fly out with an 81mm mortar, and heard the radio traffic from the whole battle broadcast live over the intercom: there was a similar system at Um al Gwarif. He recalls:

'We heard a pilot call: "I'm hit; I'm hit. No fuel: repeat, no fuel." Seconds later, as the fire trucks raced across the tarmac, the jet could be seen lining up for the runway, its tailpipe bleeding black smoke. The pilot literally slammed the jet into the ground as fire tenders, which had raced side-by-side with the aircraft, pumped foam to extinguish the fire.'

By this time the desperate situation was clearly understood at Um al Gwarif. The G Squadron relief force had already been loaded into three choppers and was rapidly heading down the coast, covering the 30 miles to Mirbat in about 10 minutes. Because of the cloud, the men of the relief force were dropped off to the south of Mirbat and instantly made contact with an adoo patrol that was covering the rear. The adoo, consisting of one older soldier and three youths, were held up in a cave and refused to surrender. Several 66mm LAW rockets slammed into the entrance, followed by fire from several GPMGs, and in this fashion the adoo picket was quickly neutralized.

With the jets taking the sting out of the adoo, Kealy had time to crawl forward and examine the gun pit. He could see that the Omani gunner was still alive and so, too, was Tobin, although his wound looked horrendous. Savesaki lay listless against the sandbags; his whole body seemed covered with blood, but he still managed a smile. Slowly, he and Kealy covered the others up and gave what comfort they could.

The SOAF jets had pushed the adoo back, and were now dropping 500-pound bombs on the Jebel Ali. Kealy and Savesaki tried to shout at the gendarmes in the fort to open the door, but it was to no avail. Then the SAS relief force arrived. Moving through the town had been difficult: as with the SAS in Mirbat, identifying friend from foe in the misty monsoon conditions was not easy. The G Squadron men had to be alert, as firqat had positioned themselves in groups of twos and threes around the town.

As the mess started to clear and the adoo withdrew, harassed all the way by the Strikemasters, concern was raised about the main firqat patrol that had been lured away before the attack. Obviously, having heard the amount of gunfire coming from the direction of Mirbat, it would immediately return to base. The problem now was whether it would run headlong into the retreating adoo. Although several of the choppers had been hit, they continued to ferry in more reinforcements, extracting the wounded in return. The seriously wounded Tobin and the Omani gunner were evacuated by the first available flight. Savesaki, who had suffered wounds from which a normal man would have died, walked calmly to the chopper without assistance. Three young adoo, captured and held in the BATT house, were also sent back for interrogation.

Meanwhile, the relieving force commander Alistair Morrison reorganized Mirbat's defences and, with the aid of two Land Rovers, started to collect the dead and wounded adoo. The final count of enemy dead was 38. They were stacked neatly in the back of a Skyvan transport and flown to the southern capital, Salalah, where they were laid out for the whole population of the city to see.

The Dhofar war was never the same after the Battle of Mirbat. The adoo had given it their best shot and failed, but only just. The chances that a second SAS squadron would be just 30 miles away at the time of the attack was something they could not have foreseen. Additionally, they underestimated the expertise and nerve of the SOAF pilots.

Shirshitti Caves Operation

Two years later the SAS fought another great battle in Oman: the Shirshitti Caves operation. It took place in 1974, more or less as the war was coming to an end. Major General Creasey, commander of the SOAF, ordered the Iranian Battle Group (an Iranian Special Forces battalion had been sent to the support of the Omani forces by the Shah) to advance from the air base at Mansion and secure the coastal town of Rakyut, some 17 miles to the south. Its mission was to clear the adoo stores complex located in the caves of the Shirshitti Wadi. These caves were said to hold tons of weapons, food and combat supplies. Their capture would help end the war.

The attack started in mid-December but did not get very far. The adoo had seen the Iranians coming, and in heavy fighting inflicted severe casualties on them. Unable to sustain the losses, the Iranians had called off the attack. At this stage of the war, though, defeat was not an option for the Omani government. Almost immediately, a decision was taken by Creasey to launch another attack, using Omani forces, SAS and firqat. There was a problem, however, in the fact that all the Omani regiments in the south were already hard-pressed with prior commitments. So it was that the Jebel Regiment was flown down from northern Oman. After some swift training, it was sent into battle.

By 4 January 1975, the force was ready. The plan was simple: seize an old airstrip called Defa in order to establish a supply point, and then secure the ridge which overlooked the Shirshitti depression, in which the adoo cave dumps lay. As always, the SAS and firqat led the advance. Defa was quickly taken and the advance rapidly continued. As the lead elements approached a landmark known as the Zakhir Tree, they met serious resistance. For some reason the firqat did not perform well, but the SAS men laid down a thick and furious fire. By mid-afternoon, they had managed to reach a clearing called Point 985, whereupon a base was established. During the night, the adoo attacked at very close range, killing four Omani soldiers and severely wounding many more. At times, it was difficult to establish the locations from where the adoo fire was coming, and as a result the Omani soldiers in the perimeter defences became extremely agitated and fired more for relief than to hit a specific target.

The next day the force advanced down into the Shirshitti. By mid-morning, the Regiment's Red Company had reached the Shirshitti Wadi, but the commander realized that he had moved too far south – navigation in the thick bush was difficult. There also seemed to be some confusion as to the location of the other two companies. At this stage, most of the SAS men had attached themselves to the various command headquarters. Red Company was with Lance-Corporal Thomas. As the lead platoons broke cover – against Thomas's advice – into an area clear of bush, the adoo opened fire. Within seconds, most of the platoon's men were dead, cut down by the ferocious adoo firepower.

The company commander and several other men rushed forward to get a better look at the tactical situation. The adoo were waiting, and laid down murderous fire. Even to the hardened SAS men, it became clear that the situation was getting out of control. As usual in such circumstances, they quickly grouped together for support. All around them, though, the surviving Omani soldiers dropped their weapons and ran, despite the desperate efforts of their British officers – many of whom were killed – to restore control.

It is not recorded in official sources, but it was only at gunpoint that order could be restored. In order to regain control of the situation, the SAS party with Red Company headquarters called in an air strike. However, such was the confusion on the ground that the first strike mistakenly hit the company headquarters, one of the rounds striking an SAS soldier in the back. Fluorescent air-marker panels were hastily pulled from belt kits and wrapped around shoulders for recognition. Eventually, with massive firepower from artillery, mortars and Strikemasters, the adoo were driven back. Amid all this carnage, there were several individual acts of great courage, as men braved the horrendous fire to rescue friends and comrades.

Although the dead were left behind, all the wounded and weapons were recovered before a tactical withdrawal was ordered. As the shaken troops made their way back to Point 985, shots could be heard coming from the wadi – the adoo were confirming their kills. To alleviate this gruesome sound, a full-blown mortar barrage was called down on the battle area.

That day the adoo had won a victory, but they were later to pay the price. As the defences at Point 985 were reinforced, it was decided to blast the adoo out of their stronghold. So it was that for each minute of the following two days, every weapon that could reach the Shirshitti Wadi was fired. Artillery, armoured cars, mortars and warplanes were involved, and a bombardment was even delivered by an Omani warship lying off the coast. The air thundered with high explosives, and the dust and phosphorus smoke hung over the Shirshitti Wadi like a permanent cloud.

At this stage, both SAS mortar men controlling the baseline at Point 985 had been wounded, and Barry Davies was one of those withdrawn to replace them. He explained:

'There were six mortars in two groups of three. Each half hour it was our turn to fire, each tube firing 10 rounds, a mixture of white phosphorus and high explosive. In the next few hours, the mortars alone consumed 8,000 rounds.

'Even with this massive barrage, the adoo still found time to carry out night attacks on our position; additionally, despite the carnage taking place in the wadi, they still found it possible to launch three giant rockets into our camp, with devastating effect. I watched in disbelief as the first one flew over our position, a great flame burning from its tail. When it fell to earth, the whole world seemed to shake. Luckily for us, only one hit the camp; just as unluckily, it hit the ammo bunker.'

In the end, the Shirshitti caves were taken and vast adoo stores were captured. And although the Oman War will be known for the Battle of Mirbat, battles such as that for the Shirshitti caves will remain forever with those who were there.

Battle Bear Zakhir Tree

The SAS returned later in the year. Together with a company of the SOAF, they intended to establish a firm base at Defa, to the north of the famous Zakhir Tree. By 15 September 1975, the base held a company of SAF, a troop of Saladin armoured cars and several 25-pounder guns. The SAS had a whole troop in the location, but due to Ramadan the firqat were very thin on the ground. There remained only one problem with Defa. During the Shirshitti operation, the enemy had pounded the position with Soviet Katyusha rockets and, despite the caves having been cleared, they now began to rain down again – this time from somewhere near the Zakhir Tree. As the monsoon provided a thick mist, especially in the morning, the SAS decided to silence the rocket fire by sending in a heavy patrol, backed by the SOAF and the armoured cars.

On the early morning of 19 September, 13 SAS and two firqat under the command of Captain Charles Delius slipped out of Defa, making their way towards the Zakhir Tree. Due to the darkness and mist, the patrol found itself on a small spur to the west of the Zakhir Tree. Delius decided to remain at the position with six men while Sergeant Rover Walker took the other six down the spur for a recce. They dropped lower into the wadi, but as dawn grew stronger and the mist patchy, it became obvious that their tactical position was not good. Walker, a highly experienced SAS soldier, moved his men and dispatched Corporal Bell and one of the firqat to proceed across the wadi bed and up the other side in search of the Zakhir Tree, in order to fix their position. Bell moved cautiously until the mist cleared and he was able to observe the landmark and take a bearing. However, as he and the firqa moved back to rejoin the patrol, they came across several sets of freshly made footprints. Moreover, there was a very strong smell of meat hanging in the damp air.

While Walker waited for Bell to return, he observed a man walking through the mist, heading roughly toward Delius's position, and quickly sent a message. Delius was still on the radio when three enemy soldiers appeared directly to their front and a rapid exchange of fire broke out. All three enemy were cut down by the SAS, but one of the enemy had time to fire, and one of the bullets found its mark, hitting Lance-Corporal Geordie Small in the thigh and severing the femoral artery. The patrol medic quickly bandaged the wound and Small was moved to higher ground. Contact was made with the SAF at Defa and an armoured car was sent to pick up the casualty. Sadly, no one realized how bad the internal damage was, and Geordie Small died while the medevac helicopter was flying him to the Field Surgical Team (FST).

On hearing the shots, Walker ordered his men to make their way up the wadi, heading north for the high ground. They had just started to climb when a burst of fire signalled an all-out contact. The men dropped and wriggled forward, using the scanty mist as cover; however, the weight of fire was so close that it seemed as if the enemy were right on top of them. Suddenly Lance-Corporal Tony Fleming was hit badly in the back; Walker at first thought he was dead, only to see his eyes open. Dragging Fleming between them, the patrol forced itself forward, but such was the enemy fire they eventually decided to stay put and defend as best they could. Walker explained to Delius his only option; they must stand and fight and wait to be relieved. Delius immediately called for mortar fire, but due to the mist and the fact that he did not know Walker's exact position, adjustment control was difficult.

Walker's men huddled together, with those able to shoot firing at anything that moved while the medics attended to the wounded. The mist cleared briefly, and one of the patrol shouted with relief; a line of smartly uniformed soldiers was advancing towards them in open order. SOAF had arrived. Walker got to his feet and shouted, indicating their position, whereupon the soldiers opened fire. Walker was hit and dropped to his knees. Another round hit him, and he fell to the ground. He tried to rise, and was hit a third time. The enemy advanced to within 65 feet, into grenade-throwing range. Still the SAS held its ground, but was forced to switch to single shots as ammunition ran low. Walker, who by this time had been given morphine, shouted for Bell to take over the patrol, when suddenly an armoured car appeared coming down the slope; the enemy started to disengage.

By 09:00 the battle was over. Captain Delius rejoined his men, only to find that every man in Walker's patrol had been wounded. Fleming and Walker were the worst, and Delius ordered that they should be placed on one of the armoured cars and carried to safety.

As with most battles, word is quickly spread to the SAS base at Hereford and from there to the sub-units operating around the world. What makes this story so good were the comments made by Fleming as they bounced along on the back of the armoured car returning to Defa. Danny had been cradling Fleming's head when the latter whispered, 'Danny I'm going off.'

'No,' replied Bell, 'hang on in there – think of those you love!'

Fleming smiled: 'No, Danny; I'm falling off the fucking armoured car.'

Tony Fleming bravely battled against the disability which resulted from his wounds. He died in 1994.

Belize

A couple of months later, the SAS was in action once again, this time in Belize in Central America. Shipwrecked English seamen discovered Belize in 1638. Over the next 150 years, more English settlements were established. This was a period also marked by piracy, indiscriminate logging and sporadic attacks by Indians and the neighbouring Spanish settlements. The area became the Crown Colony of British Honduras in 1862. Several constitutional changes were made much later to expand representative government. Full internal self-government under a ministerial system was granted in January 1964, the official name of the territory was changed to Belize in June 1973 and full independence was granted on 21 September 1981.

Throughout this time, the British Army remained responsible for the protection of Belize, and accordingly a British garrison remained in situ. This force was designed primarily to deter military advances from neighbouring Guatemala, which is much larger and lays claim to Belize. From time to time, the Guatemalans have rattled their sabres and begun preparations to take Belize by force. Much of their rhetoric was taken with a pinch of salt, but on one occasion they seriously intended to invade. This was in November 1975, and the 1,800-strong garrison was rapidly reinforced. One of the SAS soldiers takes up the story.

'It was one of those quick-move jobs. One minute we were happily doing a spot of training in Hereford, and the next we were winging our way over the Atlantic. The faithful Lockheed C-130 Hercules transport took off from Brize Norton bound for Belize, with a refuelling stop at Nassau in the Bahamas. Here, we were given permission to leave the aircraft and stretch our legs while the transport was being serviced. It was at this stage that I noticed the RAF loadmaster beating one of the engines with a broom. About 10 minutes later we were informed that the flight had gone US (unserviceable) and that we would have to spend the night in Nassau – I could have kissed him! If you've ever wondered why the sailors of old never returned from these islands, one breath of the relaxing air would explain everything.

'Forgetting the war, we were taken by a fleet of taxis to a Trust House Forte hotel. Here, the whole squadron was given grand rooms, many right on the beach: "Eat what you like, gentlemen. For you, Happy Hour has just begun," said the manager, as a way of saying that it was all free.

'Unfortunately, next morning the Hercules was fixed and we continued our journey to Belize, with most of us nursing a hangover. We arrived at about 14:00 in the afternoon, and quickly set about equipping ourselves for the jungle. I was given a seven-man patrol. This was a bit large for the jungle, but it suited our task. We were to penetrate the thick jungle in central Belize and move up to the border with Guatemala. By 16:00, we were ready to get choppered in, and that's when this guy arrived from the government. He had come to tell us about the type of jungle in Belize. The squadron sat on the floor as Major Rose introduced him. The first words he said were "fer de lance" or something like that. We looked at each other in some amusement, wondering what the hell he was going on about. He then proceeded to tell us all about this snake which could fly. It would leap out of the trees and bite your neck, and then you died. Charming. And on top of this, we still had to take care of the Guatemalans.

'We infiltrated at dusk, and after clearing the drop-off found a spot to hole up for the night. To be fair, the boys went into jungle mode straight away: no talking, no cutting, everyone alert. Next day we set off, and as two of the guys were new to the troop I decided to carry out one or two contact drills. This we did, and I'm confident that, had we hit the enemy, the patrol would have held its ground and extracted in good order.

'Three days later, as we neared our objective, I suddenly saw the lead scout, Tony, move to one side and bring up his weapon. I heard two loud bangs, followed by the cry "fer de lance!" Initially thinking that this was an enemy contact, the boys behind me had gone directly into combat mode, ready to take on the worst. Two seconds later, as the words "fer de lance" pierced the air; you couldn't see them for dust. Fighting Guatemalans is one thing; flying snakes are another.

'Our task was to observe a main jungle route which led from the Guatemalan side and stretched over the border into Belize. It was thought the Guatemalans might use this to infiltrate troops. In the event of invasion, we were to report all enemy movements and strengths. If we were compromised, the plan was to bug out and run north to Mexico [an agreement had been reached between the British and Mexican governments for the internment of all UK soldiers until the end of the war; blood money was issued to make this journey possible].

'By day five, Harriers of the RAF had arrived. They flew down the border in teams of four, stopping now and then to hover, like giant angry bees waiting to sting. In full sight of any Guatemalan forces, they flaunted their massive firepower. It was enough, and a day later the Guatemalans called off any thoughts of invasion. Once more, British gunboat diplomacy had worked and Belize had been saved from the threat of war.

'We remained in the jungle for several more days carrying out "hearts and minds" activities before being extracted to Belize City and thence home. Before I left, I purchased a T-shirt with "I fought the Guats" printed on the front and "ALL DAY" on the back.'

Northern Ireland

Back in Britain, it was announced that the SAS would be sent to Northern Ireland to curb the increase in IRA violence. True, the SAS had been in the province since 1973, but most of these were just visits with an SAS man being attached to a local regiment. In 1976, the SAS was to become a political tool. Results came quickly: on 12 March 1976, Sean McKenna, a known IRA member, was lifted from his home over the border in Eire. He was dragged from his bed and frogmarched into Northern Ireland, whereupon he was handed over to the Royal Ulster Constabulary (RUC). Less than a month later another IRA member, Peter Cleary, was lifted from the home of his fiancée, who lived just north of the border. The house had been under observation for some time, as it was known that Cleary was soon to be married, and it was just a matter of waiting. Once the suspect had been taken into custody, the SAS men moved to a pick-up point and waited for their helicopter. However, Cleary tried to escape, and was shot dead as he did so. The incident did not go down well: the IRA claimed that he had been murdered.

Several senior officers in Northern Ireland were aghast at having a bunch of men such as the SAS in their midst, but as the Prime Minister, James Callaghan, had sent them, there was little they could do. However, the situation did serve to send a message to the IRA: 'Border or not, we will come and get you.'

Tensions arose when, at 18:00 on 5 May 1976, the Eire police stopped two men in a car at a checkpoint within the Republic, and discovered that it had members of the SAS on its hands. To make matters worse, two back-up vehicles arrived to assist the first, and in total the Eire police took eight SAS men, together with their vehicles and weapons, into custody. As the news emerged all hell broke loose, and the newspapers had a field day. The men were taken to Dundalk and then on to Dublin. All were charged, and in the end it was just as embarrassing for Eire as it was for the SAS soldiers, most of whom were fined £100 each for having unlicensed weapons.

The SAS suffered another blow when the IRA killed an Intelligence officer, Captain Bob Nairac, in Northern Ireland in May 1977. Although not a member of the SAS, Bob did live and work out of the same location in Bessbrook, Armagh. He was from a unit known as 14 Intelligence and Security, a covert unit used to gather information on which the SAS could operate. For some reason best known to himself, Bob Nairac had taken to speaking with an Irish accent; it was good, but not good enough. He also had the idea that he could pass himself off as an Irishman, and to some degree he did. Two days prior to his death he had gone to a shop that sold Republican song sheets and purchased several well-known songs, then he practised singing the verses until he was word-perfect.

A highly intelligent man, and certainly enormously courageous, Bob decided to visit a local pub close to the border with the Irish Republic. The problem was that he neglected to tell anyone where he was going. He drove off from Bessbrook Barracks around 19:30, but he did not reach the Three Steps Inn, near the village of Drominthee, until around 22:00. Here, the evening was in full swing, and at first Bob managed to fit in well with the locals, all having a good time. Several people did a turn on the makeshift stage, mostly singing rebel songs. It was at this stage that Bob got up and joined in, putting himself in a position where he would be noticed. It was not so much his accent that gave him away; it was more that no one knew him.

As he attempted to make his way back to the car park, he was followed. Casually, several men inquired as to his identity. A fist fight ensued (Bob Nairac was an excellent boxer and could take care of himself) but during the tussle his Browning 9mm pistol fell to the ground. His assailants grabbed it and he was soon overpowered. What happened after this is not clear, but from various people brought into the police barracks for questioning, a rough picture emerged.

While Bob was held, a telephone call was made to members of the IRA just over the border in the Republic. Blindfolded and gagged, he was taken by car to a field on the border where the IRA members took control. He was tortured and interrogated in the corner of a field, the main instrument being a fence post, with which they beat him repeatedly around the body and head. Despite what has been called a murderous beating by the IRA themselves, Bob Nairac did not talk. In the end, they shot him with his own pistol and disposed of his body, never to be recovered. However, some years later a suspect under interrogation in Armagh Barracks offered information on the disposal of Nairac's body. It was so horrifying that it has never been made public. Strangely enough, the IRA man relating the story had nothing but praise for the way in which Bob Nairac had suffered in silence.

During the late 1970s, there were other successes and the occassional failure, but slowly the Regiment evolved its own strategy, forming stronger links with the RUC's Special Branch. This link provided more accurate information for the SAS to work on. One such operation came in June 1978, when information was received that an IRA cell was about to bomb the Post Office depot in Belfast. A member of the SAS who served in Ulster at the time takes up the story.

'It was a classic operation. Special Branch had given us the information and we would provide the solution. It was simple: a team of IRA terrorists was to firebomb the Post Office depot in Belfast. We even knew of their approach route and made our plans accordingly. The only thing we did not know was the exact time of the bombing. In the event, several observation posts were set up, the main one being located in a house. This gave us a clear view of the small alley which ran by the side of the Post Office compound where the vehicles were kept. This compound was protected by a high fence. As well as several cut-off groups positioned around the compound, a reaction team, sitting in a van, lay in wait. I hate to think how many hours I spent lying in that van – it was bloody uncomfortable. As the operation progressed over several days, it was deemed a better idea to position two guys in a large bush during the hours of darkness.

'On the night in question, the task fell to Tony and Jim (not their real names). Tony was in my troop, and a better man would be hard to find. He was solidly built, laid-back and very cool. In this incident and many others afterwards, when the chips were down, he was the man to have by your side. Jim was a little younger but not quite so level-headed.

'The SAS guy in the observation house was bored. He had sat at the window for several days and nothing had happened. Special Branch had reassured him several times that the bombing would take place, but as time went on, he had begun to entertain doubts. Then, suddenly, he saw some figures in the alley approaching the wall of the compound. Before he could raise the alarm, one of the figures moved his arm, and the first bomb was already arcing its way towards the target. Orders were screamed: "Go, go, go!" The operation was activated. With Tony in the lead, the two men leapt from the bush. The light on top of Tony's MP5 sub-machine gun sent out a beam which illuminated three figures in front of him, two of them about to throw satchel bombs. Tony fired two short bursts, and two men fell dead. The third made a run for it, retreating back down the alley in the direction from which he had come. Tony fired another short burst and the third man fell. It was perfect, except that Jim, who on this occasion was armed with an SLR, decided to confirm the kills, pumping a lot of heavy-calibre rounds into the bodies. Almost as Jim finished firing, two more men entered the alley from the bottom end. Tony immediately issued a challenge, unsure as to the identity of the men. One dropped to the ground and placed his hands on his head, but the other made a run for it. He never made it – a short burst from Tony killed him outright.

'As the situation stabilized, it turned out that the two men were just returning from the pub and had accidentally walked straight into the firefight. Had the man, a Protestant by the name of William Hanna, remained still after the challenge, he would be alive today. I can assure you a clear challenge was given. Without going into too much detail, the fun really started when the legal eagles arrived. The weapons were tagged and taken away for forensic examination. Then each man gave his story. It was all clear and simple until the lawyer asked Jim to give his account in his own words. "Well, I saw Tony move and I backed him up. He slotted two, but the third made a run for it. As Tony fired, I stepped to one side and shouted to the boys in the bottom cut-off, 'Keep your head down, Bobby.' Then I let rip with a 30-round mag." The legal eagle stared in horror, while the rest of us just rolled around laughing. Subsequently his story was corrected, and no court case followed.'

Not long after, Special Branch in Armagh asked the SAS unit in Portadown to undertake a reconnaissance of a small Catholic church in Castleford. The essence of the information was that there was an IRA meeting place in a small building at the rear of the church grounds. Special Branch requested that the SAS take a look and photograph any documents of interest that were discovered.

Two men were entrusted with the task, one of them a lock-picking specialist. They were driven to the town by two other SAS personnel, who would stay mobile in the area and act as backup. At around 01:00 on a wet and windy morning, the two men were dropped off by a gateway at the edge of the town and quickly made their way to the rear of the church. The whole church was surrounded on three sides by a 12-foot-high wall, with an iron railing fronting the road. Approaching from the rear, the two men quickly climbed the wall and, remaining in the shadow of the church, approached the meeting house. The small, two-storey building stood in one corner, with a single door providing the entrance. One of the SAS men produced a set of picks and made short work of the padlock. Once inside, they searched the ground floor. There was nothing of interest, as most of the space was taken up with church props and junk. A small set of stairs led to the second floor, the entrance to which was also barred by a padlock (which was soon picked). This upper floor had two windows, allowing the single room to be illuminated by the street lighting. The room itself contained several lockers filled with paperwork and books, with a large table and several chairs sitting in the middle. The two men carried out a search of the room and the cupboards, but little of interest was found, and certainly nothing referring to the IRA. A small trapdoor leading to the loft was discovered, and by placing a chair on the table, it could be reached. Checking the hatch for any booby trap, one of the SAS men climbed inside the loft. After he had secured the hatch behind him, he switched on his torch. What confronted him was a whole pile of large plastic bags, most of which contained bomb-making equipment. Several pounds of Semtex plastic explosive were also discovered, as were 20 ready-to-go cassette incendiaries. The information was relayed directly back to control and an observation unit organized for the next day.

Unfortunately, when Special Branch found out about it, the situation changed. For some unexplained reason, MI5 became involved; this meant the SAS wasn't allowed anywhere near with the target being electronically tagged. The two SAS men had the pleasure of taking the MI5 operative into the building, but he was so fat that he demolished half the rear wall as he climbed over it! Then he could not pick the lock, and thus became hell-bent on calling in an expert until the SAS man picked it. For the SAS, that was the end of the story, although only for three weeks. A call came from Special Branch to remove the whole explosives find and bury it in a hide. The hide was to look like an IRA job and be at least half a mile from the church. This we did, and the next day an SAS soldier stood on the site as the local Ulster Defence Regiment (UDR) unit searched the area. 'It's here, mate,' said the SAS man. The day after, the newspapers carried head-lines of a major explosives find by the UDR. There was a reason for this subterfuge: it told the IRA, which had put the explosives in the church grounds, that it was being watched, and in the eyes of the general public it also made the British Army look good.

Sadly, another SAS soldier died on 7 June 1978 while travel-ling alone from Portadown to Londonderry, when his car left the road at Shanalongford Bridge. Dave Naden was the SAS liaison officer attached to Special Branch in Londonderry. Working alone, it was his responsibility to assess work suit-able for SAS operation. As a mark of respect, the RUC Special Branch attended the funeral in very large numbers and contin-ued the wake for several days afterwards.

Lufthansa Hijack

On 13 October 1977, two men and two women belonging to the Popular Front for the Liberation of Palestine hijacked a Lufthansa Boeing 737 that was returning from the holiday resort of Palma, Majorca. What was not known was that the hijackers were working in conjunction with the Baader-Meinhof terrorist group, which had kidnapped a top German industrialist, Dr Hans-Martin Schleyer, a month before. It later transpired that both the kidnapping and the hijack were allied to the same demands.

The hijack team spent several days in Palma posing as tour-ists and selecting a flight to take them to West Germany. After having visited several travel companies in the holiday resort, they eventually booked several seats on Flight LH181, which was bound for Frankfurt. Later, it is reported, three of the group returned to the airport where they met a German woman who was pushing a child's pushchair. This woman handed over a biscuit tin to them that contained the weapons and grenades for the hijack.

Flight LH181 took off from Palma for Frankfurt at 12:57 on Thursday, 13 October. The in-flight meal had just been served when the hijackers struck. Brandishing pistols and hand grenades, they seized control of the flight and started a drama that would ricochet around the Middle East. Refuelling at Rome and at Larnaca in Cyprus, the airliner then flew on to Bahrain. Here, it refuelled yet again before making its way to Dubai in the United Arab Emirates. The terrorists were now demanding the release of Baader-Meinhof gang members being held in a top-security West German prison, as well as two other terrorists held in Turkish prisons. They also demanded $15 million. The demand note was identical to that issued for the release of the kidnapped industrialist Dr Schleyer a month earlier. During the first 48 hours of negotiation, the German government in Bonn took a firm line, refusing any concessions and holding to a strategy of continuous dialogue as a means of achieving the hostages' safe release. At the same time, the West Germans looked to Europe for support in its stand, and received assurances from both France and the UK. In response, British Prime Minister James Callaghan sent two members of the SAS to support the Germans. Barry Davies, who, along with Major Alastair Morrison, assisted the German antiterrorist team throughout the hijack, tells the story.

'During the week preceding the hijack, I was on duty at Heathrow with eight other members of the SAS anti-terrorist team. We were training on various types of aircraft, familiarizing ourselves with their basic internal layouts and the many variations employed by different airlines. Most of our work was done during the periods allowed for cleaning between scheduled flights.

On the afternoon of Friday, 14October, I returned with my crew to Hereford through the beginnings of fog, which was thickening dramatically across the country. On arrival at Bradbury Lines, we checked in all our equipment and our vehicles. Ensuring that all my men were on call, I released them for the weekend before setting off for my own home. I had only just arrived when the phone rang, ordering me back to camp. Back at the anti-terrorist team office I found the team commander, Captain Holmes, who informed me that the British and West German governments had agreed on the need for a joint anti-terrorist effort, and that the two of us were to leave immediately for London.

'As the fog was so thick we took a chopper, which flew us directly to Battersea Heliport. Unfortunately, the heliport had been closed by the fog, so that when we landed we had no option but to climb over the heliport gates to get into the street. Luckily, one of the first vehicles we saw was a police panda car, which we flagged down. We asked the driver to take us to Whitehall. He was, not surprisingly, dubious about such a request from two scruffy individuals, but our manner, backed up by ID cards, persuaded him to check with his control. They played it safe, telling the PC to give us a lift to see if we were genuine – and to bring us in if we weren't!

'When we arrived outside No 10, we were met by senior military personnel who briefed us on the current situation. Major Morrison of SAS headquarters in London joined us at this time. We were further briefed regarding the areas of national secrecy concerning the operation and the equipment employed. It was made clear that we were to give all possible assistance to achieve the release of the hostages but were instructed not to talk about some of the recent equipment advances we had developed. We got the impression that a couple of politicians from Bonn had arrived, together with two members of a unit barely known to us at the time: GSG 9 [Grenzschutzgruppe 9, a division of the border police trained in anti-terrorism].

'We attended a meeting inside No 10, at which the hijack situation was more fully discussed. Present were various heads of security departments, ministers, Major Morrison, Captain Holmes and myself. It was quickly established that the plane's position was still as reported by the media that afternoon – in Dubai. We in turn reported that there was an ex-SAS man currently in position in Dubai working under contract for the Palace Guard. We were then introduced to the GSG 9 members, and within minutes realized how much in common the SAS anti-terrorist team had with them, for we had each developed tactics and equipment which would later be of great benefit to both units. I mentioned that we had developed a new type of stun grenade which would detonate almost instantaneously when thrown, effectively stunning anyone in close proximity. The grenade emits a very loud bang and a very bright flash of light in a set sequence, not dissimilar to the effect of strobes in a disco as they flash on and off. The effectiveness of these grenades, together with our expertise and knowledge gathered from the Middle East, and our recent training on aircraft interiors, was of such value to the Germans in dealing with the hijack that we were immediately asked to return with them to Germany. They also suggested that once we had talked to the people in Germany, we could, if requested, fly on to Dubai to give further assistance.

'Major Morrison and I were selected to accompany GSG 9, and arrangements were made for eight stun grenades to be sent from Hereford to meet us at Brize Norton. We left shortly afterwards, the intention being to travel by helicopter. However, due to the very thick fog, we had to endure a very tedious drive – sometimes at not more than 10–15 mph – arriving at Brize Norton at about 04:00. Here, we met the crew of a C-130, which had been placed at our disposal and was ready for an immediate take-off. Already aboard – and under guard – were the two boxes containing the stun grenades. I checked them at once to make certain that we had operational grenades and not the training variety. The C130 then took off into weather so bad that we crossed the Channel using low-level radar, and we landed in Bonn at 06:30 on Saturday, 15 October. There to meet us were the two GSG 9 officers we had previously met in London, who immediately took us directly to GSG 9 headquarters. There we had a very short discussion with the unit's second-in-command (the commander, Ulrich Wegener, was already in Dubai), and it was decided we should demonstrate the British stun grenades to the Germans. The most convenient space, which was similar in size and shape to the interior of a plane, was a long corridor in the cellars of the headquarters building. About a dozen GSG 9 soldiers took up positions in various recessed doorways. With the lights out, I tossed in a stun grenade. The language was blue as some very shocked GSG 9 soldiers emerged from the cellar corridor, but nevertheless it proved how effective the grenades were. The second-in-command then made an instant decision to send both Alastair and myself on to Dubai by the speediest means. Unfortunately, this meant getting the 12:12 plane out of Frankfurt for Dubai, and then changing in Kuwait.

'All went smoothly until we arrived in Kuwait. As one can imagine, the entire Middle East was alarmed by the hijack in Dubai. For this reason, Kuwait Airport was on full military alert, and even passengers in transit had their luggage rechecked before being allowed back aboard the plane for Dubai. Although Alastair and I hung further and further back in the queue, it was inevitable that we had to put our bag, containing the boxes of stun grenades, through the X-ray machine. I can still envisage the screen clearly showing those grenades, and I still recall, very vividly, the commotion it caused. We were at once slapped under heavy guard and manhandled quite ruthlessly by Kuwaiti soldiers into the main Security Officer's room, followed by our suspicious hand luggage.

'The bag was opened for examination, a procedure which I had to terminate when one of the Arabs tried to remove the pin from a grenade. At this stage, realization dawned on everybody in the room that we were taking the grenades from Germany to Dubai. Luckily for us, at that moment the general manager for Lufthansa in Kuwait came into the security room. After a few moments he left the security officer in no doubt that, unless we were released immediately, together with our grenades, to rejoin our original flight to Dubai, no other Lufthansa aircraft would ever again fly into Kuwait Airport. It worked, and we were hustled across the tarmac to the waiting plane before physically being pushed into our seats. Then the bag with the stun grenades was dropped into my lap for me to nurse.

'We arrived in Dubai at around 03:00 on Sunday, 16 October – only to be arrested at the airport for lack of documentation. Our passports were taken from us, and this action allowed one of the Western news reporters covering the hijack to pick up our names. Later, he realized our true identities and that we were SAS.

Alastair made numerous attempts during the early hours of the morning to contact the British Embassy but got no further than the gate man who was manning the night phone. Then luck came our way in the form of an ex-SAS officer called David Bullig. He had left the SAS and had been seconded to work training the Dubai Palace Guard. When he saw us both, he knew immediately who we were, and events took a completely different turn. Within minutes we were able to roam freely about the airport to assess the situation. David was extremely helpful in many other ways, not least because he had already primed some of the best men of the Palace Guard to be ready to attempt an immediate assault on the aircraft should the terrorists actually start killing the hostages.

'We toured the airport and then spoke to Wischnewski, the German minister who was the acting representative for the West German government. We also met and talked to the defence minister of Dubai, who had taken charge of the situation directly (this was the second hijack he had dealt with). Having fully assessed the situation, we went with David Bullig to talk directly to Colonel Ulrich Wegener, Head of GSG 9, who was resting with several other Germans in the airport hotel. We all agreed that there was very little we could do until the morning, and we would be better off refreshing ourselves with a little sleep and meeting later that day.

'David Bullig took Alastair and myself to his home, where his charming wife plied us with sandwiches and coffee while we laid out our plan of action. David scribbled notes, listing our demands for kit and equipment. Our most expensive request was for the use of a Boeing 737 for training and practice purposes. At around 05:00 both Alastair and I fell asleep. After a couple of hours' dozing we were awakened by Mrs Bullig with the news that David had managed to fulfil most of our demands. All three of us left for the airport to meet GSG 9 and three other British officers David had found from various units in Dubai. In addition, he had selected eight of the best men from the Dubai Palace Guard.

'We set out a very quick Immediate Action drill to meet the needs of the worst possible scenario: that is, when we would have had no choice but to assault the aircraft with the limited force available. Of course, the more time we had, the more our plan would improve. By now, most of the kit and equipment we needed had arrived: shotguns, masking tape, walkie-talkies, various ladders, padding and a host of other items. We had two quartermasters standing by with four jeeps and an apparently endless supply of cash to obtain anything else required. Most importantly, a Gulf Air Boeing 737 had been given on loan and was parked at the far end of the airfield, well out of sight of the hijacked plane. I was about to start a crash course in anti-terrorist techniques.

'On the personnel side, my resources were limited to a hard core of five men who had received at least some professional Close Quarter Battle (CQB) or anti-terrorist training. These included Alastair, David, myself and the two GSG 9 officers. Additionally, I had three other British officers and the eight soldiers from the Palace Guard. I concentrated our first efforts on the Immediate Action drill needed to counter any terrorist deadline.

'The Boeing 737 is a simple little animal where anti-terrorist drills are concerned. There are only three options for entry: tail, wing and front catering area. We thought that if the terrorists began to carry out any threatened shootings, they would naturally take the precaution of covering the main doors. It seemed less likely that they would cover the two emergency exit doors leading on to the wings, so the basic plan which fell into place was to attack through these entry points. The fact that the wing emergency exits were designed to be opened easily from the outside was another strong factor in favour of adopting this mode of attack. In addition, we had also discovered a blind spot where the wing joins the aircraft body. Two men could easily sit beneath the emergency doors and not be visible from any of the plane's windows. By comparison, the entry and exit points at both the front and rear require considerable manhandling and some time to get them open.

'Although our basic plan was quite uncomplicated, we calculated that it would require a great deal of practice to get the timing right, especially the time it would take the assault teams to effect their entry and make their way to the front and rear of the passenger cabin. We reckoned that as soon as we dominated these points, the only people in serious danger would be the crew in the cockpit.

'By 08:00 on 16 October – 67 hours after LH181 had left Palma – the training and practice began. We took a break around 14:00, using the time to iron out every detail, searching for anything which might increase the odds in our favour. One thing which did improve the odds were the Palace Guards. I was truly amazed at the quality of the soldiers we had with us: they turned out to be extremely tough, very quick and could be relied upon to do exactly as they were told in what was, for them, an entirely new kind of situation. We now felt fairly confident that if the terrorists forced us into immediate action we had a better than average chance of success. We were now sure that we could approach the airliner and establish all our people in their starting positions unobserved. We knew we could put eight men – the four assault pairs – inside the airliner. We knew that the outside assault teams were fully aware of their duties regarding getting the doors open, effecting their own entry and giving assistance where necessary.

'We refined our assault plan as best we could and then started to develop external additions. We worked out a suitable distraction for the terrorists. We considered how best we could locate their positions inside the airliner – extremely valuable information if we could get it. We also gave considerable thought to the possibility of an attack at night, during which, if it came off, we would have an extra man underneath the plane to shut down the APU (Auxiliary Power Unit). This is located at the rear of the wheel housing, and one yank on the red and yellow handle would kill all the lights and power in the airliner at the moment which suited us.

'At about 15:30 the Dubai defence minister left his watch in the control tower and came to check on our progress. We went through our operation on the Gulf Air Boeing 737, and I have to admit that it looked pretty impressive. Then, just as we finished our demonstration, the unexpected happened. LHl8l's engines came to life and she took off, taking with her any hope that the hijack would end in Dubai.

'Fortunately, the Germans had a Boeing 707 for the use of the negotiators. Everybody from Germany concerned with the hijack, as well as Alastair and myself, went aboard and we took off to follow the hijacked plane. First indications were that it was going to land at Salalah in southern Oman. This sounded like good news, for the SAS had men in the area with anti-hijack skills. Our expectations were dashed, however, when we learned that LH181 had in fact landed at Khormaksar Airport in Aden. Captain Schumann, piloting LH181, had been too low on fuel to fly anywhere else, and he skilfully put the aircraft down on the hard sand alongside the runway.

'Our Boeing 707 had to fly on to the international airport in Saudi Arabia. Here, confined in the aircraft, we sat on the ground awaiting further developments. During this waiting period, the negotiating psychologists attempted to persuade the hijackers to release the hostages in exchange for the $15 million, which we held in a large suitcase on board our plane.

'Then came the shocking news which brought an immediate end to negotiations: Captain Schumann had been shot
dead aboard LH181. Now the decision more or less made
itself. Wherever LH181 was, wherever she was forced to fly,
we would make our rescue attempt. For the first time, I saw
the true determination of our German partners concerning
their own nationals. The killing of Captain Schumann decided
the matter: any further ideas about peaceful negotiation were
instantly dismissed.

'Our next news was that LH181 had again taken off from
Aden, the first officer at the controls and the dead captain still
aboard, and had flown to Mogadishu, capital of the Somali
Republic. We got airborne in the Boeing 707 and sought permission to land there as well. Our flight from Saudi Arabia to
Mogadishu took us directly across the war zone lying between
Ethiopia and Somalia. On approach to Mogadishu we were
given permission to land, but the situation was complicated by
the presence of LH181 sitting in the middle of the main runway.
Our pilot was equal to the challenge, however. Using only a
short length of runway, he brought off a superb landing, using
every inch of concrete available and rolling to within literally
feet of buildings and houses on the airfield perimeter. Even the
intensity of the overall situation could not obscure this brilliant
feat of professional skill, and everyone aboard broke into spon-
taneous and grateful applause.

'On the ground, two top Somali officials collected all passports – and were surprised to discover two of the British variety
among them, though they remained most courteous and friendly.
The German minister went off to meet the Somali Prime Minister
to discuss the developing political aspects of the hijack. The rest
of us were taken to one of Mogadishu's top hotels and given
accommodation and a meal. We were kept constantly updated
regarding the hijack situation through the Mogadishu security
services, who were extremely cordial and helpful.

'The terrorists now announced that their deadline was
15:00 on that same day: Monday, 17 October. Negotiators in

the control tower at Mogadishu airport asked for an extension, explaining that the Baader-Meinhof terrorists jailed in Germany, together with the two Palestinians held in Turkey, would be released but that they could not, however, be flown to Mogadishu in less than 10 hours.

'After prolonged discussion, the terrorist leader, "Captain Mahmoud" [Zohair Akache], agreed on a final deadline of 03:00 the next morning, Tuesday, 18 October. In the meantime, Minister Wischnewski obtained permission to bring in the German anti-terrorist team, flying to Mogadishu with the option of an assault on LH181. While awaiting its arrival, we all worked together to modify the assault plan to match it to the current situation. Joining us in our planning was a colonel from the Somali Special Forces.

'We stuck to the basic plan to approach the aircraft in a single column from the rear, breaking into four subsections, each moving to its assigned position with the intention of making simultaneous entries through both wing emergency exits, the port front and starboard rear doors. We modified the choice of ladders for the assault on the doors, using double (side-by-side) instead of single ladders. The advantage of these was that two men could go up together. At the top, the left-hand man could turn the door handle and swing his full weight away from the fuselage, so pulling the door open quickly. This made it possible for the second, right-hand man to penetrate the airliner immediately. We needed outside help for two reasons. First, before the assault began, we wanted the negotiators to start talking positively to the terrorists to ascertain as closely as possible their whereabouts inside LH181. We also thought we might encourage them to come to the cockpit by lighting a very large fire at the far end of the runway. This job was entrusted to the Somali soldiers, who were also responsible for ground defence around the aircraft.

'The GSG 9 men arrived in a second Boeing 707 at 20:05 on the evening of 17 October. Their commander briefed them immediately, and they set about preparing their equipment for the assault. We ran through a quick rehearsal, using the GSG 9 Boeing 707, which was parked out of sight of LH181. By 23:30, the whole group was in position about 225 feet to the rear of the airliner. In single file we approached the plane, and in complete silence the ladders were put in position at each wing root and against the chosen doors. Major Morrison and I were on either side of the fuselage, at the rear of the wing roots. Our initial task was to throw stun grenades over the fuselage just as the doors were opened, to achieve the penetrating effect of noise and light in the cabin. I was also to throw a stun grenade over the front of the cockpit to disorientate the terrorist leader.

'The approach to the aircraft was very slick and smooth. The only problem we had was that the airfield lighting around the control tower created long shadows. Had the window blinds been up, any one of the terrorists looking out could have seen us approach.

'The GSG 9 commander was in direct contact with the tower. Just before the operation began, he transmitted to all his assault teams that the two male terrorists had been heard in the cockpit. At this moment the fire was ignited at the end of the runway. In spite of the tension, this caused some amusement, for it was plain that the Somali soldiers had let their enthusiasm run away with them. It looked as if they had set fire to a complete tanker-load of petrol. The GSG 9 commander counted down and gave the "Go" signal. Everything happened at once: the quiet African night erupted. The front and rear doors opened as the left-hand ladder-men swung on them; their right-hand partners heaved themselves out of sight into the plane. The wing assault teams stood up, punched the emergency exit panels and vaulted in as the doors fell into the cabin – all these actions orchestrated by the bangs and flashes from the stun grenades. Immediately, the rear starboard door swung open the first terrorist was sighted, amazed by this turn of events. A GSG 9 soldier shot her instantly, then threw himself flat into the rear catering area, firing up the aisle where the other female terrorist had been spotted.

'The front assault team was involved in a brief firefight with the two male terrorists. Lasting for about a minute, it ended when they were both fatally shot. During the firefight we heard two dull explosions inside LH181. These were hand grenades exploding as the terrorists' strength drained away and their grip on the weapons relaxed. Thus, as the first few minutes of Tuesday, 18 October, ticked away, the hijacking of Flight LH181 ended.

'As soon as the firing died away, the passengers began to disembark. The GSG 9 men on the ground took swift and firm command of the exits, guiding people down the assault ladders or assisting them through the midsection emergency exits down to the ground via the wings. The passengers were in a state of sheer bewilderment: they had, after all, spent five long days cooped up in a very confined space, in hot, filthy conditions and with failing sanitary facilities. On top of all this physical discomfort, every hour would have been heavily weighted by the fear feeding on the uncertainty of their future. The climactic few minutes of the assault, involving loud explosions, flashes, smoke, rapid movement, gunfire and raw danger, must have disoriented many of them. As they disembarked they were ushered to the rear, where a fleet of ambulances and other vehicles ferried them to the passenger lounge in the terminal building.

'The casualty list showed three of the terrorists dead – two men and one woman – and the second female terrorist severely wounded. As she was taken away for medical treatment she gave the V-sign and screamed an assortment of slogans. One member of GSG 9, one member of the aircrew and five of the passengers were slightly wounded. After any necessary medical attention, the passengers were soon taken aboard the negotiators' Boeing 707, while the negotiators, the GSG 9 men and the two SAS men (myself included) and boarded the GSG 9 707 to be flown back to Germany.

'Although apparently over, the hijack of LH181 still had a twist in its tail. Questions remained to which no answers have been found. During the flight we heard on the radio that the leading members of the Baader-Meinhof terrorist gang, confined in separate cells in Stammheim Jail in Stuttgart, had committed suicide. Andreas Baader and Jan-Carle Raspe had shot themselves; Gudrun Ensslin hanged herself, while Irmgard Müller had made an unsuccessful attempt to kill herself using a stolen bread knife. How did the terrorists, locked in separate cells in a maximum-security prison, simultaneously learn of the German government's success in Mogadishu, 3,500 miles away, within a few hours of its occurrence? How did the two male terrorists obtain pistols and ammunition in that same jail? These mysteries remain unexplained.

'Upon arrival at Frankfurt, Captain Morrison and I were separated from the GSG 9 people and taken to the VIP lounge. Arriving in London at around 21:00, we were moved to a secret RV for a full debriefing regarding the operation.

'So came the final end to the hijacking of LH181, together with the SAS/GSG 9 operation to rescue the hostages and crew. The success of our joint operation was marred, for me, only by the death of Captain Jürgen Schumann, shot in Aden. He was a very brave man and, like so many other aircraft captains, upheld his professional responsibilities to the end by seeking to protect all those in his care, passengers and crew alike.'

The success was soon worldwide news, and governments all over the Western world applauded West Germany's determination in the face of an international terrorist threat.

6

1980s

NORTHERN IRELAND TO GIBRALTAR

THE 1980S DID not start well for the SAS, especially for those working in Northern Ireland. Special Branch (SB) of the Royal Ulster Constabulary (RUC) would occasionally get certain information that required the skills of the Regiment. Unfortunately, SB was always very tight-lipped about the source of this information. While this was good security practice, it didn't help those troops who carried out operations.

In one incident, SB requested the SAS Armagh unit take on three separate tasks. The first job was to watch two part-time policemen whom the IRA was planning to assassinate. The information from the SB clearly stated that they would be hit close to home. This was straightforward work for the SAS, who inserted an observation post (OP). All they had to do was sit and wait...

The second task was to protect a public house, which the IRA had threatened to burn to the ground. This was another simple operation which, once again, involved inserting an OP and waiting for the IRA to turn up. Logistically, servicing two OPs with resupply and changing over men was not too much of a problem, until the weekend came around – at which time Special Branch had an operation requiring every man in the field.

It would seem that one of the local underlings in the IRA had seriously upset the organization. The punishment for his crime was to be kneecapped, with the job being carried out by a leading IRA member. Special Branch was desperate to catch such a leading IRA figure in the act and employed a massive surveillance operation each weekend. This involved the SAS, E4A (an SB surveillance unit) and 14 Intelligence Unit in a huge stakeout of a particular Republican haunt, which ran a disco every Saturday night. The problem for the SAS was one of manpower, and in order to commit itself to the weekend operation it was forced to lift the OP on the public house every Saturday night.

On the second week, the guys in the OP watching the home of the two policemen were spotted by a local farmer and asked to be withdrawn. SB was informed of the dilemma and begged the SAS unit to stay in position. The final decision was down to the men on the ground, who opted to withdraw. However, 12 hours later, as the two police officers were returning from duty, their car was badly shot up. The IRA had positioned themselves between the house and where the SAS OP had been. Had they remained in place, they would have had the IRA gunmen. As luck would have it, only one of the two policemen was injured in the attack.

The following weekend, every available man was committed to the operation around the disco, and as usual the OP on the pub was pulled off for the night. The surveillance operation went smoothly but, as with the previous two weekends, nothing happened. At around 02:00, the operation was called off. One SAS car was to drop off the crew for the pub OP on its way back to base. They approached the public house, only to find it ablaze; the IRA had done their job during the brief moment the OP had been lifted. The SAS refer to this as 'the Paddy Factor' – needless to say, Special Branch was not pleased.

It was not just the SAS unit in South Armagh that was having bad luck; the Belfast unit was also getting its share. In early April a number of IRA weapons were discovered. Although these had originally been under surveillance, the IRA had managed to move them to an unidentified hiding place. Among these weapons was a 7.62mm M60 machine gun, originally stolen in America. It was vital that the weapons be relocated. Luckily, the weapons had been fitted with sophisticated location devices, but these only had a short range and limited battery power. After an intense search, a weak signal was discovered placing the weapons hide amid terraced houses in Antrim Road, though the exact location could not be identified. After an intelligence check by the RUC Special Branch, it emerged that the IRA had previously used one of three houses. Working on the 'best bet' principle, the SAS mounted an operation to recover the weapons.

On the afternoon of 2 May 1980, two cars containing SAS soldiers headed down the Antrim Road, screeching to a stop outside Number 367. Another vehicle, containing three more SAS, secured the rear. For security reasons, there had been no cordon or military activity prior to the raid, and the SAS team stormed straight at the house. Unknown to them, the IRA had mounted the missing M60 in an upstairs window of the adjoining house, Number 369. As the machine gun opened fire, Captain Richard Westmacott, who had been sitting in the middle rear seat of the car and so was the last to move, caught the full blast. He was killed instantly. Realizing what had happened, the whole assault was quickly switched, but by this time the IRA man had surrendered. The sound of gunfire brought the Army and RUC to the scene; additionally, a Catholic priest suddenly materialized to see that the IRA man was allowed to surrender.

The tragic events of 2 May led the SAS to drastically rethink its tactics. Today, in such a situation, the house would be put under surveillance before any direct intervention would be allowed. Captain Westmacott was the first SAS soldier to die in Northern Ireland, having joined the Regiment from the Grenadier Guards and served as a Captain in G Squadron. With curly fair hair, schoolboy looks and a love of poetry, his appearance belied his performance. He was a remarkably tough member of the SAS and in recognition of his achievements, was awarded the posthumous Military Cross.

The Iranian Embassy Siege

Tragic though it was, Captain Westmacott's death seemed to end a run of bad luck for the SAS, as a few days later the anti-terrorist team successfully stormed the Iranian Embassy in London.

The anti-terrorist unit had been in operation for more than five years, and now it had the opportunity to show what it could do. Some team members had been present when the Dutch Marines stormed a train that had been taken over by Moluccan terrorists, while others had assisted the German GSG 9 unit throughout the Mogadishu hijacking. But now the SAS was to get its own 'show'. Moreover, it was filmed on national television and was beamed around the world.

It all started when a group of terrorists arrived in London seeking accommodation. Almost inevitably they finished up in the Earls Court area, home to many recently arrived immigrants. However, like so many members of the visiting Arab community, they found the pubs and clubs of the district a temptation too good to miss. This mixture of drinking and womanizing increased to the point where they were forced to leave their accommodation and seek fresh lodgings. Eventually, they all finished up at 105 Lexham Gardens, where they remained until their departure on the morning of Wednesday, 30 April. By 11:20, having mysteriously collected several weapons, two of which were machine guns, and a quantity of grenades, the group was standing outside 16 Princes Gate, home to the Iranian Embassy in London. They were terrorists, opposed to the regime of Ayatollah Khomeini and seeking the liberation of the oil-rich province of Khuzestan – which they called Arabistan – from Iran. At 11:25, the six gunmen entered and took over Number 16.

As they took control of the Embassy, they gained 26 hostages, including the British policeman who had been on duty at the entrance. This might have gone unnoticed but for the fact that, minutes later, a burst of machine gun fire could be heard. The police were on the scene immediately – swiftness initiated by the captured policeman, Trevor Lock, who had managed to alert his headquarters before being taken by the terrorists. Armed D11 marksmen soon surrounded the building and the siege negotiating plans were put into operation.

The anti-terrorist team in Hereford was at this time practising in the Killing House, but things were soon to change. By 11:47, Dusty Grey, an ex-D Squadron SAS man who now worked with the Metropolitan Police, was talking to the Commanding Officer in Hereford. His information contained the briefest details, but it was enough to alert the Regiment. Several minutes later, the duty signaller activated the 'call-in' bleepers carried by every member of the anti-terrorist team. Although the SAS had prior warning, there can be no move before an official sanction from the Home Secretary, who at the request of the police will contact the MoD. Despite this red tape, it makes sense for the SAS to think ahead and save time by positioning the anti-terrorist team closer to the scene. Around midnight on the first day, most of the team had made its way to Regent's Park Barracks, which had been selected as a holding area. From here, information could be assembled and assessed. An order was given to construct a scale model of Number 16, Princes Gate: this task fell to two Pioneers drafted in from the nearby Guards unit. Additionally, an intelligence cell was set up to gather and collate every snippet of information that would aid any assault.

By this time the terrorists' leader, Oan, had secured their 26 hostages and issued their demands. These included autonomy for, and recognition of, the people of Arabistan and the release of 91 Arabistani prisoners. The line taken by the terrorists was hard but fair, and despite several threats to blow up the Embassy and kill the hostages, on Thursday, 1 May, they released a sick woman. Later that same day, Oan managed to get a telephone call through to Sadegh Ghotzbadeh, Iran's Foreign Minister. The conversation did not go well; Oan was accused of being an American agent and told that the Iranian hostages held in the Embassy would consider it an honour to die for their country and the Iranian Islamic Revolution.

This lack of cooperation almost forced the terrorists to seek a mediator who was more sympathetic, but it also told them that the Iranian government did not care if the staff of its Embassy were killed. Another problem had also raised its head for the terrorists. Chris Cramer, a BBC journalist who was among the hostages, had become sick with acute stomach pains. His partner, sound recordist Sim Harris, pleaded with Oan to immediately call for a doctor. This was done, but the police refused to allow him to enter the building. In the end, Cramer was released, stumbling out of the Embassy door and into a waiting ambulance.

Later that night, again under the cover of darkness, three Avis rental vans pulled up in a small side street by Princes Gate. Men carrying holdalls quickly made their way into Number 14, just two doors down from the besieged building. Within minutes they had laid out their equipment and made ready for an immediate action (IA). At first sight, this was very simple: if the terrorists started shooting, the SAS men would run to the front door of Number 16 and beat their way in – slow, primitive, but better than nothing until a clearly defined plan could be organized.

By 06:00 on the morning of Saturday, 2 May, the situation inside Number 16 was getting very agitated. Oan rang a phone that had been set up between the Embassy and Number 25 Princes Gate, the Royal School of Needlework, which now housed Alpha Control and the police negotiator. Oan's main complaint was that the media had not broadcasted any reports of the siege; how, he asked, could his cause be heard? He slammed the phone down in a rage. Late that afternoon, Oan was allowed to make a statement to be broadcast on the next news slot: in return for this, two more hostages were released, one of whom was a pregnant woman. The trouble was that Oan would not release the hostages before the statement was read out; likewise, the police wanted the hostages first. In the end, a compromise was reached and the broadcast went out on the Nine O'Clock News.

Two hours later, eight members of the SAS team had climbed on to the rear roof of Number 14 and were making their way amid a jungle of TV antennae to Number 16. Two of the men made their way directly to a glass skylight and after some time managed to get it free. It opened directly into a small bathroom on the top floor of the Iranian Embassy and would provide an excellent entry point. Meanwhile, other members secured abseil ropes to several of the chimneys and made ready for a quick descent to the lower floors, where they could smash in through the windows. Oddly enough, an enterprising television director had managed to get a camera into a bedroom window over-looking the back of the Embassy: during the assault, he filmed the whole of the action.

By 09:00 on Sunday, things seemed to be heading for a peace-ful settlement. Oan had agreed to reduce his demands and, at the same time, Arab ambassadors had attended a meeting in Whitehall; Willie Whitelaw, the Home Secretary, who was for all intents and purposes in charge of the whole operation, chaired the meeting. For the SAS anti-terrorist team, events had become much more stable. By now, access had been gained to Number 14 and efforts were being made to penetrate the wall. To aid this, various sound distractions – supplied by the Gas Board working in the vicinity – avoided the drilling being heard. On the far side, Number 17, which was the Ethiopian Embassy, had also cooperated. The basic plan had been formal-ized. It was to attack each floor at the same time and to clarify areas of demarcation to avoid overshoot. Mock-ups of the floor layouts were constructed from timber and hessian sheeting and assembled at Regent's Park Barracks.

The police, who had adopted a 'softly, softly' negotiating approach, managed to drag the siege out for several days: time which was desperately needed for the SAS to carry out covert recces, study plans, build models and, more importantly, locate the hostages and terrorists within the Embassy building. They got a major break when they talked to the released hostage Chris Cramer, the BBC journalist. In releasing him as an act of faith because of his stomach disorder, the terrorists made a big mistake: in his debrief to the SAS, he was able to give them precise and detailed information about the situation inside the Embassy.

By the sixth day of the siege, 5 May, the terrorists were becoming frustrated and the situation inside the Embassy began to deteriorate. All morning, threats were being made about executing hostages, and at 13:31 three shots were heard. At 18:50 more shots were heard, and the body of the Embassy press officer was thrown out. Immediately the police appeared to capitulate, stalling for time, while SAS plans to storm the Embassy were advanced. At this stage, the police negotiator worked hard to convince Oan and the other terrorists not to shoot any further hostages, and that a bus would be with them shortly to take them to the airport; from there they could fly to the Middle East. As the telephone conversation went on, the SAS took up their start positions.

A handwritten note passed control from the police to the SAS. Shortly thereafter, while a negotiator from Alpha Control was talking to Oan, the SAS moved in. Oan heard the first crashes and complained to Alpha Control that the Embassy was being attacked (this conversation was recorded, and one can clearly hear the stun grenades going off; Oan's conversation is cut short by a long burst of machine-gun fire). For the assault team, the waiting was over, and the words guaranteed to send their adrenaline pumping were given: 'Go. Go. Go.' At 19:23, eight men abseiled down to the first-floor balcony on ropes secured to the Embassy roof. The assault came from three directions, with the main thrust coming from the rear. Frame charges – by now they had been perfected – were quickly fitted to the windows and blown. Stun grenades were thrown in advance of the assault party and the SAS went into action. Systematically, the building was cleared from the top down, room by room. The telex room on the second floor, which housed the male hostages and three of the terrorists, was of utmost priority. Realizing that an assault was in progress, the terrorists shot and killed one hostage and wounded two others before the lead SAS team broke into the room. Immediately, they spotted and shot two gunmen; the third hid among the hostages and was not discovered until later. As rooms were cleared, hostages were literally thrown from one

SAS soldier to another, down the stairs and out into the back garden. At this stage they were all laid face down on the ground while a search was conducted for the missing terrorist.

Breaking the siege took just 17 minutes. The SAS took no casualties, other than one man, who got caught up in his abseil and was badly burned.

With the operation finished, the problem was handed back to the police. Meanwhile the SAS vacated Number 14 and went back to the barracks in time to watch themselves on television. Still dressed in assault gear, and clutching cans of Foster's lager, they crowded around, eager to see themselves in action. Halfway through Prime Minister Margaret Thatcher, who had left a dinner date, arrived to thank them in person. She circulated, as one man put it, 'like a triumphant Caesar returning to the Senate', her face glowing with pride and admiration at her Imperial Guard. Then, as the news started to show the full event, she sat down on the floor amid her warriors – there can be no greater gesture of approbation from one's leader.

In total, 26 hostages were taken in the Embassy when the siege started. Of these, five were released before the SAS assault. Two died, but the remaining 19 survived. Of the six terrorists, only one survived.

After the Siege

Back in Hereford, a few months later, the building of the new barracks at Bradbury Lines was completed. At the opening, the site was renamed Stirling Lines in honour of David Stirling, the Regiment's founder. A huge party followed, with many members of the original SAS in attendance. The buoyant mood felt after the Iranian Embassy siege continued.

Later that summer an SAS free-fall team took off from Brize Norton airbase in Wiltshire and jumped from the aircraft while over the south coast of England. Using the new High Altitude High Opening (HAHO) technique, all the team managed to make it across the English Channel, landing in France. Everyone was delighted, even though the French police arrested two men for illegal entry.

The Gambia

On 1 August 1981, Lieutenant-Colonel Michael Rose, commanding officer of the SAS, was out relaxing in the Welsh countryside, having had a busy time providing protection for numerous VIPs. A large number of Commonwealth heads of state had been in London, attending the wedding of Prince Charles to Lady Diana Spencer. The gathering of notables had presented a number of opportunities for terrorists; now that it was over, the SAS could return to Hereford and relax a little. Rose therefore arranged to take time off, enjoying the company of his children, something rare for the SAS commander. Even now, he wore an electronic beeper on his belt, which interrupted this much-anticipated interlude with an urgent summons. With all haste he made his way to the nearest telephone and made a call to Hereford headquarters. Diane, a telephonist of long standing in Hereford, switched his call to Major Ian Crooke, who was acting executive officer at the time. From Crooke, Rose learned that the small nation of Gambia, a former British colony, was in the throes of a *coup d'etat*. Launched two days earlier, it coincided with the absence of the nation's President, Sir Dawda Jawara, who was representing his country at the royal wedding. Senegal, Gambia's neighbour, with which it had a military-assistance agreement, had already sent troops to combat the rebels. Additionally, Jawara had asked British Prime Minister Margaret Thatcher for help, and it had been agreed to dispatch a couple of SAS men to the scene. The Prime Minister warned of the need for secrecy; even this modest response, if it became public, could open her government to charges of renewed imperialism in Africa.

Rose first told Crooke that he was inclined to take the assignment himself; always quick at making decisions, and ever politically minded, his skills would prove very useful in Gambia. However, getting Rose back to Hereford would require him being picked up by helicopter, and he would need to make arrangements for his children. All this would take time. Eventually, Rose conceded that Crooke himself should choose another available man, select whatever weapons and equipment they would need, and get to Gambia on the first available plane.

The Gambia covers an area of 4,360 square miles of West Africa and is the continent's smallest independent state. It is a narrow strip of land on both banks of the Gambia River, bordered by the Atlantic Ocean to the west and surrounded on the remaining three sides by Senegal.

The capital is Banjul, on Saint Mary's Island, near the mouth of the Gambia River. A low-lying country, its terrain ranges from sandy beaches along the coast to a swampy river valley in the interior. The economy is overwhelmingly dependent on the export of peanuts, which provides most of the country's earnings. The population is primarily Muslim black African, of whom the Mandingo are the most numerous tribe; English is the official language.

English merchants won trading rights from the Portuguese in 1588, and in the early seventeenth century British companies founded settlements along the Gambia River. In 1816 the British purchased Saint Mary's Island, where they established Bathurst (now Banjul), and in 1843 the territory became a Crown colony. The French, who controlled the neighbouring interior (now Senegal), failed in negotiations to acquire the Gambia River settlements, which became a British protectorate in 1894. Gambia achieved self-government in 1963 and independence in 1965, under Dawda Kairaba Jawara; it became a republic in the Commonwealth of Nations in 1970. Independent Gambia is notable in Africa as a bastion of parliamentary democracy and political stability. It has maintained close relations with Senegal, with the larger neighbour being responsible for Gambia's defence.

By 1980, the average annual per capita income was only about £140, and this was on the decline because the peanut crop had fared poorly in two years of extremely dry weather. On the other hand, tourism was on the increase and could have become an important source of revenue. However, such was the poverty in Gambia that the populace started to complain about escalating prices for basic foodstuffs; the problem was not helped by the high rate of unemployment. It soon became obvious from the number of anti-government slogans painted on walls that the government was in trouble. When slogans turned to actions and the President's private yacht mysteriously caught fire, the government finally realized that a coup was being planned. President Jawara, however, discounted the information and flew to London for the matrimonial festivities.

The revolt was the work of the Gambian Socialist Revolutionary Party, which was headed by a young Marxist named Kukoi Samba Sanyang. His given name was Dominique, but when he became a communist he changed it to Kukoi, a word in the Mandinka language, native to Gambia, which means 'sweep clean'. Sanyang was also among the African radicals who had stayed in Libya. The volatile Libyan leader, Colonel Qadhafi, envisaged a confederation of Islamic African states under his guidance. He attracted exiled African political leaders of Marxist persuasion to the Libyan capital, Tripoli, and plotted to reshape a number of African governments. Gambia, being 70 per cent Muslim, suited Colonel Qadhafi's fancied Islamic realm.

At 05:00 on Thursday, 30 July, the coup erupted. Usman Bojang provided muscle power for the attempt to overthrow Jawara. A former deputy commander of Gambia's 300-man Police Field Force – a paramilitary organization charged with preserving order in the tiny country – Bojang managed to persuade or force the contingent based in the town of Bakau to join the coup. This group, which amounted to about one-third of the organization, disarmed most of the loyal police, then quickly took over the nearby transmitter for Radio Gambia and moved into Banjul, the capital. On the way, it opened the country's largest prison and distributed weapons from the police armoury not only to the inmates but to virtually anyone who happened to come along. Not long after daybreak, citizens and former prisoners alike began rampaging through the streets and looting shops. Soon, a free-for-all erupted. Within the first few hours of the coup, scores of bodies – policemen, criminals and civilians – littered the streets of Banjul. Arriving at Radio Gambia shortly after rebel policemen had seized the station, Sanyang closed the country's borders and its airport at Yundum, some 15 miles east of Banjul. Then he proclaimed a 'dictatorship of the proletariat' and charged the 'bourgeois' Jawara government with corruption, injustice and nepotism.

Most Europeans and Americans working in business or holding government posts stayed off the streets, while other foreigners and tourists remained in the capital or kept to their hotels in the nearby communities of Bakau and Fajara. Many rebel Gambian policemen, who saw no profit in harming Western individuals, guided anxious foreigners to the residence of the US Ambassador, Larry G. Piper. The house was soon a haven to 123 nervous guests, 80 of them American citizens. A number of European tourists also sought shelter in the Atlantic Beach Hotel, on the outskirts of Banjul, along the nation's beautiful sea coast. During the trouble, two armed looters raided the hotel, ransacked the safe and took the manager hostage. As they fled the hotel, the two looters were shot dead in the hotel doorway. Fearing more looters would arrive, and hearing the constant firing outside, the hotel guests organized watches and posted guards, 'armed' with fire extinguishers.

President Jawara had made contact by telephone with his vice president, who had taken refuge in police headquarters in Banjul, where he was protected by loyalist troops. In London, Jawara wisely made himself accessible to the press; in doing so, he was able to downplay events at home. Because of this, the plight of the European and Americans trapped by the situation, never reached the outside world. Had it done so, the coup would have attracted far more attention than it did. For the first few day of the coup, Jawara controlled all news of Gambia from London. Acting as if to resume control of the government, Jawara boarded a jet bound for Dakar, capital of Senegal. In a statement before leaving, the President talked about invoking a mutual-assistance treaty that Gambia had signed with Senegal some 15 years earlier to fend off external aggression, yet at this stage no foreign agitator had been identified as having backed the coup.

By now, Ian Crooke and an SAS sergeant, Tony (not his real name), had chosen and assembled their weapons and equipment. These consisted of German-made Heckler & Koch sub-machine guns, Browning 9mm automatic pistols, and a stock of ammunition and grenades. Crooke managed to pass his little arsenal through customs, baggage checks and on to the first flight available. This plane happened to be an Air France commercial flight to Dakar. Although firearms can be carried in checked baggage aboard such aircraft, explosives are normally prohibited, but most anti-terrorist teams have direct contact with each other and after several phone calls the normal channels are ignored. This is not uncommon: during the Iranian Embassy siege in London, the German GSG 9 commander, Ulrich Wegener, had been allowed to observe the incident. Upon his return to Germany aboard a scheduled passenger flight, it was discovered that he was in possession of a weapon. Informal contacts within the British Diplomatic Service cleared the way in minutes. As always, Ian and Tony were dressed casually, bringing no attention from their fellow passengers among whom were many reporters and television camera crews.

Upon arriving in Senegal, Ian Crooke encountered his first obstacle – British diplomats. Despite the brief from Prime Minister Thatcher directly to the SAS, the diplomats refused to allow them to get involved. With fighting going on between the rebel forces and Senegalese troops, and with a considerable number of British citizens in danger, officials in both Dakar and Banjul decided that it would only complicate their duties further if the SAS got in on the act. This would allow them to applaud the Senegalese if the intervention succeeded, or to chastise them if it failed. The SAS travel on many missions around the world, normally working closely with their counterparts in

VIP protection. Accommodation and reception in the various countries is normally handled by British diplomats, who generally shudder at the thought of having SAS men in their company.

With no word from Thatcher, in whose service he had come to Africa, Ian Crooke decided to go ahead with his mission despite the remonstrations of these relatively minor officials. Adopting the policy of 'out of sight, out of mind', the two men managed to get seats on a plane bound for Gambia's Yundum airport. Upon arrival, Crooke met the Senegalese paratroop commander Lieutenant Colonel Abdourah-man N'Gom, who had established his headquarters in the confines of the airport.

Crooke also made contact with Clive Lee, a hulking 6-foot 6-inch tall retired SAS major who was employed as a civilian adviser to the Gambian Pioneer Corps, a division of the country's Field Force, which trained rural youth in agricultural and construction skills.

The SAS has a very loose connection with its ex-soldiers, most of whom are scattered around the world, mostly working in some security job or for a foreign government. In such circumstances it is expected that, should the need arise and their services be required, they are honour-bound to render all assistance to the SAS operation. As with David Bullig in Dubai during the Mogadishu hijack, so it was with Clive Lee in Gambia – and there are many other untold instances. The SAS brotherhood bond is extremely strong.

Hearing of the coup on the radio, Lee had rounded up 23 Pioneer Corps members, armed them and set off for Banjul (you can't keep a good SAS man down when he smells a fight). To get there from the Pioneer Corps base in the town of Farafenni, 60 miles east of the capital, Lee had to cross the Gambia River. Because of the hostilities, however, the ferry had suspended operations. As with Ian Crooke and the diplomats, this was no time to pussyfoot around, and soon the ferry captain had been persuaded to take Lee's men to the other side. Once across, they made their way directly to Banjul, where necessary moving through mangrove swamps to avoid rebel positions along the main road to the city. In Banjul, Lee's party made for police headquarters, where it reinforced a small contingent of loyalists and set about defending their enclave by barricading the nearby streets.

For the Senegalese troops, capturing Yundum airport had not been easy. During a fierce battle, almost half the 120 paratroops making the assault were wounded or killed. Once this task was completed, Senegalese soldiers entered Banjul; within a few hours, they had cleared the city of rebels. They had also gained control of Denton Bridge, across Oyster Creek, which would prevent insurgents from re-entering the capital from their concentrations in Bakau and Fajara. A combination of these actions secured the route from Banjul to the airport.

The Senegalese troops found the situation in Banjul little changed. Although N'Gom continued to strengthen his forces in Gambia and occasionally traded shots with the rebels, the military situation had reached an impasse. His troops were stalled outside Bakau because Sanyang had taken more than 100 hostages. The most valuable captives were Lady Chilel N'Jie – one of President Jawara's two wives – and a number of his children. In addition, Sanyang held several members of the Gambian cabinet. And although N'Gom had wrested Radio Gambia from Sanyang's rebels (the transmitter lay between the airport and the bridge), the coup leader had commandeered a mobile transmitter from which Lady Chilel appealed almost hysterically to Senegal, announcing that the hostages would be executed unless the paratroops withdrew. Sanyang repeated the threat himself. 'I shall kill the whole lot,' he warned, 'and thereafter stand to fight the Senegalese.'

On 5 August, Crooke decided to make a reconnaissance. The blue jeans-clad SAS officer and his two associates slipped forward of Senegalese outposts and set out on foot. The weather was hot; during August in Gambia, temperatures routinely exceed 90°F. The three Britons, who were carrying sub-machine guns, could hardly escape notice in Fajara, but the outing was not as dangerous as it might seem. Although there was always the chance that an encounter with an armed insurgent could end in gunfire, the rebels did not seem inclined to harm Europeans. Furthermore, Crooke observed an unmilitary laxity among the troops staffing rebel positions. Unknown to both Crooke and the outside world, Bojang had been killed during the second day of the coup. His absence, and the resulting lack of leadership, probably accounted for the apparent decline in rebel vigilance. Crooke's sortie confirmed that the insurgents were now capable of little more than token resistance against well-trained Senegalese troops.

Crook persuaded N'Gom to begin an advance on Fajara and Bakau the same day. The British officer and his companions accompanied a contingent of Senegalese troops along the hot byways of the suburbs. Peter Felon, a British engineer employed by an American crane company, saw the party when they appeared at his hotel in Fajara. 'Ten Senegalese troops and a British Army officer arrived at the hotel,' the engineer recalled. The officer, probably Clive Lee, wore khakis with no insignia. 'With him were two men whom I can only describe as the most vicious-looking professionals I have ever seen.' Upon being told that rebels were hiding along a creek near the beach, the pair set off to find them. 'There was sporadic, violent gunfire,' said Felon, 'then the two men walked calmly back to our hotel.'

A US aid worker at the American Embassy was one of the foreigners who had taken refuge in Ambassador Larry Piper's house. It was early afternoon, he remembered, when a lookout they had posted announced that soldiers were coming up the hill. 'The house,' said the aid worker later, 'was on a bluff sloping to the beach. I went out and saw a wave of Senegalese come running up the hill in full camouflage-type gear led by three whites, one of whom had on an Australian hat, khaki shorts and a knife strapped to his leg. It was literally like living in a movie.' After ascertaining that everyone was all right and leaving behind a dozen or so paratroops for security, the party disappeared.

Arriving at the British High Commissioner's offices, Crooke learned that armed rebel guards had escorted President Jawara's wife and her four ailing children – one of them an infant of only five weeks – to a British clinic the day before. Doctors at this tropical disease research facility, which stood only a block or two from the High Commissioner's office, treated the children and advised her to bring them back within 24 hours.

The interval had passed, and now Lady Chilel had returned for follow-up care. This information came by way of a telephone call to the High Commissioner from the British doctor attending the children. The official told the doctor that armed SAS men would be there within minutes, and Crooke and his two companions quickly headed for the hospital. Hearing that help was on the way, the doctor began to prolong his treatment: the wily man even convinced the woman's armed escorts that they were frightening his other patients and persuaded them to put their guns out of sight.

As Crooke approached the hospital, he noticed two armed guards posted at the entrance. Handing his sub-machine gun to his companions, the major gave them instructions to circle behind the guards, then walked up to the pair and distracted them in conversation as the other two SAS men crept up from the rear. It is difficult to imagine what Crooke could have said or how devious a plan he might have formulated in order to draw the guards' attention away from his accomplices. The SAS is mute on the topic; whatever Crooke's ruse, it worked. The two guards froze when they felt gun muzzles at the backs of their heads.

Leaving the captives in the hands of his able assistants, Crooke slipped inside the clinic. He surprised Lady Chilel's weapon-free escorts as they watched the children being treated and promptly took them prisoner. After conducting the President's wife and children to the High Commissioner's office, Crooke and his party retreated to N'Gom's headquarters at the airport.

A day earlier, Senegalese troops – who now numbered about 1,500 – had found and destroyed the mobile transmitter Sanyang had been using. Although Sanyang himself escaped, he was no longer a factor. With the silencing of its leaders, the coup's backbone was broken. Yet many hostages remained under rebel guns at a police barracks, and disorganized bands of turncoat policemen and criminals had to be rounded up.

N'Gom paced his advance slowly. Panic among the rebels might cause them to begin killing their prisoners. They had nearly done so a few days earlier, when a police officer who had been forced against his better judgement to join the coup began shooting some of the rebel guards. He was killed in a trice, but his brave act seemed to thwart a planned execution. The Senegalese paratroops edged up to one side of the barracks, leaving several exits unguarded for the rebels to flee. After a tense hour or so, the hostages walked free and the insurgents dispersed, to be captured later.

Eight days later the rebellion was all over, but it had caused more than 1,000 deaths. President Jawara was once again the unchallenged and elected head of the Gambian government. Kukoi Sanyang was eventually arrested in the neighbouring country of Guinea-Bissau, but the Socialist government there later released him, despite Gambian requests for his extradition. Senegalese troops captured more than 100 of the rebels and convicts, seven of whom were ultimately condemned to death. Libya was never connected directly with the coup attempt.

In Banjul, the President posed for reporters, hugged his baby son and announced: 'I'm relieved and happy.' His answers to questions about the rescue of his wife and children by European soldiers met with a cold shrug of the shoulders, and a comment that all such claims were much exaggerated. To make Jawara's political recovery as easy as possible, all official comment about the countercoup and rescue was reserved for African governments. The only confirmation of the SAS presence came from a Senegalese officer, who told reporters that SAS personnel had, indeed, participated in restoring order. As always, the British government remained silent.

The SAS party hung around Gambia just long enough to satisfy themselves that British citizens would be safe and then made their way home. The operation in Gambia demonstrates how a few skilled and confident soldiers can influence an event far out of proportion to their numbers. Additionally, they could disappear, as if nothing had happened, throwing yet another cloak over the SAS myth.

Ian Crooke gave a wonderful, detailed account of the whole incident to a full assembly of the Regiment. It was the highlight of an annual debrief, where other members of the SAS found out what everyone else had been doing around the world: as usual, it was for SAS personnel only. Although the British government refused to admit involvement, it was recognized that the success of the action hinged in large measure on Crooke's initiative and good judgement. That he had a lot of help is undisputed. It came partly in the form of militarily incompetent coup-makers and partly from the presence of the Senegalese. N'Gom's troops supplied the manpower needed to fight rebels who were disinclined to surrender, and to maintain security in areas which had been swept clean. Nonetheless, Crooke was the one who tipped the balance. He chose to ignore the restrictions placed on him by British diplomats and acted as he believed the Prime Minister wished. Had he been wrong, he would no doubt have suffered severe consequences. However, in those days, Margaret Thatcher held the men of the SAS with high esteem.

Major Ian Crooke was a rare exception to the normal officer serving with the SAS; he was more at home drinking with the NCOs than in the Officers' Mess. Sadly, he suffered a terrible injury during a parachute jump in South Africa.

The Falklands

The SAS continued its routine of sending soldiers around the world and performing anti-terrorist duties. That was until the Argentinians decided to invade the Falkland Islands in early 1982.

The Falklands are a group of islands in the South Atlantic that have been under British sovereignty since 1833. When the Argentinians invaded the islands on 2 April 1982, Prime Minister Margaret Thatcher announced that Britain would win the islands back, taking them by force if necessary. Under Operation Corporate, a task force was immediately put together and sent on its way south. Both Peter de la Billière, then a Brigadier, and Lieutenant-Colonel Mike Rose, the Commander of 22 SAS, fought hard to have the Regiment included in the task force. By early April, members of D Squadron and G Squadron were on their way.

It fell to G Squadron to get the ball rolling against the Argentinians. Teams from the squadron were inserted to observe the enemy in advance of the main task force arriving. Due mainly to the featureless terrain, it was a hard and diffi-cult task. The men were forced to conceal themselves in small clumps of outcropping rocks, where they would lie up during the day, braving the horrific weather conditions. By night, they would slip out of their hides and walk at least six miles in order to send their reports. This was to stop the Argentinians fixing their location when they used the radio. It was a testing time, but the SAS patrols remained hidden for three weeks before being relieved.

The weather was also responsible for an incident on the island of South Georgia. A decision was taken to land D Squadron's Mountain Troop on the island's Fortuna Glacier. A small island 310 miles south of the main Falklands group, South Georgia housed a small Argentinian garrison. The British viewed the retaking of the island as a low-risk, high-propaganda opera-tion. The SAS would establish observation posts overlooking the town of Leith in anticipation of British forces landing to recapture South Georgia.

Wessex helicopters from HMS *Antrim* and HMS *Tidespring* dropped the troops, commanded by Captain John Hamilton, with their equipment and some pulkas, on the glacier. The icy conditions hindered their progress and the situation was to deteriorate as night fell. One of the two tents was destroyed in a blizzard, increasing the risk of hypothermia and frostbite, and Hamilton, knowing they would not survive another night, requested an evacuation.

The next morning, although still hampered by the blizzard, three helicopters, led by a radar-equipped Wessex, headed for the glacier in an attempt to retrieve the soldiers. They succeeded in rescuing the whole team, but as they took off again, one of the helicopters crashed into the glacier. Amazingly, only one man was superficially injured. The other two helicopters returned to help, dumping fuel and equipment in an effort to create room for the men aboard the downed helicopter. Suddenly, the weather deteriorated even more and a second helicopter struck an ice ridge and also crashed. This left them no choice: the one remaining helicopter – named Humphrey – would have to fly back to HMS *Antrim*. Piloted by Lieutenant-Commander Ian Stanley RN, Humphrey returned later in the day to the blizzard-bound glacier, where the remaining survivors were located and rescued. However, the helicopter was now dangerously overloaded and struggled precariously back to the ship, eventually crash landing on the deck. Stanley was awarded the DSO for his bravery and professionalism.

As the first attempt to land on the island of South Georgia had ended in failure, it was decided to try again. This time the SAS, SBS and M Company of 42 Commando went in by boat rather than by helicopter. Even this proved difficult: some boats developed engine trouble, missed the island altogether and had to be rescued. Eventually, however, they succeeded, and managed to carry out their task of setting up OPs (observation posts) to gather intelligence about Argentinian strengths and positions on the island. According to one of the SBS OPs, the main Argentine force – a group of about 100 marines and the crew of the submarine *Santa Fé* – was stationed at Grytviken.

On 25 April, a helicopter pilot returning to HMS *Antrim* reported the submarine leaving port and on the surface. Immediately, helicopters from HMS *Endurance* and the frigate HMS *Brilliant*, attacked it with depth charges. The submarine was badly damaged and only just managed to limp back to Grytviken, its appearance alerting the alarmed Argentines to the fact that British forces were not very far away and on the offensive. In fact, British forces were closer than they imagined: taking advantage of the enemy's confusion, a joint force made up of SAS, SBS and Royal Marines was about to assault the base. They were inserted by helicopter two miles away and slowly made their advance towards the port. When they reached the top of Brown Mountain, they looked down to see white flags being flown from every building. Despite the order to stop and hold their ground, elements of the SAS continued forward while the others provided cover from Brown Mountain. Cedric Delves, the SAS commander, arrived in the Argentinian position (having walked through a minefield) only to be greeted with a flurry of white flags. The Argentines had surrendered and the assault force had not fired a shot. 'Lofty' Gallagher walked into the base at last light. Around his waist was a Union Jack, which he had carried all the way from England. In the time-honoured tradition, the flag was immediately raised by Lofty, giving the British forces their first victory of the Falklands War. By the next morning, a small detachment at the old whaling station of Leith had also surrendered. South Georgia was back in British hands. Tragically, 'Lofty' Gallagher was killed, along with many others, in a helicopter accident during a cross-decking operation moving troops from one ship to another towards the end of the Falklands War.

While the British fleet was a formidable force, the loss of several ships gave rise to some concern. To help balance the odds, the SAS was ordered to attack an Argentinian airfield known as Pebble Island on West Falkland. Previous reconnaissance had established that the Argentinians controlled the airstrip and that a number of ground-attack aircraft were based there. British commanders considered these aircraft a major threat to the main troop landings at San Carlos Water. The SAS was given its orders: to destroy all the aircraft and to kill the ground crew and supporting garrison on the island. The SAS forces had assistance in their task from HMS *Hermes*, *Broadsword* and also *Glamorgan*, which was to supply onshore bombardment.

On the night of 14 May 1982, the helicopters, carrying 45 members of D Squadron, landed about four miles from the airstrip. The plan was that once the mortars and LAW rockets had been unloaded from the helicopters, Mountain Troop would mount the main assault on the aircraft, while the other two troops were to form a reserve.

The attack on the airfield opened with a heavy bombardment from HMS *Glamorgan*, followed by the SAS using 81mm mortars, M203 grenade launchers, 66mm LAWs and small arms. With the Argentinians forced to take cover, the SAS moved on to the airstrip and fixed explosive charges to the aircraft. The actual assault on the airfield, led by Captain John Hamilton, destroyed six Pucaras, four Turbo-Mentors and a Skyvan transport before withdrawing again. The Argentinians were caught completely unprepared and, though they desperately returned fire, most of it missed. The only SAS injuries suffered were slight; in fact, an exploding mine caused the worst ones. It was reported that one Argentinian was killed in the firefight.

Aboard *Hermes*, the mission was hailed as a success. The aircraft had been destroyed, along with a great amount of enemy ammunition, and the Argentinians were now denied the use of the airstrip. The SAS returned to the pick-up point, from which it was exfiltrated by helicopter and returned to the fleet.

With confidence running high, it seemed as if the war would not last much longer. Then, on 19 May, just five days after the raid on Pebble Island, the Regiment suffered a tragic blow when a Sea King helicopter carrying a large group of SAS troops crashed. The helicopter had been cross-decking from HMS *Hermes* to HMS *Intrepid* when a bird strike caused the engine to fail. The helicopter plunged into the icy sea, killing 22 men. It was the heaviest lost the Regiment had suffered since the Second World War. Almost the entire senior ranks structure of G Squadron had been wiped out.

Undaunted by the loss, the SAS continued its aggressive actions, and at the end of May, D Squadron seized Mount Kent, some 40 miles behind enemy lines. Despite being heavily outnumbered, it held it until relieved by Marines of 42 Commando. Although the war was drawing to an end, the SAS did not drop its guard, conscious that the Argentinians were still a formidable force.

On 10 June, the SAS suffered another loss; this time, it was Captain Hamilton. He had taken out a patrol to recce Port Howard, on West Falkland. As it approached, it was spotted by the enemy, who engaged in a firefight. Heavily outnumbered, the four SAS men tried desperately to fight their way out. Two managed to withdraw, while Hamilton and his signaller gave covering fire. Hamilton was hit, but continued to provide supporting fire. Some time later, the overwhelming force of Argentinians killed Captain Hamilton and captured his signaller. His actions had allowed at least two of his men sufficient time to escape. Captain John Hamilton was awarded a posthumous Military Cross.

The last major SAS raid was mounted in East Falkland on the night of 14 June. This involved an attack on the Argentinian rear while 2 Para assaulted Wireless Ridge, just a few miles west of Port Stanley. A total of 60 men from D Squadron and G Squadron, plus six men from the SBS, used Rigid Raiders to assault the harbour in Port Stanley. They succeeded in setting fire to the oil storage tanks and laying down heavy suppressive fire. The Argentinians retaliated with overwhelming force and the raiders were forced to retreat. One of the Rigid Raiders took more that 30 bullet holes, but it refused to sink and managed to limp safely back to the mother ship. After a bitter battle, 2 Para finally took Wireless Ridge.

In the final stages of the war, Lieutenant-Colonel Rose, along with a Spanish-speaking interpreter, used psychological warfare methods to persuade the Argentinians of the hopelessness of their cause. Consequently, on 14 June, Rose flew into Port Stanley by helicopter to commence talks with the enemy. It was after this meeting that Rose, together with Brigadier de la Billière, accepted the Argentinian surrender, thus ending the war. As a mark of the man, there is very strong rumour that Rose offered the Argentinian commander, Major General Mario Menendez, a Harrier fire-power demonstration as the

Argentinian troops massed around Stanley. The same rumour also claims that he walked out of the building taking with him a prized statue of a horse, which had reputedly been given to Menendez by a grateful government for his capture of the Falklands. But these were only rumours.

In May 1982, the discovery of a crashed Sea King helicopter near the Chilean port of Punta Arenas caused much speculation. Many versions of the story abound, but the one most commonly accepted is that the Sea King was taking a small reconnaissance party of SAS men to a point 25 miles from Rio Gallegos, an airfield in southern Argentina close to the border with Chile. The airfield was rumoured to be the main base for the Super Etendard aircraft which, with their Exocet missiles, were doing so much damage to ships of the British task force. Despite rumours that the helicopter crash landed in bad weather, leaving the crew having to find their way to the nearest British Embassy in Chile, it is known that an SAS demolitionist placed a bomb under the fuselage to destroy the helicopter. Meanwhile, back on Ascension Island, two C130 Hercules transports were loaded with SAS troops from the recently arrived B Squadron. Although never confirmed, it is said that they were equipped and prepared to assault the Argentinian airfield at Rio Gallegos – a one-way mission for which those SAS men on the helicopter had been the reconnaissance team. Political intervention by the Americans, who feared the direct intrusion into Argentina would only serve to escalate the war, finally called a halt to the raid and the aircraft returned to Ascension. The remains of the Sea King were discovered and the news flashed around the world. Fearing that surprise had now been lost, further such missions were aborted. The SAS advance party slipped quietly out of Argentina and a few days later had rejoined the task force. Had the raid been allowed to continue, the lives and equipment lost aboard the Atlantic Conveyor, hit by an Exocet a few days later, might well have been saved.

(Note: It is fact that an SAS demolitions man destroyed the Sea King helicopter, using a bar mine. It is also a fact that almost a complete squadron of SAS did board a C130 aircraft of 47 Squadron and take off from Ascension Island. It is also a fact that the American President, Ronald Reagan, did not want Chile entering the war and risk causing a major conflict in South America.)

Disaster on Everest

With the Falklands behind them, the men of the Regiment settled down to a more peaceful routine. In 1984 both 'Brummie' Stokes and 'Bronco' Lane made a second attempt on Everest, this time leading an all-SAS team consisting of soldiers from the Regiment's various Mountain Troops. The expedition was well planned, and by 2 April the front runners were already at 22,800 feet.

Then disaster struck. A little after dawn on the morning of 3 April a huge avalanche, initiated by falling ice, swept down the mountain, heading directly for the base camp. It completely ravaged the camp, propelling it and the men down the mountainside. Corporal Swierzy was killed and several others lay badly injured, the worst being Sergeant Andy Baxter. He was returned to Hereford, but died of a brain tumour on 12 August 1985.

The Brighton Bomb

By the mid-1980s, the IRA was becoming more audacious, and while most of its activities had taken place in Northern Ireland, it also brought violence to mainland Britain and the Continent. In October 1984, the IRA made a serious attempt to wipe out the entire British Cabinet at the Tory party's annual conference in Brighton. The Prime Minister, 13 of her 20-member Cabinet and many of her senior advisers were staying at Brighton's venerable Grand Hotel, a 120-year-old Regency-style building on the seafront. In the early hours of 12 October, many of the Tory faithful were still awake, looking forward to Mrs Thatcher's address crowning the four-day gathering. She, too, was still up, having just put the finishing touches to her speech when at 02:54 the night's silence was shattered by a thundering explosion. Four floors above the cluster of suites occupied by the Prime Minister and her colleagues, a powerful bomb had detonated, blowing out a section of the nine-storey building's facade 30 feet deep and 15 feet wide, spraying broken glass and chunks of concrete through the halls and on to the street.

The gap extended from the roof to the fifth storey. Tons of plaster, flooring and furniture crashed from floor to floor, finally tearing through the Grand's elegant foyer where Tory leaders had gathered only hours earlier. Thatcher's suite, located only 30 feet below the source of the blast, was badly damaged; and the bathroom was totally demolished. Miraculously, the Prime Minister was unhurt. 'This conference will go on as usual,' she declared firmly as she emerged from the wreckage, accompanied by her husband Denis. Thatcher was fully dressed, her face flushed with anger. 'We were very lucky,' she said, putting on a brave face. Inwardly, the Iron Lady was furious.

Others were not so fortunate. Four were killed, and at least 34 were injured. Among the dead were Sir Anthony Berry, a former Tory Deputy Chief Whip; Eric Taylor, chairman of the Northwest Area Conservative Association; and Mrs John Wakeham, wife of the Chief Whip. Wakeham himself was injured, as were Alfred Parsons, the Australian High Commissioner to Britain, and Norman Tebbit, Thatcher's Trade and Industry Secretary. Wakeham lay buried for nearly seven hours before being rescued. Tebbit, who subsequently underwent exploratory surgery to determine the extent of his severe chest injuries, spent four hours under the rubble.

Some nine hours after the blast, the IRA claimed responsibility. In a telephone call to the Irish state radio in Dublin, the group asserted that it had set off a gelignite bomb in an attempt to kill 'the British Cabinet and the Tory warmongers.' The IRA promised more violence in the future. 'Thatcher will now realize,' the group said, 'that Britain cannot occupy our country, torture our prisoners and shoot our people in their own streets and get away with it. Today we were unlucky. But remember; we have only to be lucky once. You will have to be lucky always.' It was the boldest and most outrageous strike ever against public officials in Britain. The IRA had, in effect, tried to destroy the entire British government.

The scene in the hours immediately following the Brighton blast was one of devastation. As Thatcher and her husband were taken to the safety of a police station the residents of a nearby hotel, including Charles H. Price II, the US Ambassador to Britain, were evacuated for fear of a second attack. Working with the help of television lights, and from time to time calling for quiet so they could hear cries for help, rescue workers used axes to chop through the debris and brought in a crane to reach those trapped on high floors. Shocked delegates wandered along Brighton's seafront promenade in their nightclothes, while dishevelled Cabinet ministers worried about losing government papers. Lord Gowrie, Minister for the Arts, dragged canvas deckchairs from the beach for use as makeshift stretchers. Education Secretary Sir Keith Joseph, in pyjamas and silk robe, sat on his dispatch case by the shore.

Thatcher had a narrow escape. An SB officer on the security detail in her hotel said she had left her bathroom two minutes before it was destroyed by the blast. Tory Party Chairman John Selwyn Gummer also had a close call. 'I was just outside Prime Minister Thatcher's suite when I was thrown backwards by the force of the explosion,' he recalled. 'The Prime Minister came through the door and the first thing she said was, "Is there anything I can do to help?" She was totally calm and looked very angry.'

The SAS responded with a whole range of operations, requiring a full squadron to be retained in the province. The cost was high. On 2 December 1984, the SAS mounted an operation against the IRA in Fermanagh. Technical intelligence had indicated that several beer kegs containing 1,000 pounds of home-made explosive would be placed in a drainage culvert on a road leading to a local restaurant. The IRA was being continually monitored by the SAS who, due to the bomb misfiring, overheard a conversation between the bombers. When the SAS went to investigate a van parked nearby, an IRA member called Tony MacBride confronted them. As the SAS started to question MacBride, other members of the IRA opened fire from a nearby ditch, fatally wounding Al Slater. In the ensuing firefight MacBride was also killed and another IRA member, Kieran Fleming, drowned as he tried to escape by swimming the river Bannagh, which at the time was in flood. The police later arrested two more IRA members at a checkpoint as they tried to cross into the south. Slater had joined the SAS three years earlier, having served with the Parachute Regiment. He was posted to B Squadron's Air Troop, where he was known as 'Mr Angry' for his impression of a comic character on Radio 1.

A classic SAS operation took place in Loughall on Friday, 8 May 1987. Intelligence had been received indicating that the police station at Loughall was to be attacked by the method used the year before in County Armagh. In that incident, in April 1986, a stolen mechanical digger had been packed with explosives and driven into the RUC station at the Birches, causing extensive damage. A report that another JCB had been stolen in East Tyrone gave rise to the suspicion that an identical IRA operation was being planned. Every effort was made to locate the digger and identify the target.

After intensive covert searching, the weapons and explosives were located. Subsequently, the digger was also found, in a derelict building on a farm some 10 miles away. Surveillance by E4A provided more information, and eventually the target was identified as the RUC station at Loughall. This station was only manned part-time and consisted of one principal building running parallel to the main road, surrounded by a high wire fence. The time and date of the attack were eventually confirmed through an SB telephone tap.

Two of the IRA activists were named as Patrick Kelly and Jim Lynagh, who commanded the East Tyrone active service unit. When masked men stole a Toyota van from Dungannon, Jim

Lynagh was spotted in the town, suggesting that the van was to be used in the Loughall attack. Not long afterwards, the OP reported that the JCB was being moved from the derelict farm. At this stage the SAS, who had been reinforced from Hereford, took up its ambush positions. It was reported that some were in the police station itself, but this was not true – most of the main ambush party was hiding in a row of small fir trees that lined the fence on the opposite side to the station. Several heavily armed stops were also in position, covering all avenues of escape.

At a little past 19:00, the blue Toyota van drove down the road in front of the police station. Several people could be seen inside. A short time later, it returned from the direction of Portadown, this time followed by the JCB carrying three hooded IRA terrorists in the cab. Declan Arthurs was driving, with Michael Gormley and Gerald O'Callaghan riding shotgun. The bucket was filled with an explosive contained in an oil drum, which had been partly concealed with rubble. As the blue van charged past the station, the JCB slammed through the gate. One of the two terrorists riding shotgun – although at the time it was not clear which one – ignited the bomb and all three made a run for it. Back at the van, several hooded men jumped clear and opened fire in the direction of the RUC station. At this point, the SAS ambush was activated.

The sudden hail of SAS fire was terrifying. All eight members of the IRA fell under the hail of bullets. At the height of the firefight the bomb exploded, taking with it half the RUC station and scattering debris over all concerned. As the dust settled, the SAS closed in on the bodies. At that moment a white car entered the ambush area, its two occupants dressed in blue boiler suits similar to those worn by the IRA. They were unfortunately mistaken for terrorists, especially when, on seeing the ambush in progress, they stopped and started to reverse. One of the SAS stops opened fire, killing one of the occupants and wounding the other. It later transpired that the dead motorist, Antony Hughes, had nothing to do with the IRA. Several other vehicles and pedestrians soon appeared on the scene, but by this time the situation had been stabilized.

Loughall was one of the most successful operations ever mounted against the IRA, who were totally stunned by the loss of two complete active service cells. The Hughes family was compensated for its loss, and with no public inquest the matter was closed. The IRA, believing that there was a mole in its organization, went into a period of self-assessment, but it did not lick its wounds for long. Shortly after, on Remembrance Day, at a ceremony in Enniskillen, the IRA detonated a massive bomb. Eleven people were killed and more than 60 injured.

Prison Assault

The same year saw the SAS involved in a rather strange operation on home territory. On 27 September 1987, a siege erupted in D Block of Peterhead Prison in Scotland. The block held some 48 prisoners, most of whom were serving long sentences for murder and rape. The majority of the prisoners gave themselves up after a short while but a hard core of five men, holding a prison officer hostage, refused to surrender. For the following week the rioters paraded on the rooftop, in full view of the world's media. Grampian Police responded with a specialist response team and, in addition, the government ordered two SAS advisors to assist. A quick assessment of the situation indicated that an SAS team, well versed in such assault tactics, would better deal with the task.

The government finally gave its consent for the SAS assault on the morning of 3 October. At around 04:00, a four-man team – armed with batons instead of sub-machine guns – made its way from a skylight across a slippery roof to a hole previously made by the rioters. The SAS threw both stun grenades and CS gas through the hole before dropping in to confront the prisoners. At the same time, back-up teams made an explosive entry through the lower-floor walls and proceeded to follow up the roof assault. The hostage was the first to be removed, too weak to help himself. The assault team hauled him through the roof hole and carried him back to the skylight, where he was lowered to safety. The prisoners were overwhelmed by CS gas and the black-clad figures bellowing commands to 'Move' marshalled them back into captivity. The SAS assault team departed from Scotland less than two hours after its arrival, having successfully completed their mission.

Because of the Peterhead Prison riot, the government set up a specialist team to deal with such incidents; these officers were initially trained in Hereford.

21 SAS Lost in Afghanistan

Around this time, the unfortunate death of Andy Skrzypkowiak was announced in the national newspapers. Skrzypkowiak had been a cameraman and part of a British film crew covering the war in Afghanistan – Skrzypkowiak was also a member of 21 SAS.

His death was due to a tribal dispute between two Afghan factions, which were both fighting the Russians. The film crew was covering one group, irregulars commanded by Ahman Shah Massoud, as they attacked a Russian fuel convey on the Salang Pass. The rival party, Hezb-i-Islami (Party of God) was intent on capturing any Western journalists covering the Massoud raid.

Andy Skrzypkowiak was not the first SAS soldier to find himself in Afghanistan. It is rumoured that a small unit was infiltrated into the country in March 1981, its mission to extract samples of the titanium alloy the Russians were using for armour on their new helicopters. Although this was a CIA operation, ex-SAS soldiers were used to carry it out.

Gibraltar: Death on the Rock

In Northern Ireland, the continuing war against the IRA had been relentless. When the opportunity arose, the SAS would hit hard. Most of these operations ended in the same way; a quick shoot-out, resulting in several dead terrorists. As well as operating against the IRA in Northern Ireland, the SAS could be called upon to work in mainland Britain as well as overseas. Consequently, when information filtered through the security screen in March 1988 that a bomb was to be exploded in Gibraltar, the SAS was put on standby.

The IRA team consisted of three people: Sean Savage, Daniel McCann and a woman, Maraid Farrell. Each had a history of terrorist activity. The three, later acknowledged by the IRA as an active cell, had been spotted by British security services and trailed for months, and many conversations between the three had been recorded. This surveillance identified the target – the British garrison in Gibraltar – and the method of attack – a car bomb. As events became focused, the target was pinpointed to a ceremony at which several military bands would be parading. It was also known that the IRA had developed a new type of remote-control device capable of detonating a car bomb from a distance.

In late 1987, Savage, a well-known IRA bomb-maker, had been located in Spain. With him was McCann, another IRA suspect. MI5 spent the next six months watching the two, gathering vital information they were certain was leading to a bombing. When, on 4 March 1988, Farrell arrived at Malaga airport and was met by the two men, it seemed likely that the bombing was on. At this stage, the SAS was invited to send in a team (the SAS and the security services have had a good working relationship since the mid-1970s). The Gibraltar police were informed of the operation, and instructed that the IRA active service unit was to be apprehended. For a while, contact with the IRA cell was lost, but by this time the target had been defined. It was suspected that one car would be delivered on to the Rock and parked in a position along the route to be taken by the parade. This car would be clean, a dummy to guarantee a parking space for the real car bomb. It was suggested that the spot where the most damage would be caused was a plaza where the troops and public would assemble: this proved to be correct. At 14:00 on the afternoon of 5 March, a report was received that Savage had been spotted in a parked white Renault 5. It was suspected that he was setting up the bomb-triggering device. Not long afterwards, another report was received to the effect that Farrell and McCann had crossed the border from Spain and were making their way into town.

The SAS men were immediately deployed, and once Savage was out of the way an explosives expert walked past the Renault. No telltale signs were observed indicating the presence of a bomb, such as the rear suspension being depressed: however, if they were using Semtex, 30 pounds or more could be easily concealed. After consultation, it was considered probable that the car did contain a bomb.

At this stage the local police chief, Joseph Canepa, signed an order passing control to the SAS. Operation Favius, as it was known, was about to be concluded. The orders given to the SAS men were to capture the three bombers if possible but, as in all such situations, if lives are directly threatened – those of the SAS or anyone else – they had the right to shoot. It was stressed that the bomb would more than likely be fired by a push-button detonator.

The SAS men, dressed in casual clothes, kept in contact through small radios hidden about their persons. Each soldier was also armed with a 9mm Browning Hi-Power pistol. Savage met up with McCann and Farrell, and after a short discussion all three made their way back towards the Spanish border. Four of the SAS team shadowed the trio. Suddenly, for some unexplained reason, Savage turned around and started to make his way back into town. Accordingly, the SAS team split, two with Savage, two staying on McCann and Farrell.

A few moments later, fate took a hand. A local policeman, driving in heavy traffic, was recalled to the station. It was said later that his car was required; whatever the reason, to expedite his orders he activated his siren. This action happened close to McCann and Farrell, making the pair turn nervously. McCann made eye contact with one of the SAS soldiers, who was no more than 30 feet away. In response to this, the soldier – who was about to issue a challenge – opened fire. He later gave evidence that McCann's arm had moved distinctly across his body, and he feared he might be about to detonate the bomb. McCann was hit in the back and went down. Farrell, it is said, made a movement for her bag; she was shot with a single round. By this time the second soldier had also drawn his pistol and opened fire, hitting both terrorists. On hearing the shots, Savage turned, to be confronted by the other two SAS men. His hand moved to his pocket: this time a warning was shouted, but Savage's hand continued to reach into his pocket. Both SAS men fired and Savage was killed.

As the first news of the event hit the media, it looked like a professional job, but the euphoria was short-lived. No bomb was found in the car, and all three terrorists were found to be unarmed. Although a bomb was later discovered in Malaga, the press and the IRA had a field day. Allegations were made and witnesses were found who claimed to have seen the whole thing. The trio had surrendered; their arms had been in the air; they had been shot at point-blank range while they lay on the ground and so on. Once again, SAS men were held up as killers: even though they had probably saved the lives of many people, and dispatched three well-known IRA terrorists. They would stand trial.

In September 1988, after a two-week inquest and by a majority of nine to two, a verdict was passed of lawful killing. Although this satisfied most people, the story did not end there. The SAS soldiers who took part in the shooting in Gibraltar were taken to court by relatives of the three IRA members killed. The European Commission of Human Rights in Strasbourg decided by 11 votes to six that the SAS did not use unnecessary force, ruling that the soldiers were justified in opening fire as they thought the IRA members were about to detonate a bomb. However, they did refer the case to the European Court of Human Rights. Because of this court case, the British government was forced to pay compensation.

Flight Assault Called Off

In 1988, the SAS anti-terrorist team was sent to Cyprus, where it prepared for an assault on a Boeing 737 aircraft. The commercial aircraft would be flying from Lebanon into Libya. Intelligence suggested that two British lecturers who had previously been kidnapped were aboard the aircraft. On the course of its flight, fighter aircraft stationed at a British RAF base in Cyprus would be scrambled. The fighters were to force the aircraft to land so that the SAS anti-terrorist team could assault it. In the event, the aircraft never flew, and after three weeks the plan was called off and the SAS returned to Hereford.

Loss of a Veteran

In 1989 Major Dare Newell died aged 71. He was a veteran member of the SOE in the Second World War and Force 136 in Malaya in 1945. With his fighting and jungle experience, he was a welcome addition to the Malayan Scouts in the 1950s, where he assisted Mike Calvert in bringing a new professionalism to the force. He went on to become the Regimental Adjutant of the SAS and Secretary of the SAS Regimental Association, and was awarded the OBE for his services. Above all, Dare Newell is best remembered for his unswerving defence against those who would politically attack the SAS and frequently fought the Regiment's corner against its enemies in Whitehall.

7

1990s

CENTRAL AMERICA
TO THE GULF

THE DECADE STARTED with David Stirling, founder of the SAS, being knighted for his services. Sadly, he died in the same year. He will never be forgotten – as long as there is an SAS unit, his name and legend will live on.

In August 1990, the SAS started its build-up training for operations in Colombia, where the drug cartels were seen to be the new enemy. The powers-that-be had decided a British force would help train the Colombian anti-narcotics police. This would allow the Colombians to carry out their own special operations within a jungle environment. In all, soldiers from three SAS squadrons rotated through Colombia, each squadron teaching basic jungle tactics, plus a few counter-terrorist methods. The training force varied from between 20 and 35 men; however, this was deemed to be overkill, as the SAS was not allowed to take part in operations.

The decision to use the SAS in Colombia had been instigated by Margaret Thatcher. She had publicly stated that she was going to send special forces to counter this problem, and that's exactly what happened. The Americans funded a large percentage of the operation, providing an overall budget of about £2 million for the two-year period. As well as training, it included such equipment as night-sights, waterproof equipment, bergens and military-type clothing.

Despite what all the other SAS books say concerning the role of the SAS in Colombia, in truth the Regiment carried out no actual operations against the drug cartels. True, they would go out on exercises, using the areas where the cartels were most active, but no direct confrontation was planned. The nearest they got to some real shooting was when the SBS, who had accompanied the SAS, reported that they were being threatened. Their task had been to train some of the police in boat work. This would allow the Colombians to intercept shipments of drugs being moved around by boat. During this training, the SBS received news that members of a cartel were about to attack them. In response, the SAS set up an ambush using the SBS as bait; however, nothing materialized.

The only shooting to take place during the SAS operation in Colombia happened one evening in the training camp. Most of the SAS members were getting ready to go down to Bogota for the weekend when one of the policemen shot a friend. Luckily, these guys were nothing to do with the training package: they were fully trained police officers who had been messing about in the hallway playing cops and robbers. One officer pulled his pistol and had an accidental discharge; he shot his friend in the head. Two SAS medics tried administering first aid to the dying man, but the .45 calibre bullet had caused major damage to the skull and brain. It was obvious that the man would not survive unless he was immediately hospitalized. However, the Colombian police, who did not seem in a rush, bundled the wounded man on to a makeshift stretcher and ran off in the direction of the nearby medical centre. The staff there could not provide adequate treatment, so they threw him on to the back of an open vehicle and drove him 40 miles to a hospital. It came as no surprise when the SAS heard the man had died in transit.

The Gulf War

In August 1990, Iraq invaded the defenceless oil-rich state of Kuwait, creating a situation that resulted in conflict with the combined forces of the United Nations. Despite attempting to negotiate with Iraq, it became apparent that military action was inevitable and a huge task force began to make its way out to the Persian Gulf. The overall UN commander was the US General Norman Schwarzkopf, who was a veteran of Vietnam and had been involved in activity in Grenada, both theatres leaving him with little regard for unconventional warfare. As a result, it seemed unlikely that special forces and the British SAS, a unit originally created for desert warfare, were going to be used. Fortunately, the commander of the British troops, Lieutenant-General Sir Peter de la Billière, himself an SAS veteran and former commander of 22 SAS, managed to convince Schwarzkopf that the special skills of the SAS would be invaluable.

(Note: There have been rumours that an SAS operation took place just hours before the Iraqis invaded Kuwait. It is claimed that a scheduled British Airways flight into Kuwait was used to infiltrate the SAS team.

Despite the situation, the flight went ahead, with many of the passengers, mainly French, taking note of the last-minute arrivals. Although there have been repeated denials that there were any SAS soldiers aboard the flight, British Airways was forced to pay £4 million damages to French passengers after a French court gave judgement against them.

Unsubstantiated information has since emerged that several leading Kuwaitis, together with senior members of the British Embassy staff, were spirited away by the SAS teams. This is not the first time such actions have taken place.) Shortly after Christmas 1990, the SAS – which had been on standby for action for months – left for the Gulf, activating the largest deployment of the Regiment since 1945, with men from A, B and D squadrons in theatre. However, there appeared to be no immediate requirement for them, since the US Special Forces and SEALs had already taken all the border reconnaissance roles. It was proposed to use the SAS and Delta Force to rescue the hundreds of foreign nationals being held as hostages under Saddam Hussein's 'human shield' policy. However, this was a logistical impossibility, as the hostages were held in various locations all over the country, and too many lives, of both soldiers and hostages, would be lost, which would lead to bad press at home. After its previous experiences in Vietnam and Tehran the United States, understandably, wanted to avoid detrimental press coverage at all costs.

By mid-January 1991, General de la Billière decided the SAS could be effective in creating diversions ahead of the main attack, destroying Iraqi communications facilities and tracking down the mobile Scud missile launchers, which so far had eluded both satellite reconnaissance and airstrikes. The SAS was to undertake these operations on the night of 22–23 January, six days prior to the anticipated start of the main hostilities.

Many stories have come out of the 1991 Gulf War, in particular the fascinating story of the ill-fated SAS patrol Bravo Two Zero. However, there were many others that have not been so intensively documented. The following ones are written from first-hand accounts. They convey the feeling, and something of the true nature, of SAS operations.

Alpha Three Zero

The patrol call sign Alpha Three Zero was one of the fighting columns the SAS had inserted behind Iraqi lines. It consisted of a half-squadron and was equipped with eight Type 110 Land Rovers, most of which were armed with a Browning .5 heavy machine gun. Additional weapons included GPMGs, American Mk 19 40mm grenade launchers and Milan anti-tank missiles. The night-sight for the Milan, which is called a MIRA (Milan Infra-Red Attachment), was mounted on the roll bar of the leading vehicle. This proved to be an exceptionally valuable piece of technology, as most of the fighting would take place during the hours of darkness.

All the vehicles had petrol engines that fed off two 10-gallon tanks. Additionally, they carried 16 jerrycans, giving them an operating range of about 370 miles. Each wagon also carried six jerrycans of water and rations to last 14 days. The normal allocation of ammunition per man was around 1,000 rounds, four high-explosive grenades and two white phosphorus. Each vehicle also carried several bar mines. Two cross-country motorbikes were allocated to each column: these would act as outriders. The mainstay support for the column was a Unimog to act as the mother vehicle, carrying stores. The Unimog's great advantage is that it can be loaded to the gunwales and still go anywhere.

Alpha Three Zero drove from Saudi Arabia heading straight across the Iraqi border. It was as simple as that. The column moved in single-line formation with the Unimog in the middle for protection. The outriders used the bikes to scout ahead and check the flanks to prevent possible ambush. The column would drive only at night and lie up by day. They would stop about an hour before first light, usually in a depression, if one could be found, and camouflage the vehicles. Sentries would be posted, and food cooked and eaten, before the men fell asleep on the desert floor.

Alpha Three Zero progressed some 60 miles from the Saudi border into Iraq during the first week. By this time the men had sorted out a routine, coming to terms with problems of moving by night and resting by day, although one problem had been overlooked – the weather. It was bitterly cold in Iraq, unlike anything one could envisage. Iraq at that time of year is a very hostile environment.

Late in the afternoon on the eighth day, while the men sat around happily, protected by the overhead camouflage nets and lazily passing the day away, the Iraqis appeared. A sentry had seen an Iraqi vehicle heading directly towards the SAS position.

He was frantically pointing over to his right. Fist balled, with thumb pointing down, means only one thing – enemy.

This is what the SAS refers to as 'headless chicken' time. They grabbed weapons, darting here and there, tripping over each other while trying to find a good firing position. Then the professionalism took over. Weapons acquired targets and the adrenalin rushed through the body. There was nothing but the sound of the engine as the vehicle drew closer. The Iraqis had spotted the SAS position from some distance and drove directly into the camp area, stopping within 60 feet of the nearest camouflaged hump. Fortunately, they had assumed the SAS were Iraqi forces, unable to believe that enemy troops would be so close to Baghdad.

The SAS watched as both the driver and another man, who had been sitting in the front seat, got out. The driver then walked to the front of his vehicle, opening up the bonnet. One of the SAS men broke cover and walked out to meet the Iraqi, who turned out to be an enemy officer. The Iraqi was a short, slightly chubby guy in his early to mid-thirties, tidy and clean-shaven. He had dark hair and a very small moustache, characteristic of the Middle Eastern male. As the two men came together, a look of bewilderment came over the Iraqi's face. Suddenly, the SAS man threw up his rifle and fired: nothing happened. He dropped to his knees, trying desperately to clear the stoppage – and at that moment a second SAS man shot the Iraqi dead. Several other bursts swiftly followed, terminating the officer and driver instantly.

The two SAS men then ran towards the vehicle, a Russian Gaz 69, only to discover two more Iraqis in the back. One had been severely wounded as the intense SAS fire ripped through the vehicle, but a second had survived without a scratch. He later also turned out to be an officer.

The SAS pulled the wounded Iraqi from the vehicle, dropping him to the floor. An incredible amount of blood was lost from his side and soaked into the sand. He had been hit several times, with the main damage just above his hip. While still in the truck, the man's body had been in a position that stemmed the flow of blood, but once he was moved the pressure was released and the blood gushed. The SAS knew he would die shortly. Other members of the patrol pulled out the only surviving Iraqi soldier. Half-crazed, he wailed in Arabic, '*In sha'Allah*' (It is the will of God) and was obviously glad to be alive. When two SAS interpreters interrogated the man, they soon discovered that he actually had both maps and orders that clearly showed the battle plans for the area. It also transpired that these Iraqis were the lead element of a large column due to materialize at any moment.

The SAS commander swiftly issued orders for everyone to pack up and be ready to move. By this time, the wounded Iraqi soldier had died. Some of the SAS men placed him in a shallow grave along with the other two, but they had barely finished covering the bodies when their commander ordered that they be dug up and placed in the back of the Gaz. The POW was bagged and tagged, then thrown on the back of the Unimog. Then, some 15 minutes after the initial contact, call sign Alpha Three Zero started to move away from the position. As the aim was to get the prisoner and the information back to Allied Command, a course was set towards the Saudi border. The men drove for two hours before stopping to send a radio message. It was then that they discovered an Iraqi position just 300 feet directly to their front. They moved back carefully and drove off in another direction. Two hours later, they stopped again. This time there was no sign of the enemy. While a full contact report was sent back to SAS headquarters in Al Jouf, some of the men decided to bury the three dead Iraqis. The ground was so hard they could only dig down six to eight inches. In order to accommodate the three bodies they made the hole wider, covering it with earth and rocks. They had just finished when once more the squadron commander interrupted them, running up and demanding an explanation of what they were doing. Somewhat surprised, they said, 'We're burying the bodies!' Again, the commander ordered them to be dug up and put back on the Iraqi vehicle.

Once the contact report had been received the column moved off, continuing in a southerly direction. Its intention was to get to within some 15 miles of the border, where a resupply by the RAF had been arranged.

Arriving at the prearranged RV, the column started camouflaging its vehicles and set about their normal administration. The resupply was due to arrive at 04:00. The helicopter came in low and fast, the pilot flying literally 10–20 feet above the ground, using only PNGs to penetrate the darkness. As the chopper got closer it flared its rotors, kicking up masses of dust. Finally, it settled, with the rear ramp deployed. The SAS men rapidly transferred the resupply to their vehicles before putting the Iraqi prisoner on board. They were about to load the Gaz, with its three bodies, when the RAF loadmaster told them, 'No way.' The final act came when the commander of Alpha Three Zero was told to get on the helicopter; an SAS sergeant major was replacing him.

Under their new commander, the men mounted their vehicles and moved off in box formation; two groups of four with the Unimog in the middle. Between 02:30 and 05:00 they covered a distance of some 20 miles, stopping only once – to place a bar mine under the Iraqi vehicle, which still contained the three bodies, with a timer set for 05:30. At exactly 05:30 there was a bright red glow on the horizon as the explosion went off. A few seconds later, there was a very dull thud. At last it was all over for the three Iraqi soldiers, who never knew anything about their demise, as they were vaporized and became part of the desolate landscape that is Iraq.

Missing in Action

Alpha Three Zero was not the only SAS unit seeing action in Iraq. Most of the other fighting columns and observation patrols had regular contacts with the enemy. One battle took place during the early hours of 9 February, when an A

Squadron team was carrying out a CTR (close target reconnaissance) on a communications installation. The team was commanded by an SSM (Squadron Sergeant Major). The SSM was standing on the back of a Pinkie, observing through a MIRA. The team had already cut its way through the barbed wire surrounding the installation, leaving one Pinkie at their entry point to act as cover. Moving further into the Iraqi position, the SSM realized that the place was far bigger than he had originally thought. However, by this time they were committed, so he told the driver, Keith, to keep going. Suddenly, as they topped a small rise, he made out some shadowy movement through the TI. There were enemy all around, and it was just a matter of seconds before contact would be initiated. Making a snap decision, the SSM decided their only alternative was to brazen it out and drive through the Iraqi position as quietly as possible, hoping the dark would conceal their identity. Good way to do a recce! As they continued weaving their way through the Iraqi defences and accommodation, a soldier stepped out in front of the wagon and made a vain attempt to stop it by holding up his hand. John, who was sitting in the front passenger seat, aimed the GPMG mounted in front of him and opened up with a large burst of 7.62mm. The soldier disintegrated. Then all hell broke lose.

Even though it was dark, the Pinkie was pinged immediately by the Iraqis. Seconds later the three SAS guys were taking incoming fire from all directions. The SSM was hit in the first burst, a round going through the top of his knee, throwing him into the back of the wagon. At the same time Keith booted the Pinkie forwards, accelerating hard, hoping to burst through the position. They were going to make it. Swerving and driving like a maniac, Keith drove straight through the camp gates, with John blasting everything in sight with the GPMG. Then their luck ran out. Just 1,000 feet from the camp the Pinkie lurched to a sudden stop as it crashed hard into a tank ditch. Seconds before, the SSM had raised himself, hoping to get the rear gun into action. The sudden stop threw him over the roll bar, where he landed half on the laps of Keith and John and half on the bonnet. His leg was lying on his chest. Shaking themselves, they immediately made to escape. Keith threw the SSM on his shoulders and started to run away from the wagon, which was now on the receiving end of the Iraqi fire. With John covering, they attempted to melt into the darkness. Those who know the SSM would describe him as a large, well-built man, with a mental strength to match that of his body, but the damage from the bullet and the vehicle crash had left him in a critical condition. Climbing a slight rise, the three hid among some rocks where they set to work to staunch the flow of blood from the SSM's leg wound. It looked bad. The Iraqis had regrouped and made an attempt to surround the three. Keith had left his rifle in the damaged truck, unable to carry both it and the SSM, so John kept the Iraqis at bay as they finally moved deeper into the darkness.

Slipping in and out of consciousness, the SSM commanded that the others should leave; he would provide what little cover he could. It was a dilemma he has faced many times before – stay with a badly wounded man, or try to take him with you and risk the whole group being captured. Even if the Iraqis did not find the SSM, he would die, but that could take several hours. Capture by the Iraqis would mean torture and possibly death – not much of a choice.

Keith bent over the SSM and whispered. 'Shall I finish you, mate? It's your best option.'

It was a tempting offer. One quick shot and no more pain. Again, this is not unique; several times during the Regiment's history the question has been asked. There is only one known occasion where this ultimate action has been taken. The SSM declined: 'No, thanks Keith. I'll take my chances to the bitter end. Now go.' As it was highly likely that the SSM would pass out, Keith and John decided that they would be better off with the rifle. John had managed to grab a 66mm rocket from the damaged vehicle and this was left with the SSM. With the guys gone, the SSM slipped into unconsciousness once more.

However, the sound of voices down in the wadi snapped him back to awareness of his predicament. Several Iraqi soldiers were standing around a vehicle – a target too good to miss. He pulled out the 66mm rocket and aimed it at the truck. At the moment he was about to fire, two Iraqi soldiers jumped him.

'Who are you?' they asked in Arabic.

'English,' the SSM replied. Although he was a fluent Arabist, he pretended he could only speak a few words. Surprisingly, an officer appeared and a stretcher was called for. Within hours an Iraqi civilian doctor was treating the SSM, doing a wonderful job of repairing the damage to the injured leg. Eventually he was treated in hospital, while his interrogation continued. One day, the two interrogators were standing by his bed deliberating which question to ask him when, as they turned to speak, he unintentionally pre-empted their question, giving away the fact that he spoke fluent Arabic. Despite protests from the medical staff, the interrogators ripped the drips and wires from his body and gave him a beating.

When the war ended, his reappearance delighted his next-of-kin, who had been advised of his status as missing in action, possibly dead. The SSM was awarded the Military Cross, a decoration normally only given to commissioned officers. This has been done only once before: in 1965, when another A Squadron SSM, Lawrence Smith, was awarded the decoration for his work in Borneo.

Victor Two

Next came the assault on an Iraqi installation known as Victor Two. This operation was given to one of A Squadron's fighting columns. It received its orders as it lay hidden in the vast wilderness of the Iraqi desert. Everything began when the two signallers started to decode long incoming radio messages from SAS headquarters in Saudi Arabia. This feverish activity around the two signallers quickly spread to the rest of the men and soon the orders became clear: to launch an attack on an Iraqi micro-wave station that night.

The men began to prepare for the assault, with Mountain Troop putting together a model of the radar station from what-ever kit they had lying around. They built it according to the intelligence coming over the radio, which seemed quite detailed on the set-up of the station but it was confusing where enemy strengths and dispositions were concerned.

At 15:45 everyone, except for the duty sentries, made their way to the middle of the lying-up point for a briefing. The sen-tries were to be briefed on their roles later; this was not an ideal situation as, in the rush, it was more than likely that they would not get the whole story and would go into battle not completely sure of what was happening. Nevertheless, ideal or not, the column was behind enemy lines and sentries were essential.

The briefing started with the men being formed in the groups they would be in for the assault. Once they had settled, Brian, the Regiment sergeant major (RSM), and Paul, the OC (Officer Commanding) designate, joined them and the briefing began. Although Paul was a major, and the new OC for the column, it was obvious to the men that Brian was still very much in charge (SAS rank structure has little to do with who is in charge).

The target radar installation was to be known by its call sign of Victor Two. The plan was for the column to drive to within a mile of it, place the vehicles in a fire support position and then send out a recce team. Once the location had been confirmed, these men would return to their positions with the assault team and close-fire support before guiding them to the target. The aim was to destroy the facility, which was the main centre for guiding the mobile Scud launchers to their targets. It had previously been attacked by Stealth bombers, but the problem was that most of it was underground and therefore safe from aerial attack. The only way to make sure it was taken out was by an attack from the ground. Once the column had achieved this objective, all vehicles were to make their way back to the present location. Brian made himself the overall commander of the operation. There were to be three assault groups, each of three men, plus close fire support and fire support groups. The rest of the men were to assist with driving the vehicles. The objective itself was a building complex with a microwave tower about 150 feet tall. The outside perimeter wall was about 15 feet in height, while a 10-feet-high internal security fence posed another obstacle. The main gate was guarded by a sentry position. The plan was to fire two anti-tank missiles at the sentry position and the gate. An explosive charge would then be placed on the internal fence. Once this had gone off, the three assault teams were to enter the building, each taking a floor, including the floors below ground.

The floors needed to be cleared and then explosive charges laid before the teams got themselves out as quickly as possible.

The men, clear about their roles, soon got to work. They were enthusiastic about the operation despite the development of some internal politics within the group. The only piece of information which wasn't clear was how many Iraqis were at the installation and how well armed they were. The intelligence coming through was vague, but it suggested that there were more civilians than military personnel present, and so there was to be no indiscriminate firing on the part of the assault forces. A man needed to be identified as a soldier before he could be shot at. Of course, this was far from ideal in a situation behind enemy lines in the middle of a war. However, orders were orders.

It was suggested at the time that this column was being sent in because the Regiment wanted to 'blood' its soldiers; that is, it wanted to give them some experience of war and to be able to claim that one of its squadrons had led an attack in hostile territory. It was also rumoured that headquarters knew exactly how many Iraqis were at the base and how well armed they were; after all, they knew all the other details about the location. Sensing that maybe they were not being told everything, the troops started to feel uneasy.

After a final brew-up, the men formed up in their vehicles and drove for a couple of hours until they reached a main road, or MSR, as they were known. Daylight was now fading. Having checked that it was all clear, the group moved off again. Before they got themselves on to the road, however, they needed to bridge a ditch so that the Land Rovers could cross over. To do this Mobility Troop placed two sand channels supported by sandbags in the ditch, so that the wheels could roll across them without the rest of the vehicle getting grounded. Within 17 minutes all the vehicles were over, the bridge dismantled and they were on their way again.

About three miles from the target, the adrenaline started to flow. All senses were alert with the expectation of an enemy ambush at any minute; so far, it had all seemed too easy. Then the ground started to become more difficult to drive on, causing the column to make a half-mile detour to the west. Here, the ground became a mass of man-made slit trenches, but as the orders were to slow down or stop only if an enemy vehicle was spotted, the vehicles carried on at the same speed.

Closing fast now on Victor Two, the MIRA wagon came forward, needing to observe the area continually for enemy activity. When it was a mile away from the installation the column came to a halt, as planned. One of the men left his motorbike at the location, and it was logged in on the satnav so that the rest of them would have a position to make their way back to after the operation was over. The target was checked once more through the MIRA. It turned out that the site was huge – lots of buildings, vehicles and people; soldiers were positioned in both slit trenches and bunkers. There seemed to be little sign of the 'civilians' mentioned by Regiment HQ.

At this point, Brian started to change the plans made at the briefing. He decided that they should move forward immediately, without the services of the recce group. The column drove closer to Victor Two, internal politics changing the line-up as certain members of the group decided they wanted to take the lead, no matter what. Driving along a tarmac road, they soon found themselves right in the middle of the enemy position with hostile soldiers and vehicles all around. With the previous orders changed beyond any recognizable form, most of the men didn't have a clue as to what they were going to do next.

Without warning, the lead vehicles pulled over to the left side of the road and the others were obliged to form up behind them. They were now parked up alongside a small escarpment running parallel to the road. At last the recce party was sent out to do a CTR and discovered the magnitude of the site. In all, it was about half a square mile, its focus being the massive control building and the microwave tower, bristling with communication dishes. The men returned quickly and a revised plan was put forward. Now it was proposed that the vehicles would split into two groups and give cover from the flanks. Meanwhile the assault teams, together with a cover party, would go ahead on foot to carry out the process of demolishing the tower with explosives.

Their forward progress went unchallenged. On reaching the complex, 1,000 feet from the vehicles, the demolition teams went forward to lay their charges while the covering team hung back, keeping a look out for any trouble. One of the cover party, while waiting near the back of an Iraqi truck, heard a sound from the cab. He went around to investigate and opened the cab door to reveal the sleepy face of an Iraqi soldier. The soldier, surprised, reached for his gun, despite efforts to stop him doing so. Then there was no other choice – within seconds he had been shot dead with a burst from an automatic rifle.

A firefight instantly erupted, and the column felt that every gun in the compound was trained on them. Even the Russian-made anti-aircraft guns were turned on their position. The Squadron fought back, giving it everything they'd got. By now the demolition teams had placed their explosives in the tower and were moving back to rejoin the rest of the column. The order was given to move out.

As the vehicles slowly regrouped and withdrew, they drew down a heavy rain of fire from all about them. Nevertheless, they kept going, punching a hole through the opposition with their own heavy guns. Finally, after an hour of battling their way through enemy positions, they disappeared into the night. Remarkably, despite the dangerous internal political manoeuvrings and the changes of plans, there were no casualties.

A Squadron spent a total of 45 days behind enemy lines, during which time two men were killed and one was captured. Members of the Squadron received a DSM, two MCs, four MMs and four Mentions in Despatches for their bravery.

As a tribute to the SAS in the Gulf War, General Norman Schwarzkopf wrote the following commendation.

Letter of Commendation for the
22 Special Air Service (SAS) Regiment

1. I wish to officially commend the 22 Special Air Service (SAS) Regiment for their totally outstanding performance of military operations during Operation Desert Storm.

2. Shortly after the initiation of the strategic air campaign, it became apparent that the Coalition forces would be unable to eliminate Iraq's firing of Scud missiles from western Iraq into Israel. The continued firing of Scuds on Israel carried with it enormous unfavourable political ramifications and could, in fact, have resulted in the dismantling of the carefully crafted Coalition. Such a dismantling would have adversely affected, in ways difficult to measure, the ultimate outcome of the military campaign. It became apparent that the only way that the Coalition could succeed in reducing these Scud launches was by physically placing military forces on the ground in the vicinity of the western launch sites. At that time, the majority of available Coalition forces were committed to the forthcoming military campaign in the eastern portion of the theatre of operations. Further, none of these forces possessed the requisite skills and abilities required to conduct such a dangerous operation. The only force

deemed qualified for this critical mission was the 22 Special Air Service (SAS) Regiment.

3. From the first day they were assigned their mission until the last day of the conflict, the performance of the 22 Special Air Service (SAS) Regiment was courageous and highly professional. The area in which they were committed proved to contain far more numerous enemy forces than had been predicted by every intelligence estimate, the terrain was much more difficult than expected and the weather conditions were unseasonably brutal. Despite these hazards, in a very short period of time the 22 Special Air Service (SAS) Regiment was successful in totally denying the central corridor of western Iraq to Iraqi Scud units. The result was that the principal areas used by the Iraqis to fire Scuds on Tel Aviv were no longer available to them. They were required to move their Scud missile-firing forces to the north-west portion of Iraq and from that location the firing of Scud missiles was essentially militarily ineffective.

4. When it became necessary to introduce United States Special Operations Forces into the area to attempt to close down the north-west Scud areas, the 22 Special Air Service (SAS) Regiment provided invaluable assistance to the US forces. They took every possible measure to ensure that US forces were thoroughly briefed and were able to profit from the valuable lessons that had been learned by earlier SAS deployments into Western Iraq.

I am completely convinced that, had US forces not received these thorough indoctrinations by SAS personnel, US forces would have suffered a much higher rate of casualties than was ultimately the case. Further, the SAS and US joint forces immediately merged into a combined fighting force where the synergetic effect of these fine units ultimately caused the enemy to be convinced that they were facing forces in western Iraq that were more than tenfold the size of those they were actually facing. As a result, large numbers of enemy forces that might otherwise have been deployed in the eastern theatre were tied down in western Iraq.

5. The performance of the 22 Special Air Service (SAS) Regiment during Operation Desert Storm was in the highest traditions of the professional military service and in keeping with the proud history and tradition that has been established by that regiment. Please ensure that this commendation receives appropriate attention and is passed on to the unit and its members.

General H. NORMAN SCHWARZKOPF
US Army Commander-in-Chief.

The Balkans

With the Gulf War behind it, the SAS once more settled down to a routine of training and servicing the numerous requirements of the British government. One such role was to take the SAS into Bosnia. While the conflict was messy and many people were killed, the role of the SAS soldiers remained that of observers. As a result, the amount of information about SAS operations in Bosnia has been minimal, the main reason being the lack of action rather than security. Unlike other wars, the SAS was sent to Bosnia under a very different directive. Its mission was to observe the major forces in the area, with an eye to preventing trouble before it materialized. Individuals or small units were assigned to monitor the various Serbian units that sought to dominate the Muslim population. The SAS was acting as a peacekeeper, something not written in SAS doctrine; its men are trained for combat.

(Note: It is not widely known that the SAS used its R Squadron, a squadron comprising a few retired regular SAS and civilians who are basically part-time soldiers, to fulfil much of its role in Bosnia.)

The first public involvement of the SAS in Bosnia came when Major General 'Mike' Rose officially took over from General Briquemont on 24 January, two days after a mortar shell had killed six children in Sarajevo. His first task was to ensure all information was channelled directly to him. Secondly, he made it clear that the aid convoys would no longer negotiate for passage. Days later, British soldiers fired back on the snipers who sought to prevent free passage of the convoys. Rose's attitude to the Bosnian Serb leaders was clear: 'Back off or we will hit you hard.' It was a policy which would have worked had it not been for the weakness of the UN and the indecisiveness of NATO. Agreements with the Serbs were full of lies, deception and intimidation, tactics designed to win time and ground against the disadvantaged Muslims. These stop-go tactics angered Rose and, although he had employed the correct measures in reply, the politicians failed to back his response. Thus the key element of force was lost to him. Towards the end of March, the Serbs started shelling the eastern enclave of Gorazde. The hospital was hit repeatedly and the wounded were forced to huddle in the basement. As the Serbs advanced with infantry and tanks, intent on taking the city, Rose called for NATO air support, sending SAS men in to act as forward air controllers. The bombing was remarkably accurate, and the Serb offensive was halted just as the town seemed about to fall. The air support was not sanctioned, but it had worked. The Serbs called for a local ceasefire while the wounded were evacuated.

The role of the SAS was to act as independent observers for General Rose. This they did by positioning themselves in close proximity to Serbian forces. It is rumoured that two members of the Regiment were spotted by the Serbs and fired on; as a result, one was killed and the other badly wounded. That night a second SAS team moved into Gorazde to assist the wounded men and also to extract a pilot who had been shot down during the bombing: this mission ended successfully.

The Lima Embassy Siege

In many cases, the SAS is invited to the scene of a terrorist incident purely to give advice. Such a case occurred on Tuesday, 17 December 1996. In this instance, 14 Peruvian rebels of the Tupac Amaru movement, known in Spanish by the initials MRTA, stormed the Japanese Embassy in Lima. The surprise attack occurred while the building was thronged with dignitaries as diplomats, Peruvian government officials and business leaders attended a party celebrating the Japanese Emperor's birthday. In all, some 600 people, most of whom were VIPs, were enjoying the party when the assault began. According to accounts provided by hostages who were later released, the guerrillas entered between 20:15 and 20:25, as many of the guests were working their way down to the buffet table set up in a tent in the grounds. An explosion, followed by a volley of gunfire, announced the takeover.

It has never been established exactly how the rebels gained access to the Embassy, but reports indicated that most of the attacking guerrillas simply stormed the high concrete walls surrounding the Embassy compound. Other unconfirmed reports said that they entered disguised as waiters, while one newspaper described how the rebels had spent three months tunnelling their way into the grounds of the residence. While this latter method may sound totally implausible, it did in fact have a grossly distorted basis in truth.

Whatever their method of entry, the MRTA rebels had certainly researched their target and timed their attack to perfection. The hostage list read like a Who's Who of Peruvian society and included the country's Foreign Minister Francisco Tudela, Agriculture Minister Rodolfo Munante Sanguineti and the Speaker of the nation's parliament. Also caught up in the assault were Peru's Supreme Court President, Moises Pantoja, and at least three of the country's legislators, as well as Japan's Ambassador, Morihisa Aoki, and 17 members of his staff. The ambassadors of Austria, Brazil, Bulgaria, Cuba, Guatemala, Panama, Poland, Romania, South Korea, Spain and Venezuela, together with seven Americans, were also unlucky enough to have accepted their invitations to the party. Without doubt the hostage list was the most prestigious ever taken in any terrorist action, although most guests managed to avoid being taken captive during the raid. Fernando Andrade, the mayor of the Miraflores section of Lima, escaped by sneaking into a bathroom and then climbing out of a window. US Ambassador Dennis Jett had attended the party but left around 19:45, about half an hour before the attack.

Those who were taken hostage were immediately divided into groups and ushered into rooms on the second floor of the residence. The various ambassadors were separated from the other guests and held together in one room, which was heavily guarded by the rebels.

Despite a pitched gun battle during the takeover and the guerrillas' threats, by nightfall the siege had resulted in no deaths and only minor injuries. Once the siege had settled down, the rebels issued their demands via a telephone call to a local radio station. They were:

1. Release of some 300 imprisoned rebels, including Tupac Amaru's leader, Victor Polay, who had been in solitary confinement for the past four years.

2. Transfer of the freed prisoners and the hostage takers to a jungle hideout with their hostages; the hostages were to be released once they had reached their destination.

3. Payment of an unspecified amount as a 'war tax'.

4. An economic programme to help Peru's poor.

Although the demands centred on the release of imprisoned rebels, there was also strong reference to what the rebels called Japan's 'constant interference with Peru's internal politics'.

In response, the Peruvian government and President Alberto Fujimori, who is of Japanese descent, reminded the world that they had sworn never to negotiate with terrorists. Fujimori, who was elected President in 1990, had managed to severely weaken the guerrilla movements, capturing most of the leaders and jailing thousands of militants and sympathizers. The take-over of the Japanese Embassy now put Peru's image at stake. It was because of President Fujimori's hard-line action in the past that Japan had invested so heavily in Peru, leading to the Tupac Amaru's resentment of Japanese influence on its country.

With so much in the balance, Fujimori spent most of his time presiding over a closed-door meeting of his Council of Ministers, including the chief of police, Kentin Vidal, a legendary figure who had led the successful operation to capture the rebel leader Abimael Guzman.

When medicine was delivered to the Embassy 24 hours into the siege, the rebels released four diplomats – the ambassadors of Canada, Germany and Greece and the French cultural attaché. The freed men read out a statement in which they said they had been sent to 'search for a negotiated solution' that would avoid deaths. During the next few days, the rebels released more hostages including President Fujimori's mother and sister. In return, Christmas turkeys were delivered to the besieged Embassy. Fujimori, however, rejected an opportunity to make a separate deal for other relatives trapped in the Embassy and flatly refused to release Peru's guerrilla prisoners. Instead, he offered the terrorists safe passage to some location outside of Peru as an incentive for them to lay down their arms and free all their hostages. The rebels refused this offer and set several deadlines, each accompanied with the threat to kill hostages. All these deadlines passed without the loss of life. By 6 January 1997, the rebels were becoming agitated and refused to release any further hostages until the government started negotiations.

Within minutes of the attack, Peru's security forces had started flexing their considerable muscles, but they couldn't dislodge the guerrillas. They did, however, start to implement anti-terrorist procedures. All services were disconnected and the government refused to allow fuel into the residence for the generator, which had provided power to the rebels and hostages after the electricity had been cut off. The Peruvian authorities ignored repeated demands to restore running water and telephone connections.

As the weeks went by, the Peruvian intelligence services started to monitor activities in the Embassy, setting up a series of listening devices. The CIA sent a US Air Force RG-8A aircraft with a forward-looking infrared camera to monitor the remaining 72 hostages and their 14 rebel guards. The 29-foot, single-engine aircraft makes very little noise and, in addition to an infrared camera, it carries several high-resolution television cameras. The information gathered through these and other observation techniques was vital before any planned assault could take place. It is also believed that one of the hostages, a former military officer, was using a concealed two-way radio to supply information about the rebels.

While both the US and Britain deny having had any direct role in the rescue operation, both have supplied experts in anti-terrorism training to Peru. And, remember, this was no ordinary terrorist incident. The taking of so many foreign nationals forced many countries to become involved. Some openly offered help. The British Ambassador to Peru, John Illman, voiced Britain's concern, saying: 'We are ready to respond and are, in fact, making preparations in advance to respond to any such request. And we've made it clear that the experience that we have is totally at the disposal of the Peruvian authorities should they require it.'

This response came in the guise of four members of the British SAS – four specialists with unparalleled expertise in the world of counter-terrorism. Their brief was to evaluate the situation and offer solutions. Ultimately, all of their solutions involved an assault of some form. In this case there was a choice of two primary actions: assault the Embassy or assault the rebels while in transit to freedom.

While the military planned and gathered information, the politicians tried to work out some form of compromise, one of which was to release the rebels and give them asylum in Cuba. To this end, President Fujimori had talks with President Fidel Castro of Cuba. Some 11 weeks into the siege, a basic agreement was in place whereby a military aircraft would take the rebels to Cuba. Whether or not this was a deception or a plan to assault the rebels en route, we will never know, for while these discussions were taking place another plan was being conceived by the shadowy figure of the unofficial head of Peruvian intelligence, Ivan Vladimiro Montesinos.

Montesinos is a cashiered army captain with a frightening reputation, and a figure who inspires fear and fascination in Peru. He has not appeared before news cameras for several years but the fact that, wearing dark glasses, he strode victoriously into the liberated Japanese compound with the army chief of staff once the siege was over was an obvious indication of his involvement. In reality, it was Montesinos who had raised the 150-man commando unit to carry out the hostage rescue mission. Using his strong personality, he was able to recruit a combination of the best of the elite special forces units from the police and army and get President Fujimori's permission to use them in a daring plan.

Montesinos's plan was to tunnel under the embassy from several different directions. Then, at the right moment, the assaulting force would blast its way through the floor and walls. To facilitate the plan, 24 miners were brought in from the government-owned Centromin mining company. Over a period of several weeks they excavated several tunnels from nearby buildings, each running to a precise position under the Japanese Embassy. This was not an easy task, as the work was done in secret, with both noise and vibration diversions having to be devised and put into operation. The end result was a series of tunnels, all equipped with electric lighting and ventilation. While the tunnels were being dug, the assembled group of elite commandos was undergoing painstaking training at a crude wooden replica of the ambassador's home constructed in the hills outside Lima.

There remained, however, one small problem with the method of entry into the Embassy. The final flooring, which was solid concrete, had to be breached. If explosives were used, the blast in the confined space of the tunnel would leave none of the assault force in any fit state to jump out and close with the rebels, added to which was the great danger of a cave-in. The SAS has, for many years, contemplated such a problem and has researched and developed a wall-breaching cannon. This ingenious device not only creates a hole, but can do so with the assaulting force standing within a few feet. There is no violent shock wave to tear the assault team limb from limb or cause a cave-in that would bury them alive.

Montesinos's plan was to make a sudden breach into the Embassy from five different directions. While 20 of the commandos would enter rapidly through the floor, the remainder would enter at ground level through the compound walls. With the entire assault force in position, the plan was initiated.

At 15:00 hours on 22 April 1997, after four months of captivity, the hostages heard several explosions, rapidly followed by blistering gunfire. The rebels had become lethargic, and at the moment of the assault half of them had been playing football in the main hall, while others were sleeping upstairs. Those rebels outside the building were killed instantly, while those inside met their fate as the commando team carried out room-by-room clearance. In all, the assault took some 15 minutes.

During the assault only one man, Supreme Court Judge Carlo Giusti Acuna, died after being shot, and this was the result of a heart attack. Two police officers involved in the assault also died, one being a member of the security detail assigned to protect the President's son. In all, 25 hostages received minor wounds, with two others requiring surgery.

Above: Two SAS soldiers drinking in the SAS bar at Bessbrook. For security reasons the SAS rarely shares military facilities with other units of the British Army. Note the long hair and casual clothes, all done to fit in with the local Irish community.

Below: Sean Savage, Daniel McCann and Mairéad Farrell were all shot dead by the SAS after a suspected car bomb alert in Gibraltar.

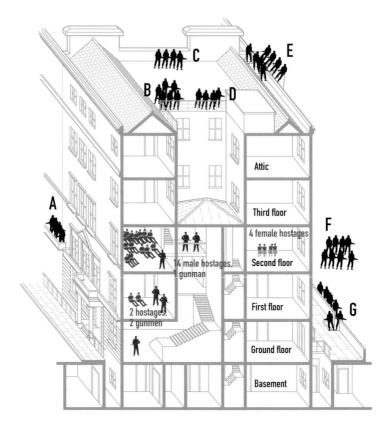

Attic

Third floor

4 female hostages
Second floor

14 male hostages
1 gunman

First floor

2 hostages,
2 gunmen

Ground floor

Basement

A Four-man assault team (Bravo) – *front*
B Six-man assault team, third floor – *roof*
C Four-man roof security, distraction charge – *roof*
D Four-man assault team, fourth floor – *roof*
E Two four-man assault teams (Romeo) – *roof*
F Eight-man hostage reception – *rear of building*
G Ten-man assault team (Bravo One, Bravo Two, Bravo Three)
   – *ground floor and basement*

Call Signs
BRAVO (Blue Team)
ROMEO (Red Team)
JULIET (Sniper Team)

Operational Code Words
"Road Accident" (Move into position)
"London Bridge" (Top [main] charge
ready)
"Bank Robbery" (Ready to Move)
"Stand by, Stand By, Go, Go, Go"
From Officer Commanding

Embassy Siege Personnel

Support HQ, Regents Park Barracks
Lt Col. AA
Major. AB
WO2. AC
WO2. AD
Sgt. AE
S/Sgt. AF
Cpn. AG
Cpl. AH (IC Signals)
Sgt. AI
Pvt. AJ 'B' Squadron Company Clark

Sniper Group, Regents Park
Sgt. BA
Sgt. BB (D Sqd attached)
L-Cpl. BC (D Sqd attached)
L/Cpl. BD (A Sqd attached)
L/Cpl. BE (A sqd attached)
L/Cpl. BF (A Sqd attached)

Reserve Outside Embassy – BRAVO
Cpn. CA (Blue Team)
Cpl. CB (Blue Team)
Tpr. CC (Blue Team)
L/Cpl. CD (Red Team)
Tpr. CE (Blue Team)
Cpl. CF (Blue Team Signals)

Support Base. Regents Park Barracks
Sgt. DA (Helicopter Pilot)
L/Cpl. DB. REME
L/Cpl. DC REME
Sgt. DD
Sgt. DE
Sgt. DF

Reception/Smoke
L/Cpl. EA (Reception)
L/Cpl. EB (Smoke)
L-Cpl. EC (Reception)
L/Cpl ED (Smoke)
Tpr. EF (Smoke)
Tpr. EG (Smoke)

HOSTAGE RESCUE FORCE
CSM. FA (Distraction charge planner)
Cpl. FB (Distraction charge)

Basement – BRAVO
Sgt. GA (Blue Team)
L.Cpl. GB (Blue Team)
Cpl. GC Blue Team)
L-Cpl. GD (Blue Team)
Cpl. GE (Blue Team)

Ground Floor – BRAVO
Tpr. HA (Blue Team)
Cpl. HB (Blue Team)
Cpl. HC (Blue Team)
Tpr. HD (Blue Team)

First Floor (Balcony Front) – BRAVO
Tpr. IA (Blue Team)
L-Cpl. IB (Blue Team)
L/Cpl. IC (Blue Team)
Tpr. ID (Blue Team)

Second Floor Abseilers – ROMEO
S-Sgt. JA (Red Team)
L-Cpl. JB (Red Team)
Tpr. JC (Red Team)
Cpl. JD (Red Team)

Second Floor Abseilers – ROMEO
Cpl. KA (Red Team)
Cpl. KB (Red Team)
Tpr. KC (Blue Team)
L-Cpl. KD (Blue Team)

Third Floor Abseilers – ROMEO
Sgt. LA (Red Team)
Tpr. LB (Red Team)
Cpl. LC (Red Team)
Tpr. LD (Red Team)
Trp. LE (Red Team)
Tpr LF (Red Team)

Forth Floor. Roof Ladders – ROMEO
S-Sgt. MA (Red Team)
Cpl. MB (Red Team)
L/Cpl. MC (Red Team)
Cpl. MD (Red Team)
Cpl. ME (Red Team)
Cpl. MF (Red Team)
Capt. MG (Red Team)
Sgt. MH (Red Team)

Above: A member of the SAS hugs the earth in the Falklands. The fire in the background is one of the town houses set on fire by mortar shells. The Argentinians were only a few feet in front of where the SAS man is crouching.

Left: Members of the assault team make ready to abseil down the Iranian Embassy in London.

Below: As every SAS man knows, to win a firefight you have to use a lot of weaponry. These SAS soldiers are practising anti-ambush drills.

Left: After the prisoner had been extracted back to Coalition headquarters the Gaz 69 was destroyed. An SAS demolitionist placed a bar mine under the vehicle, which still contained the dead Iraqi soldiers.

Below: Alliance Commander, US General Norman Schwarzkopf, personally thanks SAS troops at the end of the Gulf War.

Above: Walk up and run down is the only way to get to the RV (rendezvous) on time. At the end of Test Week comes the endurance march – 40 miles with a 55-pound Bergen in 20 hours.

Below: An SAS fighting column prepares to cross the border into Iraq during the Gulf War.

SAS Victoria Cross awards

Clockwise from top left: Major Anders Lassen, Corporal Ben Roberts-Smith, Corporal Mark Donaldson, Corporal Bill "Willie" Apiata.

All 14 of the rebels were killed. Although at least two dropped their weapons and were seen by several hostages surrendering to the commandos, in the event the government reported that all the rebels had been killed during the assault. TV footage later showed that some of their bodies had been mutilated and even dismembered by the soldiers. The bodies of the rebels were buried in unmarked graves to prevent closer examination.

Operation Tango in Bosnia

On 10 July 1997, the SAS was back in Bosnia, where it initiated Operation Tango. This action called for the arrest of two war criminals in Prijedor. Prijedor, which sits in the forested mountains, saw some of the worst ethnic crimes in the whole Bosnian war. Chinooks of Special Forces Flight 47 were used so the SAS unit could infiltrate into the area.

The two men, Simo Drljaca and Milan Kovacevic, were wanted for war crimes, and the International Criminal Tribunal for the Former Yugoslavia had issued an arrest warrant. Both were suspected of involvement in some of the worst excesses of ethnic cleansing in Prijedor, where thousands of Bosnian Muslims were imprisoned, starved and tortured in 1992.

The men were identified and tailed covertly before being challenged by the SAS men, who were dressed in regular army uniform. Kovacevic, who worked as a director in the hospital at Prijedor, did not offer resistance when he was arrested. Drljaca, who was Prijedor's chief of police, pulled a pistol when confronted, shooting one of the SAS in the leg. The SAS responded, killing Drljaca. An American helicopter transported Drljaca's body, along with the wounded SAS man, to its base at Tuzla. Kovacevic was taken to the tribunal's headquarters in The Hague.

The SAS was also deployed to arrest General Stanislav Galic, the Serb commander who had rained down death and destruction on Sarajevo, killing thousands of innocent civilians. Galic, branded 'the Butcher of Sarajevo', commanded the Bosnian

Serb army's Romanjia corps. This unit laid siege to Sarajevo for almost three years. From 1992, the Serb army simply used the city as a killing ground. Snipers would shoot women as they queued for bread or children as they played. Whole families died as their homes were shelled or mortared. This was not a secret war: horrified viewers around the world watched the deaths on television. In February 1994, a mortar bomb hit the central market, killing 68 people and injuring 200. In all, the siege cost the lives of 10,000 people, most of them Muslims, with thousands more wounded.

Galic, who had left the army in 1997, did not expect to be arrested. He was not to know that the SAS had attached a sophisticated satellite tracking device to his vehicle and had been monitoring his movements for some time. On 21 December 1999, as he drove through Banja Luka, the largest city in the Serb part of Bosnia, he found his car boxed in by other vehicles. The box closed and he was forced to stop in a crowded street. Seconds later, his car was surrounded by two squads of SAS. As morning shoppers watched, bewildered, the windows of Galic's car were smashed. Strong arms dragged him to the ground while one soldier fitted Plasticuffs to his wrists. He was then thrown head first into the back of a waiting car. As swiftly as they arrived, the SAS were gone. Two hours later, Galic was on board a NATO aircraft bound for The Hague. Galic, aged 56, was arrested on an indictment issued secretly by the UN war crimes tribunal. He was sentenced to 20 years, extended to life imprisonment in 2006.

8

2000s

THE SAS TODAY

I N ORDER TO appreciate the actions of the SAS, one must first recognize what makes the SAS so special. '22 Special Air Service' is the designation given to the present SAS regular regiment, now based in Credenhill, Herefordshire. The Regiment consists of around 200 men divided between four Sabre squadrons: A, B, D and G. In addition to these, the Regiment also supports Training Squadron, 264 Signals Squadron and HQ Squadron.

There are also a number of smaller units, such as Operations Research, Demolition, Parachute Section, Boat Section, Army Air Corps Section and a host of sub-units responsible for the daily running and administration of such a large organization. In total, the new camp at Credenhill houses almost 1,000 service men and women.

Many people often wonder why there is no C Squadron in the SAS. The answer is simple. During the Second World War, a handful of Rhodesians opted to serve with David Stirling. In 1951, about 100 volunteered to serve with the SAS in Malaya; these were called C Squadron, Special Air Service. After the conflict the unit was disbanded, but in 1961 C Squadron was resurrected to fight on its own soil. For the next 17 years, Rhodesia fought a losing battle against factions of the African National Congress. (The courage of the SAS during its battles against ZANU and FRELIMO insurgents can be read about in *The Elite*, a book by Barbara Cole.) In June 1978, C Squadron became 1 Special Air Service Rhodesia.

The war ended in April 1980 when Robert Mugabe was elected Prime Minister of an internationally recognized, independent Zimbabwe. In December of the same year the Rhodesian SAS was disbanded, at which time it received a telegram from the Commanding Officer of 22 SAS in Hereford: 'Farewell to a much-admired sister unit. Your professionalism and fighting experience has always been second to none throughout the history of the Rhodesian SAS. C Squadron still remains vacant in 22 SAS orbat [Order of Battle].'

It should also be made clear that the SAS is not a machine; neither is it a clinical force cloned for warfare. It is what it has always been: a collection of dedicated soldiers. They are men who love military life and wish to reach the pinnacle of their chosen profession. Above all, they are men who have found the true meaning of self-discipline. True, they seek adventure in the SAS and thrive on the adrenaline rush, experiencing the same ecstasy as those who participate in high-risk sports. The standards for entering the SAS have been honed ever since the Regiment's conception and standardized since the mid-1950s. To reach this standard, every soldier must pass SAS selection, possibly the most stringent military enlistment course in the world.

SAS selection is hard; there is no other way to say it. The basis of the selection system is to ensure that the valuable training time is spent on only the very best volunteers. Ideally, candidates for the SAS need to have had at least three years' service with a parent unit of the armed forces. This ensures that the basic training requirements and disciplines are already in place. In practice, most of the volunteers come from the airborne regiments and infantry units.

Selection is a funny word to use. The verb 'select' means 'to pick out the best or most suitable', while the adjective means 'chosen for excellence'. The problem is that nobody picks or chooses the volunteers; they must earn their place. It is more a case of the individuals selecting themselves. And it is this single factor that makes the SAS so unique; a whole bunch of individuals, but with the capacity to act as one. All volunteers who pass selection must give up whatever rank they held in their original regiments and revert to that of trooper. Each individual must then work his or her way back up the promotion line. In fairness, everyone keeps their original pay, plus after a specified period they also receive additional SAS pay – something not to be sniffed at.

The physical side of selection takes place in and around the Brecon Beacons in South Wales. Although not a high range of mountains, they are treacherous, exposed and battered by constant weather changes; death by hypothermia is seldom far away. Numerous SAS volunteers have suffered a slow death while lost and disorientated. It is therefore essential that the candidate has undertaken a diligent, self-imposed training schedule prior to arriving at Hereford.

The overall course, which was originally devised in 1953 by Major John Woodhouse, has changed very little over the years. More emphasis was placed on safety after a series of deaths in the late 1970s and early 1980s, but the tests remain very similar.

Since the mid-1990s, the SAS has run the Special Forces Briefing Course (SFBC) to ensure that prospective candidates are fully aware and prepared before they attempt Special Forces selection. It is also an opportunity for the Regiment to look at prospective candidates, making sure they like what they see.

Students are given a series of briefings and presentations about the role of British Special Forces in general and specifically that of the SAS. It normally starts with a brief from Training Squadron OC, prior to being briefed on what selection is all about and how best to prepare themselves. Those who return to attempt selection must attain the required stamina and fitness; the ability to read an Ordnance Survey map also helps.

Test Week comes at the end of the first phase of SAS selection. The week consists of a series of tests designed to push the individual to the very limits of endurance, hence the name of the final test: 'Endurance March'. Little prepares the volunteer for it. With a rifle and bergen (rucksack) weighing 55 pounds, they are expected to walk 25 miles in just 20 hours. No problem, one might say – until one realizes the route runs up and down the Brecon Beacons mountains. The endurance march starts early in the morning, and the volunteer needs to make good time by maintaining a steady pace; walk uphill, run downhill. Energy expenditure is high and food stops are required every three hours, but these rest periods last a maximum of 20 minutes. Most make a brew of tea and eat a small amount of high-calorie, light food. Eating too much food will cause the volunteer to vomit. Time during the rest break is spent checking the map and memorizing the route. During summer selection, the candidate must watch for signs of salt deficiency through sweating, while in winter he must guard against hypothermia. Simply being too hot or too cold will severely affect the individual's performance and overall route timings. Irrespective of what the weather looks like when you set off, the candidate should always carry a complement of clothing to cater for all climatic conditions. The weather over the Beacons can change rapidly, from sunlight to thick fog. Accurate compass-work is needed in order to prevent the candidate from staggering around aimlessly when visibility is down to arm's length. In addition to map and compass navigation, the volunteers also require a working knowledge of the Global Positioning System (GPS). The lucky volunteers who find their way to the final RV inside the allocated time can rest assured that, physically, the worst is over. Yet there is no time for relaxation: there is still a long way to go before the volunteer enters into the ranks of the SAS.

Continuation training follows, and all the necessary basic skills required of the SAS soldier are taught and practised. For many of the Paras and infantry candidates it's back to basics: weapons training, patrolling skills, SOPs, escape and evasion exercises, parachuting and finally five weeks' jungle training. Then, for those who cannot swim or drive, there is a crash course in both before the volunteer is allowed to enter an SAS squadron. Finally, before this is done, the candidate will receive a beige beret with its famous winged dagger – and, as any SAS person will tell you, it is a special moment and a fabulous feeling!

There is an orbat of the SAS at the back of this book but, briefly, the SAS consists of four Sabre (fighting) squadrons, R Squadron being held in reserve.

(Note: R Squadron is a Territorial unit directly attached to the SAS, officered and manned by a mixture of both ex-members of 22 SAS and volunteers from civilian life. These volunteers go through the same form of selection as regular soldiers, many having already served in the regular British Army. Members of R Squadron are highly professional and take their soldiering seriously, often training with the regular squadrons on various exercises. The aim of the Squadron is to add extra manpower support for 22 SAS. The Squadron was used operationally for the first time during the Gulf War, when 15 members volunteered. They fought alongside men of the regular squadrons, showing great courage. When the Iraqis compromised one of the fighting columns, they were forced into a series of shoot and scoot firefights, in which seven SAS soldiers, including a member of R Squadron, became separated. With their vehicles destroyed, this group – whose number included a soldier shot through the stomach – was forced to exfiltrate itself on foot. After two days of dodging the enemy, the R Squadron soldiers managed to slip into the Iraqis' rear and steal a truck, in which the survivors made their way to the Saudi Arabian border. Days later, they were re-equipped and sent back into Iraq.)

Organization and Kit

Each of the four squadrons is divided into four Troops, each with a small headquarters section. The Troops are designed to operate in all terrains and environments, providing the different methods of insertion: Mobility, Mountain, Air Insertion and Boat. Each patrol within a troop is made up of six people:

this was increased in recent years from four, due to the amount of communications equipment and firepower carried by each patrol. Within each troop, every SAS soldier will learn an individual skill such as medics, languages, demolitions or signals.

All SAS soldiers learn CQB (close quarter battle). This is a standard requirement, the basics of which are taught during the final stages of continuation training. The wider role of the SAS demands that each person be proficient with a pistol and sub-machine gun. These skills are the very essence of the SAS soldier – the weapon must become an extension of the person's hand and feel as natural as holding a knife and fork.

In the old camp at Bradbury Lines, these skills were practised in the famous 'Killing House': today, they use a highly advanced facility in Credenhill, to which many refer by the same name. Due to the high number of personnel practising at any one time and the number of rounds fired daily, safety is of the utmost importance. Weapon training starts from the very basics of pistol work and encompasses all the problems of movement and weapons stoppages. It then progresses to the more advanced techniques using automatic weaponry. The famous SAS 'double tap' is learned; this involves firing two shots in rapid succession from the SIG Sauer P226 pistol. It takes several years to become comfortable with this method of shooting, but the results have proved themselves time and again. Two rounds stop a terrorist far better than one.

Another favourite skill practised by the SAS is the famous hostage snatch. This drill forms part of the anti-terrorist hostage rescue scenario. The SAS plays host to an endless procession of VIPs who visit Hereford, and many are keen to view the anti-terrorist team in action. All VIPs are possible future terrorist targets, and the demonstration normally involves the visiting VIP sitting in the hot seat, surrounded by silence, not knowing what possessed them to volunteer in the first place. Abruptly, the door bursts open. A stun grenade explodes inches away. The VIP watches as laser beams of light penetrate the blackness. Those in the hot seat dare not move, fearful that any movement might bring them into contact with the hail of bullets now spitting within inches of their body. Seconds later, they are grabbed by the black-clad figures and literally thrown out of the room. Most VIPs are surprised to discover not a single hair has been harmed, though when Princess Diana volunteered to sit in the hot seat, the odd bit of hair was singed.

Apart from the Killing House, the SAS has a vast variety of equipment and training aids in close proximity to Hereford (called Camp 1). Most are in constant use. Several aircraft types are available to practise both aircraft entry and assault: there is also access to a complete two-storey building known affectionately as 'the Embassy'. Railway carriages are positioned to construct train hijack scenarios and there are plenty of roads to simulate coach and vehicle ambushes. Each move is practised time and time again, guaranteeing is attributable to the success of the SAS; there is no substitute for hard work, constant practise and attention to detail.

SAS training and operations are generally dictated by threats to the British sphere of influence around the world. For example, on 5 September 1972, at the Munich Olympics in Germany, eight Palestinian terrorists forced their way into the quarters of the Israeli team in the Olympic village. Calling themselves Black September, a name signifying the Palestine Liberation Organization's (PLO) defeat and withdrawal from Jordan in September 1970, they killed two Israelis and took nine others hostage. There was an abortive gun battle to free the hostages between the terrorists and the West German police. The nine Israeli athletes died, along with five of the Palestinian terrorists. This was seen as the climax of a whole series of hijackings and assassinations carried out by Palestinian militants.

Following the hijacks at the Munich Olympics, world governments became determined to combat this new breed of terrorism. At the G7 talks the following year, the various heads of government made an agreement to establish dedicated forces capable of dealing with any terrorist situation. In Britain, the SAS was tasked with equipping and training the new force, known by a variety of names including the Anti-Terrorist Team, SP (Special Patrol) Team and the Pagoda Team. New equipment was purchased and the SAS responded to the training with unmatched keenness.

Today, the SAS anti-terrorist team is housed at Credenhill, in a purpose-built building which is manned 24 hours a day by two teams, Red and Blue. An alert device is issued to each team member and their movements are restricted, to allow for a quick response. On call-out, their vehicles are loaded with a vast array of weapons and equipment before a briefing is given on the operational requirement. The anti-terrorist team will only move into position when requested by the Home Office. The SAS anti-terrorist team is considered by most of its peers to be the best in the world.

At some time during the SAS operational cycle, all SAS soldiers have the opportunity to serve on the anti-terrorist team. Normally, the skills of the individual will dictate whether a soldier is to be part of the assault group or a sniper. All assault team members wear a black, one-piece, fire-retardant suit; on top of this go the body armour and the weaponry. This is normally a Heckler and Koch MP5 sub-machine gun, which clips flush across the chest. Additionally, a low-slung Browning Hi-Power pistol is strapped to the leg for backup or use in confined spaces. In the past few years, the SAS has evaluated many hand weapons: the models of choice entering the 2020s is the Glock 17 (which largely replaced the Browning High Power) or the Sig Sauer P226. Respirators are normally carried in a container strapped to the back, but it is more likely that during the actual assault the pack will be discarded and the respirator shoved up the left arm, held by its straps and ready for immediate use. Most actions now involve wearing the respirator, for it not only protects against gas but also presents an evil-looking, anonymous mask of menace to the terrorists. Boots are non-slip, similar to professional climbing boots.

Snipers' dress will frequently be identical to the assault teams, but excellent camouflage clothing is also used. Again, the same weaponry is issued, but additionally each person will each have two sniper rifles, one for daytime use and one fitted with a night scope.

The main sniper weapon used when I was last on the team was a Finnish Tikka M55, but this has since been changed for the British Accuracy International PM sniper rifle.

Training for the team can be very exciting, but it is also exhausting. Abseiling down the side of a building in full gear is not as easy as it sounds. The entanglement of ropes, harness, weapons and stun grenades has to be cleared rapidly so that the soldier can close with the terrorists. The drills are very repetitious, but the end result produces a team that can challenge any terrorist act, from a hijacking to the seizure of an oil rig.

Most members of the general public see the SAS as a land operational unit, with its talents directed towards such things as embassy or aircraft assaults. They would be wrong, as a quarter of the SAS is trained for seaborne operations. That said, the SBS takes on the primary role in tackling problems at sea, although if required the SAS will become involved in the actual assault.

SBS

In 1975, the Royal Marines were given the task of providing Britain's Maritime Counter-Terrorist Force; 1 SBS was thereafter dedicated to this role. In 1979, 5 SBS was deployed to Arbroath in Scotland in support of Comacchio Company, the quick-reaction force for the protection of nuclear weapon sites and convoys and for counter-terrorist operations on ships and offshore installations. Thereafter, 1 SBS concentrated on operations involving ships. In 1987, 1 and 5 SBS were amalgamated and located at Poole in Dorset, where they were redesignated M Squadron SBS and remained dedicated to the maritime counter-terrorist role.

In 1982, at the start of the Falklands War, 2, 3 and 6 SBS were deployed in advance of the task force, landing on the islands some three weeks before its arrival. SBS reconnaissance teams played a major role during the campaign, keeping enemy positions under constant observation and carrying out beach reconnaissance tasks.

In 1991, elements of the SBS (formerly the Special Boat Squadron, but redesignated post-1983) were deployed to Saudi Arabia during the Gulf War, carrying out Scud-hunting operations in the eastern sector of southern Iraq and attacking a major enemy line of communication. Two years later, SBS personnel were deployed to Bosnia on reconnaissance tasks and remained there until 1996 as part of the British Special Forces element serving with the NATO Allied Rapid Reaction Corps.

Today the SBS, together with the three SAS regiments and two SAS signals squadrons, forms one of the elements under the command of the Directorate of Special Forces, which was established in the early 1990s.

The current role of protecting shipping is likely to be increased as the threat heightens. Oil rigs provide the British nation with vital fuel and revenue. For the most part they are unarmed, poorly protected and isolated, leaving them vulnerable to terrorist attacks. Likewise, a cargo ship laden with explosives could access central London via the Thames. In such a scenario, dock areas such as Canary Wharf would suffer the same fate as the Twin Towers.

Both SBS and SAS divers have used a wide variety of diving equipment over the years, and they have generally kept up to date with the latest technology. Divers are used in many roles, such as sabotage on shipping, covert entry to offshore facilities and underwater searches prior to VIP visits. The present diving equipment used by the SAS is the German-made Drager system, which is a lung-governed, closed-circuit breathing apparatus for use with pure oxygen. This small, compact unit is easily operated and maintained, giving the diver up to four hours of submersion, depending on the underwater activity. The Drager is ideal for covert operations, as it uses a semi-closed circuit with a soda-lime cartridge to provide air purification: it leaves no trace of bubbles either below water or on the surface.

Since 1970, the normal delivery system has been a Rigid Raider assault craft, which replaced the inflatable Gemini. It facilitates speedier disembarking for the people on board. Fitted with four lifting points, the craft can be transported by helicopter and is powered by one or two 140hp Johnson outboard motors, giving it a top speed of 37 knots. It is capable of carrying nine fully equipped soldiers plus a coxswain.

The Rigid Raider is claimed to be almost unsinkable, although one of the craft actually achieved this feat at the end of the Falklands campaign, when 1st Raiding Squadron planned a diversionary raid on Port Stanley. All four Raiders were hit, yet only one sank, and even then not until the others had managed to limp clear of the danger. Both SBS and SAS have recently taken delivery of 16 new Rigid Raiders, which were specially adapted for them and are constructed of Kevlar, giving them a hull weight of less than 660 pounds. This means that a four-person patrol can carry the craft, even when it is fitted with twin 40hp motors.

In January 2002, the MV Nisha, a cargo ship inbound for London docks, was seized off the south coast of England. In a dramatic dawn raid by Royal Navy units, including the SBS, together with Customs and Excise officers, the ship was stopped and boarded. The ship, flying the flag of St Vincent and the Grenadines in the West Indies, was then escorted to Sandown Bay on the Isle of Wight.

Once in dock, Customs officers started their extensive search, but no explosives or ammunition were found; in fact, the vessel was carrying raw sugar to a Tate and Lyle refinery on the Thames. The seizure was due to an intelligence tip-off warning the British authorities that such a ship could be carrying 'terrorist material'. The ship had called in at Djibouti on its voyage, so it is entirely possible that al-Qaeda was involved. The British government played down the incident, claiming the search was part of the nation's tighter security measures since the 11 September bombings.

'Hearts and Minds' in Oman

Many believe the SAS to comprise swift and deadly killers; and for the most part, it does. However, the SAS soldier must also learn skills to prevail on the hearts and minds of people. Although not new, this concept has been exploited by the SAS, which has refined the skill into a tool of warfare. The SAS 'hearts and minds' philosophy is the responsibility of all its members, but the practical side falls to the medics and linguists. The system is simple: befriend and win the hearts and minds of an indigenous people through communication and practical help. The following example is just one of many.

After the abortive raid on the northern coast of Oman and the free-fall descent into Wadi Rhawdah, some of G Squadron set off on a 'hearts and minds' campaign. The trip was to take them by Arab dhow (a small sailing ship) around the Strait of Hormuz, where they would visit the tiny coastal villages of northern Oman. The dhow was crewed by three Arab soldiers from the Trucial Oman Scouts (TOS) and three SBS Marines who operated a Rigid Raider. As many of the smaller villages had no docks, the Raider was used to put the party ashore. The story continues in the soldiers' own words.

'It wasn't until we reached our first village that the full term "hearts and minds" really came home to me. I say "village": it was nothing more than a few stone huts and half a dozen people. A party of eight SAS went ashore, two of them medics, of which I was one. I've seen poverty, but compared to this place poverty was The Ritz. Apparently, the family had committed some crime in the past and had been banished by the Omani Sultan to this remote and barren island. No one could remember the crime, or how long the family had been there, but it was several generations ago. They had one small boat – well, more a canoe – fashioned from a dead tree trunk. The fish they caught, and a little rice, was all the food available. A well had been dug at the furthest point from the seashore, but due to the rocky features of this desolate place, this was no more than 150 feet from the water line. I tested the water: it was so salty none of us could drink it.

'The head of the village, an old man who looked 80 – yet I doubt if he was 40 – welcomed us to his home. We were the first white visitors they had ever received on the island, and he celebrated with typical Arab hospitality: the best food in the house was offered. This turned out to be a 20-year-old can of pineapple; the label had long gone, and the contents had turned to mush. We sat there in our clean combat uniforms, healthy and well fed; we were all humbled by the old man's gesture and ate the fruit. I later examined one of the women who was complaining of toothache; she looked old but gave her age as 25. I couldn't believe the state of her teeth: many were missing, and her gums were a rotting mess of blood and pus. Gripping one of her teeth with a pair of forceps, I was dismayed to discover that it was very loose – a gentle tug and it came out. In the end, I took out all her teeth and did my best to sterilize her mouth. We remained on the island for three days, and I continued to treat the woman. I have always been amazed by the speed with which penicillin injections worked on these people. Before we left for our next destination, all the ration packs were stripped of jam, butter and biscuits and presented to the old man – likewise, spare clothing was given to the children. A signal was sent requesting that the family be repatriated to the mainland.

'In a somewhat larger village along the coast, we found a worker who had fallen off the top of a building. His fall had resulted in a large, square piece of his skull becoming detached. Together with the medic, we removed the festering skin and the skull bone from around the wound; the brain was clearly visible. In order to protect the brain, we took the lid off a large tin of beans from a ration pack. This was then beaten flat and placed in boiling water. Once it had cooled, it was placed over the hole in the skull and secured in place by healthy skin. Suturing the lid securely in place, we treated the wound with penicillin powder. Several months later, I had the opportunity to revisit the village.

As I walked up the beach, the man was paraded in front of me; smiling, he bent his head and tapped the tin lid. The wound had healed extremely well, but a small section of the tin could still be seen: the letters 'ans' from 'beans' were still clearly visible.

'However, "hearts and minds" is not just about water, food and friendship; it is also concerned with the enemy. If some of the enemy can be persuaded to change sides, there is much to be gained. During the Oman war, leaflet drops were made in an effort to explain what the new Sultan was trying to achieve. Many adoo left the communists and returned to the fold. Likewise, many adoo were taken prisoner: these, too, were given the choice of being shot, going to jail or joining the firqat. Those who joined us were quickly put in a chopper and flown over the territory of the adoo: all the guy had to do was point to his old hiding places. These flights were know as "flying fingers", as the chopper was normally followed by several jet fighters which would then bomb the indicated area with 500-pound bombs.'

When 'hearts and minds' tactics are used properly in warfare, a brotherhood and kinship with the indigenous people develops. The basics of life in most war-torn areas are always difficult; any effort to improve them is generally welcomed. The rewards for the SAS, are shelter, trust and information.

Sierra Leone

The dawn of a new millennium did not change the world; for the SAS, it merely added to its burden. The Regiment continued to operate in major wars, and conflicts surfaced around the world, the majority of which were sparked by various terrorist organizations. On 25 August 2000, the SAS became involved in Operation Barras, which took place in Sierra Leone. Soldiers from the Royal Irish Regiment were sent to Sierra Leone as part of the 200-strong British training team assisting the country. On 25 August, for reasons unknown, 11 of the soldiers in two vehicles left a safe road and entered rebel territory controlled by a renegade militia known as the West Side Boys. As they drove along an isolated jungle track, the soldiers were stopped and taken hostage. Once it became obvious that the men were overdue, other British forces in the country launched a search operation using helicopters, but they failed to locate the missing soldiers. Two days later, an exchange offer was received from the West Side Boys asking for the release of their leader General Papa from prison, along with food and medicine. One of the soldiers was allowed to meet and negotiate on behalf of the rebels. He assured the British commander that they were being well treated and that no one was injured. On Wednesday, 30 August, the situation looked somewhat better when five of the British soldiers were released in exchange for a satellite phone and medical supplies. The remaining six soldiers would not be released until the demands were met.

As negotiations continued, the British government, not keen to show weakness, ordered 120 soldiers from the 1st Battalion, Parachute Regiment, to Sierra Leone. It was also rumoured that a small force of British SAS had also been sent to the region some days before; both units were there as a possible military solution to the problem. The SAS unit supplied deep penetration patrols to locate the West Side Boys' camp in the area known as Rokel Creek. It was there that the six remaining hostages were being held. One of the patrols witnessed several mock executions of the hostages where they were lined up in front of firing squads. This prompted the British government to sanction a rescue attempt.

At dawn on 11 September, the plan was put into operation. Three Chinook helicopters and two Westland Lynx gunships headed directly towards Rokel Creek. By 06:30 they were overhead, and the two Lynx helicopters began strafing the banks of the river. Moments later, one of the Chinooks landed, dropping the paratroopers directly at the rear of the rebel huts. A firefight broke out immediately with rebel guards, who had been alerted by the approaching helicopters. As the rebels were taken care of, a special hostage rescue unit of SAS men ran to the hut containing the hostages. At that moment, a heavy machine gun opened up on the assaulting forces, killing one of the paratroopers. This served only to rally the British, who moved forward, overrunning the position and forcing the West Side Boys to retreat. By this time the SAS had moved the hostages, who were hustled into one of the helicopters; it immediately took off and flew directly to the warship *Sir Percival*, which was anchored off the coast at Freetown. As the hostage rescue was taking place, the remaining two Chinooks landed at a secondary camp south of the first position where, with support from the Lynx gunships, the paratroopers engaged in a vicious firefight with the rebels. The fighting continued for several hours, but by mid-afternoon mopping up operations were complete and the rescue party was airlifted out.

The British had lost one man, with another seriously wounded and 11 more slightly injured. In addition to the six rescued hostages, the British had captured one of the rebel leaders, Foday Kallay, killed 25 West Side Boys and captured a further 18.

Afghanistan

On 11 September 2001, two hijacked airliners crashed into the twin towers of the World Trade Center in New York City. Soon after, a third struck at the Pentagon. A fourth hijacked plane, suspected of being bound for a high-profile target in Washington, crashed into a field in southern Pennsylvania. Almost 3,000 US citizens and other nationals were killed as a result of these acts. The prime suspect for these attacks was the organization al-Qaeda, headed by Osama bin Laden.

Al-Qaeda has bases and supporters in many countries, and embraces and supports radical Islamic movements worldwide. The organization was formed in 1988 by bin Laden, a radical Islamist from a wealthy Saudi Arabian family. Travelling to Afghanistan in 1979 to support the resistance movement against the Soviet invaders, he saw that the Muslim fighters were ill-equipped to carry out a sustained conflict against a technically superior enemy. Not only were they lacking in numbers and skills, but also the infrastructure necessary for the fight. Using his wealth and influence, he brought both workmen and construction plants to Afghanistan and, together with the Palestinian Muslim Brotherhood leader, Abdallah Azzam, began to organize an international programme of conscription through a new recruiting office: Maktab al-Khidamet (MAK – Services Office). As new recruits from such countries as Saudi Arabia, Yemen, Algeria and Egypt arrived, their transportation paid for by bin Laden, he began to build training facilities. Specialists were brought in from around the world to coach the men in guerrilla warfare tactics. Ironically, bin Laden was probably aided by the Western powers in his struggle.

By the end of the war, with the Russians gone, bin Laden now had around 10,000 well-trained, well-equipped and warhardened veterans under his command. Some dispersed back to their former lives and families, deciding they had done their duty and could now live in peace. Others had become so fanatical about Islamic fundamentalism that they returned to their countries ready to organize their own terror groups and overthrow what they saw as secular governments.

Bin Laden's new fight started with his own country of origin. After the Afghan war, he returned to Saudi Arabia to raise an insurrection against the government. This plan, however, was thwarted, and bin Laden was thrown out of the country and his citizenship revoked. Undaunted, he moved his centre of operations to Sudan, using his wealth to create farms and factories, supplying jobs for his followers. He also improved the infrastructure of the country – building roads and an airport. His many business interests included a bank, a construction company and an import-export business. More training camps were set up and former Afghan comrades were encouraged to move to Sudan.

However, Sudan's friendliness towards its guests soon began to crumble when its government started to bow to pressure from the United States. Not wishing to be subject to sanctions or other methods of persuasion, the Sudanese asked bin Laden to leave. This he did in 1996, returning with his followers to Afghanistan.

While many terrorist acts were attributed to al-Qaeda, bin Laden's involvement in the bombings of two American embassies in Nairobi, Kenya and Dar-es-Salaam, Tanzania, on 7 August 1998, was incontrovertibly proved. At the time, it seemed as if al-Qaeda could commit any atrocity it liked while hiding under the protection of the Taliban rule in Afghanistan – that was, until the attacks on the United States.

America fought back. However, armies take time to assemble and intelligence needed to be gathered. The Afghans had a ferocious reputation for fighting, especially in their own country. The first people to enter Afghanistan were a special unit of the CIA called the Special Activities Staff. The team was made up of retired members of Delta Force and Seal Team 6, all experienced field operators. They arrived on the ground in Afghanistan at the end of September 2001 in order to prepare for a major Special Forces operation.

A squadron of SAS troops arrived soon after and began operating in the mountainous country. Their first task was to concentrate on finding Osama bin Laden and Mullah Mohammed Omar, the Taliban leader. Later they would help train and lead the soldiers of the anti-Taliban Northern Alliance in their push south towards Kabul.

It is also widely believed that the SAS took part in an incident at Qala-i-Jangi where hundreds of Taliban soldiers were killed. On Saturday, 24 November, some 400 Taliban soldiers had surrendered to the Northern Alliance a few miles to the north of Mazar-i-Sharif, having fled the American bombardment of Kunduz. The prisoners were then shipped by lorry to a holding area in Qala-i-Jangi. This is a sprawling nineteenth-century prison fortress to the west of Mazar where the Northern Alliance warlord, Dostum, stabled his horses.

None of the Taliban soldiers were searched until they were inside the prison, at which time one of the prisoners produced a grenade and pulled the pin, killing himself and an Alliance commander called Nadir Ali. A second incident occurred later the same night when another prisoner killed himself and a Hazara senior commander, Saeed Asad. Despite these attacks, the Alliance guards did not seem too disturbed; neither did they arrange any extra security.

Around 10:00 the next morning, two CIA officers entered the prison with the purpose of identifying any al-Qaeda members. The senior of these two Americans, Johnny Michael Spann, had operated in Afghanistan since the beginning of the war; his colleague was identified only by the name 'Dave'. Alliance guards took them to an open area outside the cells where a group of Taliban prisoners had been assembled. As they were being interrogated, one prisoner leapt forward to grab Spann's neck. Spann drew his pistol and shot the man dead. A fight then broke out, resulting in the two Americans and the guards firing at the prisoners. One prisoner managed to grab an AK-47 from an Alliance guard and opened fire. With this, Taliban fighters launched themselves at Spann, knocking him to the ground. Spann continued to fire his pistol, killing two more before he disappeared under the crush. Dave beat a hasty retreat as the Taliban overpowered the remaining Alliance guards, taking their weapons in the process. This group then ran to free the other prisoners before assaulting a nearby armoury, where they obtained AK-47s, grenades and a mortar. A firefight then ensued, with the Alliance soldiers holding the south-east quarter of the fort while the prisoners held the south-western quarter. Some three hours after the incident had started, two vans and a pair of SAS Land Rovers arrived at the fortress gates. This force consisted of nine American Special Forces and six British SAS. There was a quick conference with the Alliance commander while one of the newly arrived Americans talked to Dave on the radio. Dave outlined the position: he was stuck with a German television crew and had run out of ammunition. He confirmed that the Taliban prisoners were armed and Mike Spann was missing in action (MIA). Dave was told to stay put while they dealt with the Taliban, assuring him that he would be rescued. While the fighting continued unabated, the Special Forces called for air cover. Shortly afterwards two American fighter aircraft arrived overhead. At 16:00 the first missile hit, sending shock waves around the whole prison. The fighters continued to fire missiles for the rest of the afternoon, reducing much of the prison to rubble. Later that night, Dave and the German journalists managed to escape over the north wall.

By Monday morning, most of the Taliban had been killed or wounded and the Alliance had retaken much of the prison. Then disaster struck. At around 11:00 another air strike was called and, while the previous strikes had been close, this one was too close. The explosion killed a number of Alliance soldiers as well as wounding several Americans and members of the SAS. The firefight subsided as the casualties and walking wounded were loaded into makeshift transport, which sped off to the US base. In all, nine men were airlifted out. The next day, the Pentagon said that there had been no military deaths but that five US service personnel had been seriously injured and had been evacuated to Landstuhl Regional Medical Centre in Germany. Four SAS were also reported wounded, but the British government never comments on its Special Forces.

Towards midnight, an American AC-130 gunship arrived over Qala-i-Jangi. Having identified points of Taliban resistance, it proceeded to strafe the area: at some point, one of its cannons hit an ammunition dump, creating a massive explosion which could be heard 10 miles away.

By Tuesday morning, only a handful of Taliban were continuing to offer resistance and the Alliance started to move in and clear the prison. One prisoner, who had escaped during the night, was caught by local residents and hanged from a tree. The rest lay dead or dying in their hundreds, some still with their hands bound behind their backs. In one of the basements, five Taliban fighters were trapped alive. The Alliance soldiers threw in grenades before entering under a barrage of AK-47 fire. In the end, 86 filthy and hungry prisoners emerged; one of them was an American who had converted to Islam. Mike

Spann's body was recovered, but only after a specialist team had been flown in to remove the booby trap set under it.

There are two opposing views of the incident: some say the Taliban at Qala-i-Jangi fought to the death, while others say they were massacred.

The SAS had been in Afghanistan for several weeks when they were ordered by the American Central Command in Florida to raid an opium storage plant to the south-east of Kandahar. The target location was said to hold pure opium worth some £50 million and to be heavily guarded. In addition to the opium, it was believed, due to the large number of guards on-site (estimated at 80-plus), that al-Qaeda might have some interesting intelligence documents at the location.

Unfortunately, maps of the area were virtually non-existent and the SAS was forced to rely on aerial photographs taken by an unmanned US spy drone. The American command requested that the site be attacked almost immediately, leaving no time for a CTR. This would have enabled the SAS assaulting forces to better determine the strengths and weaknesses of the al-Qaeda position and refine its strategy accordingly. Timing also meant that the attack would have to go on during daylight hours, abandoning the element of surprise and the use of technically advanced night-vision equipment.

The SAS mustered two full squadrons: almost 120 men, the largest force it has fielded in a single operation for many years. The final assault was to rest on firepower. To this end, the SAS used some 30 'Pink Panthers' (Type 110 Land Rovers especially made for desert warfare), all armed to capacity with ferocious weaponry. The Pinkies carried both front- and rear-mounted GPMGs, while the roll bar was mounted with either a Milan anti-tank rocket system or Mk 19 automatic grenade launcher. Big 2.5-tonne ACMAC lorries acting as 'mother' vehicles supported them. Just prior to the assault, the US Air Force would carry out two precise air strikes. These would be close enough to destroy the drug warehouses but leave the headquarters building intact.

The journey to the target started long before dawn; it was a long one over dreadful, rocky terrain. As the area was hostile, the column was forced to stop at regular intervals and send out scouts. For this, they used off-road bikes, just as they had done in the Gulf War.

Dressed in light order, which means no rucksack, each SAS man carried his personal weapon, which was either a Colt with an underslung 203 grenade launcher or a Minimi weapon. During such an assault, the SAS prefers to forego any body armour, depending instead on speed of movement. However, in this case both body armour and Kevlar helmets were used. Belt equipment consisted mainly of grenades, ammunition, food, water, and emergency equipment, such as a SARBE (Surface-to-air Rescue Beacon) to call for help.

By 10:00, the force was within a mile of the al-Qaeda camp but the going was slow due to soft sand. This meant an on-the-spot change of plan.

Midday saw the start of the action, as half the SAS lined up their Pinkies and started to lay down covering fire ready for the other half to assault. The ground was not suited to a direct assault and the al-Qaeda rebels had chosen their defensive positions accordingly. By 13:00, a serious firefight had developed, but the attack continued to push forward. The assault was helped at this stage by the arrival of US F-16s. The first pass caused massive explosions in and around the compound, but, as requested, it didn't touch the building serving as the headquarters. The second air strike came close to wiping out the assaulting force. However, by this time the air was thick with the drug-laden dust resulting from the destruction of the warehouses and nobody really cared very much.

Despite the horrendous attack from the SAS, the al-Qaeda fighters refused to give ground, preferring to die. However, by 14:30 most resistance had been overwhelmed and the headquarters was raided for laptops, computers, papers and maps. The ground was absolutely covered with dead al-Qaeda fighters, with those who were wounded screaming for Allah. On the SAS side, several men had been hit but, thanks to the body armour and Kevlar helmets, most of the wounds were to the limbs. That said, several were extremely serious and required all the skills of the SAS medics to keep them alive.

Finally, the word was sent to 'bug out'. Everyone jumped back into their vehicles and headed south. The first port of call was an RV at a makeshift airfield where a C130, complete with doctors and medics, evacuated the wounded, flying them directly back to Britain for treatment in the Centre for Defence Medicine in Birmingham. The worst hurt of the four was hit in the stomach, arm and the top of one leg. He was in a stable condition but still faced the prospect of losing his leg. This aside, the mission had been accomplished without the loss of a single SAS soldier.

Following the Afghan war, the papers reported that a dispute had developed between the government and the SAS over the award of gallantry medals. Senior members of the government were said to want the names of decorated SAS men to be made public, along with detailed citations. The Regiment challenged this because it did not want to compromise the identities of its soldiers. In any case, the SAS was the only British unit to fight in the conflict, and any military award for gallantry in Afghanistan would be automatically linked to it.

Perhaps the greatest praise the SAS received came from US Secretary of Defense Donald Rumsfeld: 'Special forces in the US and Britain are not comparable. There are huge numbers of Special Forces in the States. In Britain, they are an elite force, able to put down an astonishing level of firepower, allowed to think for themselves and with incredible intelligence-gathering skills, prepared to hide up for days.'

Although there is no record of it anywhere, one other story has emerged from Hereford. It is believed that an SAS unit saved the life of an American CIA agent who had been captured by the Taliban. The agent was moved to a house surrounded by a high wall and protected by at least 30 Taliban fighters. According to the story, the American military were pondering the problem when an SAS officer happened to hear of the situation and chimed in, 'We can do it!' The surprised Americans were asked for a helicopter in order to perform the rescue.

It is rumoured that about eight SAS men then boarded the helicopter and flew directly to the building in question. Landing on the roof, half the team then proceeded to kill any Taliban stupid enough to show his face, while the other four entered the building in order to carry out the rescue. They found the CIA agent strapped to a chair, suffering after a serious bout of physical interrogation. Again according to rumour, the SAS killed everyone in the room, grabbed the agent and made their way back to the roof. The area was fairly secure at this time, as just about every Taliban within sight had been killed. The extraction went off without anyone getting injured.

This story has never been validated, but shortly afterwards several members of the SAS were invited to visit the White House where they received medals. Additionally, the CIA, whose praises for the SAS know no bounds, have sought to use them in other operations.

The Second Iraq War

On Thursday, 20 March 2003, at approximately 17:35, the first salvo of missiles fell on Iraq. After the Gulf War of 1991, when Saddam Hussein was left in change of Iraq, he was said to have failed to comply with UN resolutions to destroy weapons of mass destruction. The process of monitoring by UN weapons inspectors had come to an embarrassing end and the United States, together with the UK and its other allies, decided to invade. It was not the war the world expected: the UN and NATO failed to support the Americans and took no part in the conflict. In the end, it fell to US and UK soldiers alone.

The SAS were deployed on several operations into Iraq prior to the main air campaign, with small teams being infiltrated to ascertain information. *The Telegraph* disclosed that a team of

35 SAS men was operating in and out of western Iraq as part of a 100-strong allied force looking for Scud missile launchers, which could be used to attack Israel. However, most of the teams were operating inside Baghdad in support of CIA and MI6 operations. These teams were intent on locating Saddam Hussein and confirming the satellite imagery by taking a GPS fix directly at the actual target. This accounts for pinpoint accuracy during the first wave of bombing, when Saddam Hussein was the target. SAS teams also monitored the oil fields, making sure they were not being prepared for demolition by the Iraqis and that they could be quickly seized intact once the war began. It is also believed that an SAS unit captured Watban Ibrahim Hasan al-Tikriti, Saddam Hussein's half-brother. Watban was included on the deck of cards issued to each soldier showing the 55 most wanted members of Saddam Hussein's regime. He was apprehended close to the Syrian border, where SAS units had been waiting in ambush. Watban, a presidential adviser, was accused of overseeing executions, deportations and torture. However, he fell out of favour when he argued with Saddam's son Uday – it is rumoured that Uday shot Watban in the leg at a party back in 1995. The SAS handed him over to the Americans. Other than the odd report by journalists who stumbled across SAS units, there has been no information concerning SAS operations in the second war against Iraq.

The only story that relates to British Special Forces is one concerning the SBS. The story first emerged showing two SBS men as heroes, when a captain and a sergeant trekked hundreds of miles through treacherous countryside in order to reach the Syrian border. On the surface, this looked very much like a replay of the Gulf War story of SAS patrol Bravo Two Zero. It is thought that two groups of about 30 men were inserted into Iraq, their mission to carry out reconnaissance and sabotage operations around Mosul. They were to operate using Land Rovers similar to those used by the SAS. One of the patrols is reported to have been lying up waiting for a resupply when it was spotted by an Iraqi Republican Guard reconnaissance unit. The Iraqis were quickly reinforced and a firefight broke out. Although the SBS were only outnumbered two to one, they decided to abandon the vehicles and make a run for the emergency RV. All the men made it to the ERV, where a Chinook helicopter picked them up. However, the captain and sergeant in question are reported to have taken a quad bike and made their way to Syria. The Land Rovers, which were left behind, contained a wide variety of sophisticated equipment and weaponry. An American A10 Tankbuster later destroyed them. Although this story was reported in the *Mail on Sunday* and various Internet sites, there was no confirmation from the Ministry of Defence as to its authenticity.

The SAS had infiltrated Iraq almost two weeks before the main assault, which began on 1 April 2003. Operation Row was intended as a diversion in order to convince the Iraqis that the main invasion was coming from a different direction, mainly the north and west. The Middle Eastern news channel al-Jazeera showed video of what was thought to be a Special Forces Land Rover captured by Iraqi forces. The media also highlighted the fact that two men, again claimed to be Special Forces, had crossed the border into Syria after a contact close to Mosul in northern Iraq. While these rumours abounded, Operation Row was a reality. The SAS and its Australian cousins, together with American Special Forces, were indeed laying down a deception. Members of B Squadron SAS came in from the west in lightly armed Land Rovers, searching and pursuing any targets that might pose a threat to the Coalition troops. Meanwhile D Squadron SAS was tasked with seizing an Iraqi airfield, which would later be used to bring in more troops.

Most of the Iraqi targets, especially the airfields, were heavily defended, but the SAS had done its planning well. Using the latest satellite imagery and intelligence gained from a host of unmanned aerial vehicles (UAVs), the raids had gone smoothly. The assaults started with a series of air strikes to soften up the defenders. These were followed by the SAS driving directly on to one airfield and clearing the building. The Iraqis were overwhelmed by the speed of the Special Forces assault, allowing them to take control. While covering teams laid down a barrage of Mk 19 and heavy machine gun fire, the main assault made directly for the airfield buildings before separating to attack the control tower, hangars and barracks. Within the hour most of the airfield was secure, with hundreds of Iraqi prisoners being rounded up. Once secure, regular troops were brought in to secure the perimeter and get the airfield up and running so the runway could receive Coalition forces.

As the main invasion started the SAS, headed by Brigadier Graeme Lamb, then Director of Special Forces, made its way to Baghdad. The idea was to set up a firm base with all speed and assist other security units in rounding up as many prominent Iraqi military leaders as possible. Fighting was still raging in the city, with mortar and artillery shells still falling even as the SAS Chinook landed. In addition to the Special Forces, several members of the Secret Intelligence Service (SIS) had also joined the party, as the first function was to help MI6 set up a new station. Once the offices were established, MI6 needed the SAS to assist by gathering timely intelligence. At this juncture, the hunt was on for the infamous 'weapons of mass destruction'. Getting this intelligence meant smashing down doors and raiding complexes on a nightly basis. The workload and stress placed on the SAS were enormous. Once the Special Forces headquarters had been established in Baghdad, G Squadron was embarked, while both B and D squadrons, including the Regimental Command Group, returned to Hereford.

In order to gain as much intelligence as possible, many G Squadron members had been trained to speak Iraqi Arabic and act as interpreters. This meant that the moment they captured a high-ranking Iraqi official or officer they could carry out an initial interrogation immediately; this tactic was to produce some excellent information, as intelligence gained from an immediate arrest was of a much higher value that that extracted once a prisoner had time to reflect on his situation. This proved effective when, on 16 June 2003, information gained from one captured Iraqi indicated that Lt Gen Abid Hamid Mahmud al-Tikrit could be located hiding out in Tikrit. Due to swift action by 23 Troop of G Squadron, together with elements of the US Delta Force, the Ba'ath Party member was easily found and arrested.

G Squadron continued its intelligence-gathering operations and also provided a quick reaction force when required. Such was the case when, on 24 June 2003, six members of the Royal Military Police were slaughtered after an angry mob overran the police station in Majar al-Kabir. The SAS deployed to the town and soon found itself in a hotspot; due to lack of support from other British troops, the team was unable to extract the suspected ringleaders and was forced to withdraw. This action occurred prior to the SFSG being raised (see page 281).

October 2003 saw the arrival of A Squadron to replace G Squadron. A Squadron decided on a diverse role and instead of uniform, took to wearing local clothes bought from the markets and driving around in locally purchased civilian vehicles. While the latter proved excellent for surveillance, they offered little or no protection and were prone to breaking down on a regular basis. However, A Squadron did have some luck when two RAF Chinook helicopters were put at its disposal.

The first operation carried out by A Squadron was code named Abalone. It took place on 31 October 2003, when they assaulted two houses in Ramadi with the aim of capturing a number of foreign Jihadists from the Sudan. The SAS and SBS assault teams were supported by American Special Forces in Bradley armoured vehicles. Things went well in the first building assault, but the moment they entered the second building they came under heavy fire. One member of the SBS team, Corporal Ian Plank, was killed, the first Special Forces member to die in the second Iraq War, and another corporal was seriously wounded; he was rescued by other members of the Special Forces as he lay in the open. Due to the stiff opposition the operation was curtailed, but it had detained four non-Iraqi fighters.

Around this time the battles in and around Fallujah started, and A Squadron went out on a series of both day and night raids. The battles in Fallujah lasted throughout October and November 2003. It was just a series of firefights, from one street to the next; as one SAS soldier put it, 'You were just as likely to be shot by the Americans as the enemy.'

The new year was only hours old when two SAS members met their deaths. Major James Duncan Stenner and Sergeant Norman Patterson had been at a New Year's Eve party in the heavily forti-fied Green Zone for British and American officials, an area that also encompassed many of the embassies and diplomatic resi-dences. As they drove home, both having been drinking, their car drove into a concrete bollard. They were killed instantly.

Having completed 85 raids in a four-month tour, A Squadron was relieved by B Squadron in February 2004, and the replace-ments started as they meant to go on, launching Operation Aston, once again designed to locate and arrest foreign fighters. Several were killed and some arrested; the latter were from a group called Lashkar-e-Taiba and provided valuable intelligence.

For the SAS, the second Iraq War settled into a routine of one Squadron replacing another, but it was not all plain sailing. On 30 January 2005, an RAF Special Forces Hercules aircraft had just taken off from Baghdad airport on its way to Balad, when only a few minutes away it was shot down by small arms fire. Six minutes after take-off the radio operator reported a fire on board and the aircraft was reported missing 24 minutes later. Investigation of the wreckage revealed that a projectile had pen-etrated the fuel tank in the starboard wing, causing a fire; the ensuing explosion caused the aircraft to crash. Of the 10 people who died, one is believed to have been a member of 264 SAS Signals Squadron. G Squadron mounted an operation close to Baghdad airport to hunt down those responsible.

However, despite this hard work, 2005 also saw the length of the SAS tour in Iraq increase from the normal four months to six. Six months is a long time for a married soldier with children, and this change did not go down well within the

Regiment, resulting in a number of resignations. For those who did continue to serve, two new threats had raised their heads. The introduction of improvised explosive devices (IEDs) meant travelling by vehicle or simply on foot became extremely dangerous, though this threat was somewhat reduced when the SAS acquired a pair of Puma helicopters in the early part of the year. The other problem was kidnapping.

Sangin

Although a small town in the northern part of the Helmand province of Afghanistan, Sangin has been an area of operations for the British Army on more than one occasion. The town itself was Taliban controlled as well as a haven for drug-trafficking warlords. In an attempt to further efforts and take control of the area, a unit of SAS soldiers was tasked to snatch four senior Taliban leaders from a stronghold just south of the town. Along with some soldiers from 3 Para, the 'snatch squad', under the cover of darkness, successfully apprehended the four men, all of whom were on the Most Wanted list.

The plan was to RV with a nearby quick-reaction force consisting of troops from 7 Para, the Gurkhas and the Royal Artillery. However, as the two units met, around 70 Taliban fighters – who had obviously learned of the assault – ambushed them. The Taliban had a firm advantage. Familiar with the terrain, they had chosen well-hidden positions from which to launch an attack with AK47s, machine guns and rocket-propelled grenades.

The British forces suddenly found themselves in the middle of a fierce battle, during which two of their four prisoners were killed while the other two escaped. Hemmed in by enemy forces, the men held their ground, with a bit of help from the artillery's 105mm light guns. During the firefight, which lasted more than an hour, two unnamed members of the SAS were killed defending their positions. The assault ended when an Army Air Corps Apache attack helicopter and an RAF Harrier

GR7 from Kandahar responded to a request for air backup and targeted the Taliban positions. It is thought that the Taliban sustained up to 30 casualties.

In April 2006, Operation Larchwood started, with the aim of hitting al-Qaeda targets involved in making vehicle-borne IEDs (VBIEDs). One lead had been identified via his mobile phone by 18 Signal Regiment, which had managed to get a position reference showing his location. The SAS, supported by Special Forces Support Group (SFSG), moved to surround a farmhouse on the outskirts of Yusufiyah in south Baghdad. While gunships circled overhead, the main SAS assault force landed to the north-east of the farmhouse. The assault did not go as planned and the terrorists put up strong resistance, wounding three members of the SAS in the first few minutes. One terrorist detonated his suicide vest, injuring two more SAS soldiers, but the SAS pressed home its attack and ultimately overpowered the defenders, five of whom were killed. The al-Qaeda member responsible for making the VBIEDs was arrested after being found hiding with half a dozen terrified women and children. OC B Squadron received a medal for his conduct during the mission.

D Squadron's Sergeant Jonathan Stuart Hollingsworth CGC QGM, a highly experienced SAS soldier, died of wounds on 24 November 2006. Although Sergeant Hollingsworth was killed while carrying out a successful SAS operation, his loss to the Regiment was immeasurable.

In 2007, Special Forces started the move from Iraq to Afghanistan. It was to be the largest-ever deployment of Special Forces, with two squadrons from 22 SAS, M Squadron SBS, elements of Special Reconnaissance Regiment (SRR) and two companies of SFSG, the total force being close to 500 personnel.

The Rescue of Norman Kember and Members of the CTC

On Saturday, 26 November 2005, 74-year-old Professor Norman Kember, a British peace activist and member of the

Christian Peacemaker Teams (CPT) was kidnapped in Baghdad along with three colleagues: American Tom Fox and Canadians James Loney and Harmeet Singh Sooden. The group responsible, calling itself the Swords of Truth, claimed the men were spies and threatened to execute them unless all Iraqi prisoners were released by 8 December. Despite pleas to release Professor Kember due to his age and frail health, the kidnappers refused to relent, instead sending several video-taped messages showing the hostages to the al-Jazeera television station. In one of them, Kember called for all British troops to be pulled out of Iraq.

On 8 December, the day of the kidnappers' deadline, Kember and Fox were paraded on another video broadcast blindfolded, chained and dressed in the orange jumpsuits made infamous by Guantanamo Bay. The deadline was extended by two days. This passed without incident and the Swords of Truth continued to provide more footage of the men over the following weeks, repeating its threat that the hostages would be killed unless demands were met.

On 10 March 2006, the body of Tom Fox was found in the city. He had been executed. It was at that point that it became clear that negotiations had failed and the only choice was to set up a multinational rescue mission and go in by force. The unit tasked with the actual rescue consisted of SAS troops, backed up by 250 men from the British, American and Australian counter-kidnap group as well as 100 soldiers from the SFSG. Huge resources had already been poured into intelligence efforts to locate the men and finally on the night of 23 March, the SAS was able to storm its way into a building within Iraq where they were being held. The kidnappers had already fled, leaving the men tied together in a ground floor room. The rescue was completed without a shot being fired or any casualties taken. Although Kember later thanked his rescuers privately, the peace activist resisted a public display of gratitude as a forced rescue had been against his principles of non-violent action.

Ethiopia

The SAS was called in for another hostage rescue, this time in Ethiopia in March 2007. Five British nationals, connected with the British Embassy in Addis Ababa, together with their Ethiopian guards, were overpowered and kidnapped by members of the rebel Afar Revolutionary Democratic Front in a remote area close to the Eritrean border. Their Land Rovers were left where they were stopped, still full of personal possessions and riddled with bullet holes, while the hostages were marched across the region's salt lakes and into Eritrea.

Fearing a possible compromise of national security, the British government convened an emergency Cobra meeting, deciding to have an SAS troop on standby in the UK in case it was needed for a rescue mission. Meanwhile, as negotiations continued, two SAS soldiers flew to Ethiopia in a liaison role and to reconnoitre the ground in case of action. However, in this case negotiations proved successful and the rebels released the hostages without harm.

SAS Conspiracy?

While the SAS has been quietly getting on with its normal business, there have also been some oddball stories that have made the news. In September 2005, the Iraqi police in Basra apprehended two British soldiers, thought to be from the SAS. The two men, dressed in Arab clothing and wearing black wigs, were driving a car and were about to be stopped by the police for a routine vehicle search. Instead of pulling over, they drove at the police and started firing weapons. The men were finally arrested, and, according to a BBC report, the car was found to contain radio gear, assault rifles, a light machine gun, an anti-tank weapon and medical kit. Another report also stated that explosives had been found.

The soldiers were taken to a nearby prison. However, the

purpose of their mission was already being speculated upon, with some suggestions that they were to stage a car bombing in the city that would be blamed on Iraqi separatists and thus cause further tension. Certainly this was the theory in most of the Arab world, which generally points the finger at the occupying forces for fomenting unrest for their own purposes. Another factor adding to the conspiracy rumour mill was the sudden reluctance of the British press to cover the story.

The incident, though, did not go away. Despite high-level discussions between government officials of both countries, the governor of Basra refused to release his prisoners. On 20 September, the British took the matter into their own hands after receiving reports that the police were about to hand the men over to a militia group. Warrior Armoured Personnel Carriers broke down a wall of the jail, thus liberating the SAS men, as well as accidentally freeing 150 other Iraqi prisoners, causing a riot in which one Warrior was set alight.

There is another explanation. Although Whitehall has kept any details of the incident secret, it is possible that the men were on a close observation mission when they were stopped. As they had been told not to stop when challenged, due to their undercover role, they attempted to escape. A gun battle ensued and they were arrested. It is also possible that some of the equipment 'found' in the car could have been planted. It is one of those situations that we may never know the truth about.

Colin Berry

An ex-SAS soldier, Colin Berry had been working undercover for the Afghan government when he was involved in a shoot-out in his hotel bedroom in Kabul in January 2003. Two Afghans were killed and Berry was wounded before being arrested and thrown into jail. Afghan television broadcast the event as a row between business partners.

Berry, however, claimed he had been providing intelligence to the Afghan government, as well as MI6, about illicit arms trafficking. His investigations centred on the CIA initiative to buy back the weapons it had supplied the Afghan rebels with in the 1980s in their fight against the Russian invasion. However, he found that some of the weapons were being resupplied to anti-government forces in both Afghanistan and Pakistan. He also stated that he was not responsible for the two deaths in his room and that it was, in fact, a set-up, the killings being done by US Special Forces operatives, who then covered their tracks. President Karzai released him after six months in a general amnesty for foreign prisoners.

Afghanistan

The SAS has proved invaluable in the fight against the Taliban and al-Qaeda in Afghanistan, both during the first phase of the fighting in 2001 and later. As well as collecting intelligence, SAS patrols have also killed dozens of enemy fighters during search-and-destroy missions in the rebel-held mountains in the south-east of the country. The Regiment's strength in Afghanistan in 2001 was high, consisting of two squadrons, backed up by troops from the SRR, the Australian SAS and members of the Parachute Brigade.

One typical incident occurred near Kandahar in November 2001. Two squadrons, A and G, attacked an al-Qaeda stronghold in a cave complex near Kandahar. Air Troop performed the Regiment's first ever High Altitude Low Opening (HALO) jump over enemy territory and established a landing zone for the C130s that were bringing in the rest of the soldiers. In the ensuing battle, which lasted four hours, four SAS were wounded – one seriously, but the operation resulted in 20 enemy casualties and the gathering of important intelligence.

The seek-and-destroy role of British Special Forces in the war on terror has been aided by the use of the latest warfare equipment. For example, during the invasion of Afghanistan, the SAS was equipped with a hand-launched unmanned aerial vehicle (UAV) the size of a toy glider, as well as laptop computers able to link to satellite imagery from the larger American UAVs, Predator and Global Hawk. Sophisticated signals equipment meant that enemy communications could either be intercepted or jammed by remote electronic jammers.

Protecting Iraq's Borders

An important role that the SAS were involved with in Iraq was protecting its borders against Arab insurgents crossing from neighbouring Syria. It is thought that most of the bombings in Iraq were the work of these foreign terrorists as they fought what they saw as a holy war against the West.

In one such encounter, the SAS battled with a group of 12 insurgents that they had tracked crossing the border from Syria. A brief firefight followed in which all 12 were killed. The SAS took no casualties. In another incident, an SAS patrol arrested two insurgents, who later gave details of their training under questioning, therefore providing valuable intelligence. The important role the SAS played in Afghanistan was rewarded when 12 of them were awarded military honours. Although the men were unnamed, it is thought that four of the awards of the Conspicuous Gallantry Cross were bestowed upon the SAS soldiers wounded in action against an al-Qaeda base in November 2001.

The increased need for Special Forces' skills in Iraq and Afghanistan has led to a shortage of manpower, with the Regiment being stretched to operating capacity. In order to fulfil operational commitments, the SAS has been forced to call up reservists from its two territorial arms: 21 SAS (Artists') Volunteer, based in London and 23 SAS (Volunteer), based in Birmingham, making another 60 men available.

The territorial units receive the same training as those in the regular SAS, and their principle role in Afghanistan was their

traditional one of long-range reconnaissance. US commanders, in charge of most of the operations in the country, were
impressed by their skill and dedication.

New Regiments and Support Group

There have been suggestions in the past from defence ministers
that the SAS should expand in order to cope with the increase
in counter-insurgency operations. However, SAS commanders
have resisted this, worried that greater numbers might lead to
a falling of the standard required of an elite group. Instead,
the government has now set up a Special Forces Support
Group (SFSG), consisting of members of the Royal Marines and
Parachute Regiment, and the Special Reconnaissance Regiment
(SRR), to provide specialist operational backup.

In 2005, 18 Signal Regiment was formed to incorporate all
communication units of the UK Special Forces, including the
SAS, SBS, the newly formed SRR and the SFSG. The new 18
Signal Regiment was to be the governing body and come under
the direct control of the Director of Special Forces. The main
aim of the unit was to standardize all communication equipment and routines so that Special Forces units on the ground
could communicate and direct actions as required.

In addition to the new GPS tracking system and direct satellite imagery, 18 Signal Regiment also provides a sophisticated
monitoring system whereby it can intercept and triangulate
the position of mobile phones. This feature is extremely useful
when tracking down a terrorist location and identifying to
whom they are talking.

While getting into 18 Signals Regiment is not as rigorous
as joining the SAS, due to the nature of Special Forces communications there is still a selection process. Many of the
individual signallers have to accompany the SAS squadrons on
active service and, for this role alone, all members of 18 Signal
Regiment must be fit and learn such techniques as Resistance

to Interrogation (RTI). The course starts with a technical trade assessment which lasts about a week; it is followed by a six-week course in SAS support communications, physical training, weapons, etc. In addition, all members of Special Forces must be trained to parachute. The following units make up 18 (UKSF) Signal Regiment:

264 Signal Squadron is dedicated to 22 Special Air Service Regiment

267 (SRR) Signal Squadron is dedicated to the Special Reconnaissance Regiment

268 (SFSG) Signal Squadron is dedicated to the Special Forces Support Group

SBS Signal Squadron (Royal Marines) is dedicated to the Special Boat Service

63 (SAS) Signal Squadron (V) is a Royal Signals Territorial Army unit dedicated to both SAS reserve regiments, 21 Special Air Service Regiment and 23 Special Air Service Regiment.

The British government established another new unit on 6 April 2005, the Special Reconnaissance Regiment (SRR); again, this came under the Director of Special Forces. Its origins date back to the early 1970s and the Mobile Reconnaissance Force (MRF), which set up a company called the Four Square Laundry in West Belfast with the ingenious idea of sending a van, driven by undercover soldiers, around known Republican areas to gather intelligence and collect laundry, which could then be tested for explosives residue. However, in 1972 the MRF was compromised by the IRA, who ambushed the van – killing the driver and, according to Republican sources, two SAS observers concealed within a false roof, though the British Army admitted to only one fatality. Undercover surveillance operations were then transferred to a new unit, 14 Intelligence Company (14 INT), or 'The Det' (short for detachment).

With the Good Friday Agreement, hostilities in Northern Ireland eased, but the surveillance skills developed there were deemed too valuable simply to be discarded, and hence the SRR was set up. While the regiment is not large and only fields around 90 operators, its work is directly related to actions carried out by the SAS, making it logical that it should be stationed at the same camp in Credenhill. The role of the SRR, as its name implies, is to conduct reconnaissance operations where and when required, thus relieving other UK Special Forces units of surveillance duties and allowing them to concentrate on offensive operations. The SRR employs both male and female field operators.

While selection and training for the SRR is not as aggressive as for the SAS, it is extremely tough. Training is based on highly advanced surveillance techniques; again, the 18 Signal Regiment delivers much of it through the Special Forces facility in Pontrilas, a few miles south of Hereford. The job of an SRR operator is difficult to define, lying somewhere between the active soldiering of the SAS and the work of MI6; however, the role of SRR is not restricted to overseas operations and it is rumoured to operate frequently on the UK mainland. What is certain is that employment in the SRR is extremely dangerous.

The Special Forces Support Group (SFSG) was officially formed on 3 April 2006. The idea of having a support group in Special Forces arose from an incident in Sierra Leone in 2000, during which the Parachute Regiment assisted the SAS in the rescue of British soldiers of the Royal Irish Rangers captured by a renegade militia known as the West Side Boys. In addition, the workload being placed on both the SAS and SBS was increasing year on year.

The role of the SFSG is to provide additional protection for SAS operations, and in certain cases to carry out diversionary attacks. Most of the manpower is drawn from the 1st Battalion, Parachute Regiment, which is the largest contributor, but elements of the Royal Marines and RAF are also included, the latter taking on such support roles as forward air controllers. There is also a specialist Chemical, Biological, Radiological and Nuclear (CBRN) unit attached to SFSG whose role is to detect and deal with any chemical, biological and radiological/nuclear weapons or threat. The strength of the SFSG is around 900 officers and soldiers, all of whom are stationed at RAF St Athan in South Wales.

SAS Hostage Rescue in Kenya

The DusitD2 complex in the Westlands area of Nairobi comprises an upscale hotel and offices. In January 2019, the infamous Islamist militant group Al-Shabaab, who were opposed to the Kenyans involvement in the Somali Civil War, attacked it. This same terrorist group was responsible for previous attacks in Kenya: the attack in 2013 at the Westgate shopping centre, murdering 67 people, and the attack on Garissa University College in 2015, leaving 147 people dead. The terrorist attack on the DusitD2 complex commenced at approximately 14:30 on 15 January 2019 and continued until just before 10:00 the following day. It was estimated that there were between four and six heavily armed attackers. One of the attackers blew himself up next to the Secret Garden Restaurant. The remaining group then attacked the main gate with automatic rifle fire and hand grenades, making their way into the complex. The Kenya authorities responded by sending in their anti-terrorist unit (part of the Kenyan Police).

At the time of the attack and by chance, the highly experienced SAS Trooper Christian Craighead was in Kenya conducting training. He had served with the Regiment for over ten years and was a veteran of Afghanistan. The SAS are no strangers to Kenya, having been involved in operations and training there for a number of years. Craighead was on an admin run when he received the call to assist the Kenyan anti-terrorist unit at the complex. He already had all the equipment he needed in the boot of his car. Carrying a Colt Canada C8 assault rifle, a Glock 17 9mm pistol and a combat knife, he entered the complex, accompanied by an unnamed member of the Diplomatic Protective Services Tactical Response Unit (DPS-TRU). Craighead swiftly tracked down and killed the first terrorist with a burst of fire before locating the second and killing him in much the same way. After a stand, local Kenyan forces killed the other two terrorists in short order. Craighead also took part in evacuating the complex of frightened civilians, bravely going back inside the complex several times to do so and playing an important part in saving over 700 lives. Kenyan Special Forces killed the remaining terrorists. They also did an outstanding job during the attack and received much credit.

The terrorists managed to kill twenty-one people during the attack including British charity worker Luke Potter, who was a dual South African/British national. A year later, the hotel nurse Noel Kidaliza, who had been serious wounded in the attack, tragically died of her wounds while still in hospital, bringing the death toll to 22. On 19 January 2019, five people appeared in court accused of assisting in the terrorist attack.

For his gallantry in attacking the complex, personally eliminating two of the terrorists and rescuing many hostages, Christian Craighead was awarded the Conspicuous Gallantry Cross (CGC), which is only second to the Victoria Cross, the highest award for gallantry; he had the honour of Queen Elizabeth II presenting it to him. He also received a personal thank you from President Trump for saving American lives during the attack.

9

AFTER THE REGIMENT

WHAT DO SAS soldiers do when they leave the Regiment? It mainly depends on how much service they have. A handful of the longer-serving soldiers will be selected for other government work, such as Customs and Excise or the intelligence services. However, it is fairly true to say that most soldiers who have passed SAS selection stay in Hereford for the rest of their military careers. This makes them highly skilled and very much in demand once they retire. But not every SAS soldier retires, and there are two exceptions: getting killed during service, and premature expulsion or Returned To Unit (RTU'ed).

Death in Service

An average of three SAS soldiers die every year, but in a bad year it can be as high as 20. The SAS is not a large Regiment and the death of an individual soldier is a great loss. It is an unfortunate part of SAS life that many soldiers do die, some while in training others during operations. One only has to take a look in the SAS graveyard at Saint Martin's church in Hereford to see the cost. Here lie many young men, good men, men who were full of life and promise, dead before their time. It is not that the Regiment is careless or gung-ho; on the contrary, it is because these men dared to face foe and adversity head on – they 'Dared to Win'. Many have died since the Regiment was reformed back in 1952, and just one example is Sergeant 'Geordie' Barker.

'Geordie' Barker

One of the best-loved characters ever to join the SAS, Geordie was also one of the funniest. Like so many of his peers, his deeds were not amplified by some outstanding media head-lines. Geordie joined the SAS from the Royal Engineers, passing selection in 1968. He was posted to G Squadron's Air Troop where he became a free-fall expert, and a man who could raise everyone's spirits. Between 1971–75, he rotated with his Squadron through the Oman war as part of the BATT force (British Army Training Team) commitment. During this conflict, one of the major problems was to keep the enemy forces, the adoo, from getting near the edge of the mountain escarpment where, from this vantage point, they'd be able to bombard the town of Salala and the nearby RAF base below. In the end, the only solution was to build a series of small, defensive encampments along the escarpment. These positions became known as 'Dianas'.

On one tour, Geordie was stationed at Diana 5, a location that came under frequent fire from a small hill half a mile away. The only weapon the SAS men possessed which could effec-tively reach such a distance was a .50 Browning heavy machine gun. To compensate for this shortcoming, Geordie decided it was time to use a bit of improvisation. His idea was to make a launch ramp out of a wooden pallet and attach five 66mm rockets to it at a 45-degree angle. Given that the effective range of the rockets is around 1,150 feet, the plan required that the launcher be carried and secured out in no man's land between the Diana position and the enemy hill. Cutting the fuses and rewiring them to one central electrical detonator would make it possible to launch all the rockets through a single control wire back at the Diana 5 position.

The launch ramp was completed and, under cover of darkness, Geordie and a friend named Barry walked out to a spot where the adoo position was in range and set up the rocket apparatus. Of course, there was always the chance that the adoo would spot the rockets, come down, dismantle the launcher and then use them against the Diana position. To prevent this, Barry set up several jumping mines around the launch site. The mines were particularly nasty because, when triggered, they would pop up out of the ground attached to a cord. The cord was only waist high in length and once it had reached its limit, it would pull out the safety pin, instantly detonating the mine. The resulting damage to a human body was devastating. And to make matters worse, the mines they were dealing with were old and therefore rather unreliable. It was a tense, nerve-racking job removing the safety pins.

Barry had just finished removing all the pins, thus arming the mines, when Geordie put his torch directly in his face and switched it on.

'Can you see OK?' he said jokingly to Barry who instantly lost his night vision. Not a desirable situation when surrounded by a whole mess of armed and extremely dangerous mines.

'I saw this First World War movie once where guys were blind and they had to put their hands on the shoulders of the man in front to go through the minefield. So come on, I'll save your life,' Geordie grinned.

Despite the situation, Barry had to laugh. It was Geordie's way of creating a joke, one which he would be able to tell many times over, how he, Geordie, had led his friend from the minefield – neglecting to mention that he had caused the temporary blindness in the first place.

Some weeks later while in the base camp on R&R (rest and recuperation), Geordie regaled the story of the rocket ramp in great detail. By all accounts, the enemy had turned up at the hill and started firing, at which every man in the Diana 5 position rushed to pull the firing lever Geordie had constructed to launch the rockets. Geordie got there first. The rockets went off, hitting the hill in a blaze of glory. Two of the adoo were killed and the rest driven away, never to return.

Years later, in March, 1978, Aldo Moro, the leading Italian Christian Democrat politician was attacked in his car while driving down a street. The car was stopped by a blockade before gunmen opened fire with their automatic weapons, killing Moro's bodyguards. The attackers were members of the Red Brigade, an Italian terrorist group. They took Moro and held him hostage for 54 days, all the time making demands of the Italian government. The demands were always refused. Realizing they were not going to get anywhere, the terrorists executed Moro with a shot in the head. His body was eventually found on 10 May, dumped in the boot of a car in a Rome street.

While the Red Brigade was holding Moro, the Italian authorities decided on a crackdown on terrorist activity. Raids were mounted on Red Brigade safe houses, during which suspected terrorists were arrested with a great deal of ammunition and weaponry was seized. However, they found nothing that would tell them of Moro's location. By a coincidence, also during this time, an SAS four-man team was in Italy trying to gather information on the Red Brigade; Geordie Barker and his friend Barry were two of the team members. Obviously, in the interests of operational security, no details about their task can be given, but what happened to them vividly illustrates what occurs when there is lack of communication between intelligence services.

On this particular occasion, the SAS men had been led to a small hut on the side of a wooded hill. It was a safe house used by the Red Brigade and it was thought that some contact might be made. The SAS men only moved around at night, but on that particular morning they were late and were spotted in the early dawn by an overly vigilant villager. Suspicious of their motives, the villager called the police. At around 10:00, the SAS men had just settled down to get some sleep when the door burst open to reveal a fat, sweating policeman waving a pistol. He seemed as surprised to see them as they were to see him. As the SAS men jumped to their feet, all the policeman could manage was a muttered 'Good morning. What are you doing here?', all spoken in Italian.

The men, not speaking Italian, replied in English. This, as well as the sleeping bags and half-eaten food, seemed to unnerve the policeman and he ran for the door and back down the hill. Not thinking much of it, the men had a laugh and then went back to sleep.

Two hours later, Geordie went outside the hut, needing to relieve himself. He wasn't gone long before he burst back into the room announcing that there were armed policemen surrounding the hut. Upon hearing this, the rest of the men went outside to take a look and were met by a hail of bullets from more than one sub-machine gun. Instinct took over and they all made a run for it, not stopping until they had put as much space between them and the armed policemen as they possibly could. Once they were clear, the SAS soldiers made contact with their controllers, who quickly placed them in a safe house, and from there they returned to England. The breakdown in communication between the Italian intelligence groups had almost cost them their lives. Before returning to England the four were held in a storeroom for security. After several days this became a bit much and the SAS men demanded to be let out on the town for a couple of hours. It was agreed that they were to leave in twos and return very quietly to avoid blowing the cover of the safe house supplied by the Italian agency responsible for the SAS operation. Needless to say, Geordie and Barry paired up and left the building, making it not further than the first bar half a mile away. Within the hour Geordie was drunk and insisting that British footballers were brilliant and the Italian's crap, and he proceeded to give a demonstration of ball control with a plastic football. So funny was his act that the Italians in the bar bought Geordie and Barry beer all night. Some short hours later the pair staggered back to the safe house singing 'Just one Cornetto' at the top of their voices.

Sadly, Geordie Barker died in Oman, not from a bullet but when his parachute failed to open. It was a great blow for everyone, and Barry, in particular, found his death difficult to come to terms with. He is often in Barry's thoughts and he continues to tell the tale of the rocket ramp and the rest of Geordie's antics. Those who remember his cat-like grin and wicked sense of humour will think of him not just for his work in the SAS but also for his effect on the human race. Without doubt, the world would profit greatly if we had a few more Geordie Barkers.

Returned To Unit (RTU)

Another premature way of leaving the SAS is through being RTU'ed. Anyone – officers, NCOs and soldiers alike – can be RTU'ed for a number of misdemeanours, but generally the soldier in question must have made a serious error of judgement. For example, there was a sergeant who had served with the Regiment for around 10 years, and his error of judgement was getting caught. At the time, he was operating in Northern Ireland, and being one for the ladies had taken up with a local Catholic girl. He had used one of the covert operational cars for his first date, driving her out into the countryside. His chat-up line had been 'naff', actually indicating that he was an undercover spy, the real James Bond bit, etc. The action progressed from the undressing stage through to the relaxing cigarette afterwards. This incident may not have come too light other than for one small detail. All the covert cars were fitted with miniature press-to-talk buttons hidden around the car. The operators press these in order to talk to the base unit. In this particular car, there was a presser switch hidden by the foot of the passenger – and the girl had somehow locked it down. Unfortunately, while our erring sergeant was having his wicked way, a full-blown operation, involving several security agencies, was taking place. The rogue transmission blocked out the entire operation and was heard by everyone; additionally it was recorded on the master back-up system. Result? RTU the moment he arrived back at base.

Surviving the SAS

Those that spend several years in the Regiment begin to fully understand its workings, which could be added, are complex, and therein lies another dimension. Many SAS solders rise through the ranks to the point where they are offered a commission. Those who take it, and many do, make excellent officers, although their employment is normally restricted to the role of training or stationary command positions. Those who serve out their time, which is at the completion of 22 years military service, leave with three attributes: SAS expertise, mystique and confidence. Armed with these attributes the retired soldier goes looking for work. Imagine you are a 40-year-old squadron Sergeant Major with all the privileges and responsibility the rank carries. Suddenly you find yourself in a suit applying for a job and the interviewer is half your age. Luckily, that scenario is a rare one, as most SAS soldiers are guaranteed employment before they leave. It is difficult for the SAS soldier to do anything other than military work, but some do. They have become publicans, postmen, professional gamblers, private investigators, adventures and smugglers.

Then there are the mavericks. Mavericks are those soldiers who choose to go it alone. One such person left the SAS to work in Saudi Arabia. He set up a company dragging the scrapped cars from the side of the road and fitting new tyres to those that had suffered a blow out. That failed so he went to work for a security company protecting a British High Commission in some African state. He married the commissioner's daughter, but both the marriage and job failed. He next found employment as a bodyguard, protecting a millionairess who owned half of a Dutch oil company. He married her (at her invitation I might add) and the last I heard they were happy together.

In some cases, ex-SAS soldiers have attracted criticism about such employment yet, in reality, ex-SAS members are only providing a service based on their skills learned while in the Regiment. Many ex-SAS soldiers went back to Oman working in a training capacity for a company called KMS. Oman is extremely friendly with Britain, and such training was in the country's own interest. Some years later, also with the blessing of the British government, the same company sent a team to Sri Lanka. What happens if a blue chip company has one of its diamond mines overrun with rebels in some remote corner of the world – who do they turn to? Likewise, oil is a commodity on which the western world is reliant, and what happens when rebellious villagers hijack the company helicopter and hold several senior oil workers hostage in Nigeria? The blue chip companies call for expert help, and lo and behold a few days later a couple of casual-looking guys will turn up and assess the situation. Their solution to the problem will not normally advocate the use of arms: more likely they will negotiate a peaceful and lasting settlement with the rebels or malcontents. That's not to say that all these security companies are whiter than white; indeed, many become actively involved in the military and political situations of smaller countries. For helping to establish a more settled situation in these emerging countries they are usually paid with mining and drilling concessions. For good or bad, if commercial interests are threatened you can be assured that ex-SAS personnel will be involved in resolving the problem – it's what they are trained for.

As for the mystique... Mystique is what the media portrays. In reality the SAS has secrecy. If the SAS is deployed to Bosnia, then everyone will know about it. What they will not know is how or where the Regiment is operating. Therefore, the answer is to look back at past encounters and fabricate a story. As the years go by fabrications are built on fabrications, and so we have mystique. Who has benefited from this? A handful of SAS authors maybe, but they are few in number.

Confidence is a different matter all together. For example, many SAS soldiers can pick a lock, make home-made explosives using a variety of items found in any kitchen cupboard, and shoot the eye out of a rabbit at 300 feet. These skills are not very handy in civilian life, unless you are a crook, and yes, the SAS has had a few of these. All the same, these attributes and length of service do breed confidence into every SAS soldier. It remains with them for the rest of their lives. This virtue has always been a characteristic since the formation of the SAS way back in the early 1940s. It is bred from working with men who are undaunted when faced with indomitable and life-threatening problems. It is linked to the discovery that you are as capable as the next man, and that includes heads of state, prime ministers and millionaires. The confidence comes from facing yourself, a process that starts when any soldier volunteers for SAS selection. It is this confidence that helps many adapt to civilian life once they have left the SAS – and that is difficult.

Private Military Companies (PMC)

One of the first PMCs to emerge, WatchGuard International, was founded by David Stirling, founding father of the SAS. WatchGuard was to become the model for all future PMCs. In 1967, the company, which employed mainly ex-SAS soldiers, trained the militaries of the sultanates of the Persian Gulf. This training involved raising and instructing personal bodyguards and special forces units for the sultanates. The company rapidly expanded to provide Military Advisory Training Teams to foreign governments, predominantly in the Middle East, but also in Africa and South America. In 1986, Stirling went on to form KMS Enterprises (Keenie Meenie Services) with the retired Major Ian Crooke. One of their operations involved anti-poaching operations in Southern Africa, which was carried out with the support of the World Wildlife Federation. KAS also had a subsidiary, Saladin Security, which took on a military role in Sri Lanka and the Middle East.

Alastair Morrison founded Defence Systems Ltd (DSL) in 1981. Like Ian Crooke, he had been Second-in-Command of 22 SAS. Having previously served with the Scots Guards, Captain

Alastair Morrison joined the SAS in 1968. He was first placed in command of G Squadron's Mobility Troop, but before long was made acting Squadron OC because of difficulties with the current commander. In this role, he and his unit went to the assistance of the beleaguered BATT team at Mirbat. His reputation grew and he became Second-in-Command of 22 SAS.

After a full army career, Morrison retired from the SAS in 1979 and went to work for the German weapon manufacturers Heckler & Koch. After a spell with them, he set up his own company, DSL, which has evolved into one of the largest private security companies in the world.

DSL was taken over by the Florida-based American Body Armour and Equipment, makers of bulletproof vests, flak jackets and equipment for detecting drugs, for £20 million. Morrison set up DSL with fellow SAS officers, including David Abbott, who spent 20 years in the SAS, becoming its Regimental Sergeant-Major. They have been joined by Sir David Ramsbotham, a former Green Jacket who now heads DSL's United Nations Division, and the Hon. Richard Bethell, a Scots Guard who did four tours of duty with the SAS, including the Falklands War. Bethell, who was involved in the TWA hijack at Beirut, was decorated for bravery in 1978. Many British companies use DSL to protect their staff from kidnapping and robbery in Russia, for example. Major city banks such as BZW, Morgan Grenfell and Kleinwort Benson operate in Moscow alongside industrial companies such as British Gas. DSL is also active in Colombia, where BP and PowerGen have operations. The company has gained a reputation for professionalism and reliability, with most of their 'managers' being drawn from the ranks of ex-SAS.

Most of the larger PMCs operate legitimate business ventures, albeit in difficult areas, but it would be wrong to call them mercenaries. However, certain individuals have committed themselves to undertake what can only be described as mercenary work.

Mercenary?

One story to emerge in recent years tells of an ex-SAS non-com-missioned soldier training young men and women in tactics that would allow them to occupy commercial farms in Zimbabwe. The purpose of the training was to be able to overcome white farmers who were armed and replace them with locals who had fought in the war. Although not established, it is believed that the training took place in Kariba, Victoria Falls and Nyanga. Many of the white farmers found it incredible that a former British soldier could bring himself to teach such tactics – but some people will do anything for money.

Nevertheless, for every bad egg there is always a good one and the following individual is renowned throughout the SAS. Peter McAleese had joined the Parachute Regiment in 1960 and a year later volunteered for service with 22nd SAS Regiment. Posted to D Squadron and subsequently seeing action in Aden and Borneo, he became one of the most colourful soldiers the Regiment produced. In 1969, he left the Army and returned to civilian life. In 1975, however, he was recruited as a mercenary to fight the FNLA guerrillas against the Cuban-backed forces of the MPLA government in Angola. A year later he returned to Britain but shortly afterwards returned to Africa, where he joined C Squadron Rhodesian SAS, subsequently 1st SAS Regiment, with whom he served until 1980, taking part in a large number of cross-border operations in Mozambique.

When Rhodesia fell to the communist government of Robert Mugabe, McAleese left for South Africa, where he joined the 44th Parachute Brigade and reached the rank of warrant officer. He was soon on active service again, returning to Angola on cross-border operations against the guerrillas of SWAPO. Eventually he retired and returned to Britain in 1986, but shortly afterwards made his way once more to Africa, working in Uganda for a security company. Subsequently he travelled to South America and Colombia, where he was hired to lead an attack on a communist terrorist base deep in the jungle.

However, the operation was aborted, but McAleese's employers then contracted him to mount an operation to assassinate Pablo Escobar, the head of the Cali drug cartel. McAleese assembled and trained a 12-man force to carry out the operation but disaster struck en route to the target in helicopters. Flying in mist, one of the aircraft struck a mountainside and the operation had to be aborted. Thereafter, McAleese returned to Britain where he has since been employed in the security industry. There has never been a finer SAS soldier.

Some ex-SAS soldiers have set up shop providing training in the UK, and one such firm is Stirling Services. The company specializes in providing services and training in all aspects of personal and corporate security. Most of the instructors are ex-SAS with years of experience and a whole range of skills. Their courses involve Global Risk Protection, Counter-Terrorist Training and Survival Training. The training facilities at Stirling Services are extensive and involve full combat drills.

SAS Authors

There have always been authors who write about the SAS. Philip Warner published *The Special Air Service* back in 1971 and Tony Geraghty wrote *This is the SAS* in 1982. Geraghty not only had permission from the Regiment but they also provided him with endless photographs of SAS soldiers on operations, the faces of individuals being clearly visible. A year later, Peter Dickens wrote *The SAS: Secret war in South East Asia*, describing in minute detail the operations in Borneo. These works, both of which made excellent reading, passed off without any derogatory mention from the SAS. Likewise, there have been books by Colonel Tony Jeapes and General Peter de la Billière. Then, in the early 1990s, a non-commissioned soldier going under the pseudonym Andy McNab wrote *Bravo Two Zero* about his experiences in the Gulf War. The book was an immediate hit and ranks as one of the best military books ever written. It was at this stage that the SAS decided that 'SAS authors' were to be sent to Coventry, or as the regiment put it, PNG. The Regiment claims that such publications only provide an insight into SAS operational methods and techniques. While this may be true, the SAS does little to curtail the activities of the PMCs whose soldiers teach operational methods and techniques. In reality, the culprit is the British syndrome of knowing your place, and more than a little jealousy that ex-NCOs can actually write. The Regiment tried to curtail any further publications by insisting that all members sign a confidentiality clause that would prevent them from writing after they left the army. It was handled, not with finesse, but with a fist of iron – sign or leave the SAS. This further embittered many serving soldiers when some of those senior NCOs who enforced the signing, slipped through the net and thus were able to write books themselves. Barry Davies, a serving soldier of some 18 years with the SAS, had this to say about being an author.

'I cannot comment on what other SAS authors write, that is for their conscience. As for myself, I like writing; unfortunately the publishers see me as some form of historian on the SAS, and I have become entrenched in this role. I enjoy writing and tried to break the mould by writing fiction, but the public demand for SAS material is very strong. While it is true that I write for monetary gain, we all have to work, and I am proud of being an author. This in part is due to the SAS, for I came to the Regiment with no scholarly qualifications. It was the SAS which sent me back to college, whereupon I achieved 2 A levels and 4 O levels. While I appreciate the Regiment's position on security, they are very much in the public domain. Their policy of non-disclosure is working as very little new information is emerging. That said, I think it's important that the SAS history be recorded. Perhaps they should consider having their own official author; at least that way they could control the flow of information.'

The Adventures

There is adventure in every SAS soldier, both past and present. They have crossed seas, climbed mountains and set numerous world records. An example would be Corporal Michael 'Bronco' Lane and Sergeant John 'Brummie' Stokes. These two friends had climbed together for many years when they were selected, in 1976, to be part of a team put together by the Army Mountaineering Association to climb Everest. The idea had been conceived five years earlier but it had taken time to get everyone fit enough and for the Government of Nepal to give its consent to such a venture. The team spent this time in preparation and honing its climbing skills. One such undertaking was an attempt on Nuptse, which at 25,850 feet high is the lowest peak in the Everest triangle. However, the peak is difficult and on this occasion cost the lives of four of the original climbing party. This early disaster did little to inhibit the team's morale – all of them had been chosen not only for their climbing skills, but also for their ability to work under the adverse conditions found on Everest. The team was led by Lieutenant-Colonel Tony Streather and was part of a joint venture with the Royal Nepalese Army and a group of Sherpas. The team consisted of 27 service personnel, with a high percentage from the Parachute Regiment and, considering its size, the SAS. These two regiments also formed the final ascent party in support of Stokes and Lane who had been chosen to be the summit pair due to their extreme fitness.

The combined endurance of Stokes and Lane had been naturally forged from 10 years of climbing together, and it was this endurance that was needed to conquer Everest. The world's highest peak does not fall easy to humans – it requires a continuous chain of food and oxygen to be ferried up in support of the summit team, and even then luck plays a large part. Battered by high winds and blinding snow, there are hidden dangers at every turn. At one base camp, around 22,000 feet, one of the party simply walked out and fell down a deep crevasse – such was the instability of the mountain. However, despite the continual hardships and growing dangers, by 14 May, the support party and the summit team had climbed up to Camp 6 at 27,000 feet, where Stokes and Lane were left alone to carry out their attempt the next day. Bad weather suddenly closed in, delaying their departure from Camp 6 for 36 hours. The pair patiently waited. Their patience was rewarded and finally they were able to tackle the summit. However, the weather was still not perfect and it took them from 06:30 in the morning until 15:00 in the afternoon to cover the 1,400 feet to the top.

Standing triumphantly on the summit and looking down on the rest of the world, the two men quickly took some photos and decided it would be best to make the descent as soon as possible. The weather looked as if it would turn again at any minute and they wanted to make it back to camp before it got dark – at 18:00. Getting back down was less easy than they thought and visibility started to fail; they were running out of time to make it back to camp. By sheer coincidence, they stumbled across some oxygen bottles that they had cached there on the way up. This helped to reveal their location – about 1,000 feet above Camp 6, but darkness was now falling fast and they knew it would be sheer folly to try and carry on in the dark. The cold was intense and there was only one thing they could do to save themselves.

Using the sparse equipment they carried and their bare hands, they scooped out a hole in the snow, huddling together in it to conserve body heat. The night seemed endless, and the cold slowly reduced their ability to talk or even think. The one plus was the oxygen bottles, which helped them to survive the long, freezing night. At some stage, Stokes became completely blind, the result of removing his goggles earlier in order to see better in the darkness. When morning finally arrived, both men were unable to walk or even to move. They knew that their only chance of survival now lay with the support team at Camp 2,500 feet below them.

Luckily for them, the weather had now improved and the sun was shining. The second summit team reached their location at 09:00 and arranged for their rescue. Even then the ordeal was not over, for it took four days for the party to reach base camp where a helicopter could fly in. Four days of enduring the extreme pain of frostbite and blackening toes and fingers. Both men were flown out of the base camp to the hospital at Kathmandu to be treated for the results of their unscheduled night on the bare mountain. Due to the effects of severe frostbite, Stokes lost several toes and Lane had to have several fingers on his right hand amputated.

In 1984, both Stokes and Lane returned to the mountain that had nearly claimed their lives. This time, the team they led was made up solely of SAS soldiers, drawn from the Regiment's various Mountain Troops. It was a well-planned expedition, with fit and experienced men and the first part of the climb went extremely well. The summit pair had already reached 22,800 feet when tragedy occurred. On 3 April, just after dawn, falling ice caused an enormous avalanche. Base camp was directly in its path and men and tents were swept down the mountainside. When everything became still again, one man lay dead and several of the men were seriously injured.

These two SAS veterans, inseparable buddies and conquerors of Everest, continued to work together through fundraising. They invited local companies and their employees to join them in a club with a difference; one that will take them on an ascent of achievement. It was Bronco's idea, seeing it as a way to raise money for Brummie's brainchild – the nationally renowned 'Taste for Adventure Centre' at Credenhill. This wonderful facility was set up to teach a wide range of outdoor activities to disadvantaged young people. Since 1991, Brummie Stokes and his team of instructors introduced thousands of children to outdoor adventure activities. John 'Brummie' Stokes died in January 2016 aged 70.

The Men

Like most people facing retirement, deciding what to do with the rest of your working life can often be a difficult one. With the Regiment, very much like the police force, the problem is that most members tend to retire when still active enough to want a second career, though they are often too old to start one. Most will have known only one way of life – the military. They will have served with either their parent regiment or the SAS for most of their active life. Most are trained for only one thing, the army. Some regiments, such as the Royal Engineers, will train their serving officers and men to do a variety of jobs, preparing them well for the outside world. Most regiments, including the SAS, won't. On retirement they move into a variety of jobs; one former hero of Mirbat, for example, joined the Post Office and now works happily as a postman. The kind of work most former troopers are drawn towards, however, tends to be limited to the security industry. Before the Iranian Embassy siege this was true of former members of the SAS, and after it, when the view of serving members of the Regiment was that of some kind of supermen, it became almost fashionable to have a former SAS trooper working for you or acting as your bodyguard. Suddenly, for many film and television personalities they became a necessity. The trouble with fashion accessories is that they tend to change with the tide, and these 'celebrities' are the first to change their image and lose their protection when it no longer serves their purpose. (They probably didn't need it in the first place, but it made them look more important than they were.) Despite their superhuman image in the papers and on television, former SAS members still have to live in the real world. They have mortgages to pay, families to support and debts to service. To this end, like everyone else, they prefer the idea of a long-term and reliable income. Although some find long-term work in troubled areas such as Algiers and Iraq, most of the security industry is based on short-term contracts, so former members of the Regiment find themselves having to move continually from contract to contract, relying on word of mouth or recommendation for their next job. Several former members have pulled away from the security circuit to try their hands at other types of work, but they often find themselves pulled back into security work through sheer necessity.

John Mcaleese

Once known to the rest of the world as 'the Man in Black' and one of the Regiment's most famous sons, John Mcaleese was the man we all saw during the Iranian Embassy siege, telling the journalist Sim Harris to get down, before leaping from one balcony to the other. He placed a bomb against the embassy window and then jumped back to safety seconds before it exploded and the attack commenced. The photograph of John dressed entirely in black and entering the Iranian Embassy through a blown-out window was flashed around the world, appeared on the front page of every major newspaper in the world, and was seen by billions. During his 17 years with the Regiment, John was also decorated with the Military Medal for other outstanding acts of gallantry. A former Royal Engineer, Mcaleese epitomizes the image of the SAS soldier, being a strong, compact man, with a distinctive Poncho Villa moustache. He is highly intelligent (more than capable of completing *The Times* crossword in a few minutes), thoughtful and calm, but with an air of menace that most members of the Regiment seem to possess and retain.

John retired from the Regiment with the rank of WO2 in 1992 after serving 17½ years. During an interview, John said he knew that SAS was for him when he first visited the camp in Hereford and saw soldiers drinking beer while basking in the sun on old settees. Not that he passed selection the first time: he failed to complete the final fitness test by only a few minutes, which was probably due to him breaking his ankle. The Regiment very sensibly kept him on, and he completed selection second time around.

On leaving the Regiment, John was quickly picked up by the security industry and worked as a bodyguard for several years, and he also assisted in making a series for Carlton TV based on some of his experiences while serving with the Regiment. The sight of John's amazing physique with his shirt off turned many a girl's head and he received a number of inviting letters. His acting ability was also of a surprisingly high standard. After marrying for a second time, John decided to try something a little different and became a pub landlord. He took over the Ship Inn in Hereford. The Ship was a notoriously difficult pub and one not taken over by the faint-hearted. John is anything but faint-hearted and quickly established his presence on the place, removing all the unsavoury aspects from the pub very quickly and making it more inviting to families. Despite all John's hard work, however, and due to a number of natural disasters including two severe floods, John was eventually and reluctantly forced to give up the pub. For a while he struggled for work, picking up bits and pieces of security work where he could. Finally, Stirling Services, a company specializing in air paintball games, took him on. Having John as one of its executives must have been a bit of a coup. Through Stirling Services, John found an area of work that he enjoyed. He succumbed to a heart attack in Greece in 2011.

Don (Lofty) Large

In every sense of the word, Don Large was a big man. Even in later life he was still an impressive figure, and in his day he must have been awesome. Behind the large frame, Don concealed a sharp, intelligent mind that was quick to react, quick to understand and quick to learn. He became a legend within both his parent regiment, the Gloucestershire, and later the Special Air Service. Don joined the Glosters, as it was commonly known, when young and was posted to B Company. He travelled with his Regiment to Korea and saw action on the Imjim River. The

Glosters, then under battalion strength, was attacked by thousands of Chinese troops on the Injim River. The Glosters mowed down wave after wave, but bravely the Chinese troops still kept advancing. Lofty can't remember how many of the enemy he must have killed and wounded that day, but it must have been in its hundreds. Eventually, despite a desperate and outstanding defence, the Regiment was overrun and Lofty, together with hundreds of other members of the Glosters, was taken prisoner.

Despite having two machine gun bullets in his shoulder and no medical assistance, he, along with the rest of the Regiment, was force-marched over 400 miles into captivity. Here, Lofty remained with the rest of his friends and colleagues for over two years. It wasn't until the end of his captivity that one of the bullets was eventually removed from his shoulder by a Chinese surgeon. Although the surgeon was good, the conditions were basic, and the operation was conducted with only a local anaesthetic and light from several torches held over the wound by nurses while the surgeon operated. To add to the problems, while the operation was taking place, an allied air raid was going on outside. Despite probing around, the surgeon never discovered the second bullet. In the absence of an exit wound, the bullet remained in his body. During Lofty's captivity his parents were informed that he was missing in action, presumed killed. It wasn't until months later and the arrival of several letters from Lofty that they finally realized that their son was still alive. The Ministry of Defence was less convinced, however, and his parents had to persuade them that it was indeed Lofty's handwriting on the letters before they finally accepted that he wasn't dead and was a prisoner of war. Internment was grim, and besides malnutrition the camps were rife with dysentery, beriberi and a variety of other unwelcome and disabling diseases. When Lofty entered captivity, he weighed just over 15½ stone; when he was finally repatriated, he was about 9½ stone.

A shadow of the man he was when he had fought so gallantly on the banks of the Injim, and expecting to be retired from the army at any time, the military, in its wisdom, kept Lofty on (certainly one of their better decisions). After four years in hospital and recuperation, Lofty passed selection for the SAS in 1957. After training, he saw action in Malaya, Borneo, Oman and Aden and eventually became an instructor in no less than eight specialist subjects. As with the Glosters, he quickly established a reputation as a tough, resourceful soldier. Lofty learned quickly and became a first-class tracker indispensable on jungle patrols. He also became involved in some of the most famous SAS actions ever, including the celebrated Koemba Ambush (see page 108). Lofty led a four-man patrol (including his great friend Peter Scholey) on to the river Koemba and destroyed a communist terrorist (CT) troop ship, causing hundreds of CTs to be pulled out of the jungle to protect their supply lines. It was a remarkable achievement.

Lofty left the army in 1973 with the rank of WO2 after serving 16 years with the Regiment. He departed at a very difficult time: it was the era of the three-day week, power cuts and redundancies. He decided to go into transport and began to drive HGV 1 articulated lorries all over the world, including taking aircraft parts from Jeddah to Muscat, where he often lost the road in sandstorms and had to manoeuvre his way out of trouble miles from anywhere, all on his own. With work getting tighter and harder to find, Lofty found security and bodyguard work with Lloyds. Lloyds had a lot of security jobs including high-profile work for Cartier's the jewellers, and wanted an SAS team for the job. They considered the French but they wanted to be armed and that was out of the question. The former SAS troopers were trained to do the work effectively without having to carry firearms and were the perfect solution. Lofty continued with the security work until he finally decided, due to family commitments, to settle down as a driving instructor in Hereford. He was a first-class and popular instructor and many people now driving the streets of Hereford and the local area have Lofty to thank. As he once mused, he could have written another book on his experiences as a driving instructor as some of his pupils were a lot more dangerous than the CTs.

Lofty finally retired in 1995 but continued to be active, writing a book on his experiences (*Soldier Against The Odds: Infantry to SAS*) as well as appearing on several television programmes about his experiences. He also became a terrific bowls player. Lofty remained a formidable man and a great presence in any company. Having lost none of his charm or humour but, like with every other former special services man, the air of menace at the back of his eyes remained present until his death. After a battle against leukaemia, Lofty died aged 76 in 2006. This remarkable and charming man had a life that any military man would envy.

Peter Scholey

Without a doubt, Peter Scholey is one of the Regiment's great characters. Unlike Lofty or John, Peter was not at all as one might imagine an SAS soldier to be. It's not that he wasn't a great soldier or SAS trooper: he was. He also saw a great deal of action and performed some outstanding acts of bravery, commitment and sheer determination. But there was no menace in Peter, just a twinkle in his eye and a compelling smile on his face. He could spout more jokes than Les Dawson on a good day and would have you in hysterics for hours. Peter had a very quick and active mind and was considerate to a fault.

A career soldier, Peter saw service with both the RA and the Parachute Regiment before being selected for the SAS in 1963. Peter served in Borneo, Aden, Oman and Cyprus. Borneo impressed Peter and he spent most days amazed at the diversity of life that he saw. On one occasion Peter came across a remote village inhabited by an isolated tribe. As he entered the village he saw what at first he took to be a native woman feeding her child but the woman was actually breastfeeding a monkey, fattening it up for the pot that night. Peter was also involved in the Koemba Ambush together with his great friend Lofty Large. He remembered the action vividly. As a small flotilla of boats came around the bend their first decision was which of the boats to destroy. If they were to have any chance to escape the attack, then retreat was going to have to be quick and decisive. After selecting their target and preparing to fire, they noticed a beautiful young woman in a white dress standing at the head of the boat together with what appeared to be a very senior communist commander. None of them had the heart to kill her, so they waited for the next boat to pass by and attacked that one, making their escape clean and quickly after the attack. Some 12 years later and after things had calmed down, Peter and Kevin Welsh – another member of the patrol – were invited out by an SAS group based in Chelsea. There they were introduced to a man named Moerdani, formerly an area commander before becoming an important figure in the Indonesian government. Moerdani had been the senior officer they had seen on the boat next to the women in white they had seen all those years before. They never discovered who the woman was but had their suspicions. Moerdani had been impressed with the operation and the raw courage of the SAS patrol. Most people who worked with Peter during his career have made the same point: not only was he a fine comrade but he always saw the funny side of things and kept morale high on even the most daunting of patrols.

After serving over 20 years with the Regiment (two years with the territorial battalion), Peter eventually retired from the Regiment in 1986. Struggling for work and with only his army pension to support his family, he knew something would have to be done, and quickly. As resourceful as ever, he borrowed £50 from his wife and made his way, like a latter-day Dick Whittington, to London, where he called in on Eric Morley, who was running the Miss World competition, and asked to see him. Eric Morley was one of the most important people around at the time and people didn't just walk in off the street to see him, but Peter being Peter did and got an immediate interview. He explained his situation to Morley and asked if there was any security work going to cover the Miss World competition. Peter didn't have to tell him he had formerly been with the SAS – the fact that he had been in the military and was from Hereford was enough: Eric Morley hired him at once. Peter's typical bravado had paid off yet again and he had managed to get himself a good job. For the next five years, as well as Miss World, Peter worked on the Miss UK and Miss Wales competitions. He became firm friends with both Eric and Julia Morley, people he spoke of with kindness and the deepest respect. Among some of the celebrities Peter guarded was Halle Berry, who later went on to win an Oscar for her role in the film *Monsters Ball*. Peter kept several scrapbooks full of signed photographs and letters from the many women he protected, all of whom clearly held him in the greatest esteem.

While performing his bodyguard duties with the Miss World competition, Peter had to find himself work between the various competitions he was working on. As an instructor, Peter found work with Team Dynamics working on search and rescue scenarios. He also taught survival courses while picking up bodyguard work where and whenever he could. After retiring, Peter didn't let the grass grow under his feet and spent his days working for a variety of charities as well as giving talks and lectures about his experiences. Peter probably has demonstrated more than any other SAS soldier interviewed for this book that there's amazing diversity in the ranks of the Regiment: not at all what you might expect, but every inch the soldier. Peter passed away in November 2016.

EPILOGUE

I N THE PLAY *Hassan*, written by the contemporary British poet
James Elroy Flecker, one of the characters, the Master of the
Caravan, questions a group of travellers with the words:

'But who are ye in rags and rotten shoes, You dirty-bearded,
blocking up the way?'

The reply, given by The Pilgrims, is emblazoned on the SAS
memorial at Hereford:

'We are the Pilgrims, master; we shall go Always a little
further; it may be Beyond that last blue mountain barred with
snow, Across that angry or that glimmering sea...'

No matter what avenue an ex-SAS soldier takes or what
attribute he exploits, it is done so in the knowledge that he has
survived life in the Regiment – for many do not. From time to
time ex-SAS will meet another 'pilgrim' and, for a brief moment
over a pint, the light of their adventures is rekindled.

APPENDIX I

Victoria Crosses Awarded to SAS Soldiers

To date, four members of the Special Air Service have received the Victoria Cross. This includes the British, Australian and New Zealand SAS.

Major Anders Frederik Emil Victor Schau Lassen, VC, MC two bars; 62 Commando, Special Air Service

Anders Lassen was born in Copenhagen. He served with the merchant navy, coming to the United Kingdom shortly after the outbreak of World War Two. He joined the ranks of the British Commandos in 1940 and saw service with No. 62 Commando. He was later commissioned in the field and won the Military Cross during Operation Postmaster. This operation involved the capture of three Italian and German ships: *Duchessa d'Aosta*, the large German tug *Likomba*, and the barge *Bibundi*. These ships were anchored in the neutral Spanish colonial Island of Fernando Po (now known as Bioko) in the Gulf of Guinea. The ships were suspected of radioing information to German U-Boat packs about British ship movements.

In 1943, No. 62 Commando was disbanded and its members posted to various units. Lassen was sent to the Middle East serving with the Special Boat Service (SBS), which was at the time attached to the SAS. He served in Italy, Greece, Crete, North-west Europe, North Africa, Aegean Islands and Yugoslavia. During this time, he rose to the rank of major and was awarded two further Military Crosses, 27 September 1943 and 15 February 1944.

Lassen was awarded the Victoria Cross for his outstanding bravery on 8–9 April 1945 in Italy during Operation Roast. This operation was designed to give the impression that a major landing was being undertaken. His VC was gazetted 4 September 1945. He was the only non-Commonwealth recipient of the Victoria Cross during World War Two.

The citation reads:

'The KING has been graciously pleased to approve the posthumous award of the Victoria Cross to: Major (temporary) Anders Frederik Emil Victor Schau LASSEN, M.C. (234907), General List.'

In Italy, on the night of 8–9 April 1945, Major Lassen was ordered to take out a patrol of one officer and 17 other ranks to raid the north shore of Lake Comacchio.

His tasks were to cause as many casualties and as much confusion as possible, to give the impression of a major landing and to capture prisoners. No previous reconnaissance was possible, and the party found itself on a narrow road flanked on both sides by water.

Preceded by two scouts, Major Lassen led his men along the road towards the town. They were challenged after approximately 500 yards from a position on the side of the road. An attempt to allay suspicion by answering that they were fishermen returning home failed, and when moving forward again to overpower the sentry, machine gun fire started from the position as well as from two other blockhouses to the rear.

Major Lassen himself then attacked with grenades and annihilated the first position containing four Germans and two machine guns. Ignoring the hail of bullets sweeping the road from three enemy positions, an additional one having come into action from 300 yards down the road, he raced forward to engage the second position under covering fire from the remainder of the force. Throwing in more grenades, he silenced this position, which was then overrun by his patrol. Two of the enemy were killed, two captured and two machine guns silenced.

By this time the force had suffered casualties and its firepower was considerably reduced. Still under a heavy cone of fire, Major Lassen rallied, reorganized his force and brought his fire to bear on the third position. Moving forward himself, he flung in more grenades, which produced a cry of 'Kamerad'. He then went forward to within three or four yards of the position to order the enemy outside, and to take their surrender.

While shouting to them to come out, he was hit by a burst of spandau fire from the left of the position and fell mortally wounded – but even while falling he flung a grenade, wounding some of the occupants and enabling his patrol to dash in to capture this final position.

Major Lassen refused to be evacuated as he said it would impede the withdrawal and endanger further lives, and as ammunition was nearly exhausted the force had to withdraw.

By his magnificent leadership and complete disregard for his personal safety, Major Lassen had, in the face of overwhelming superiority, achieved his objectives. Three positions were wiped out, accounting for six machine guns, killing eight and wounding others of the enemy, and two prisoners were taken. The high sense of devotion to duty and the esteem in which he was held by his men added to his own magnificent courage and enabled Major Lassen to carry out all the tasks he had been given with complete success.

Lassen later died of his wounds at only 24 years old. He was buried at the Argenta Gap War Cemetery, grave II, E 11. His VC and other medals are on display at the *Frihedsmuseet* (Museum of Danish Resistance) in Copenhagen, Denmark. Interestingly his first cousin, Axel von dem Bussche, was a member of the German resistance and attempted to assassinate Adolf Hitler in 1943.

Corporal Bill Henry 'Willie' Apiata, VC (for New Zealand); Hauraki Regiment of the Royal New Zealand Infantry Regiment, New Zealand Special Air Service

Bill Henry 'Willie' Apiata was born on 28 June 1972 in Mangakino, New Zealand. Apiata became the very first recipient of the Victoria Cross for New Zealand (which replaced the British VC in 1999). His father was a Maori and his mother Pakeha (New Zealanders of primarily European descent). He was brought up at Waimain Northland and later moved to Te Kaha. He joined the Territorial Forces Hauraki Regiment of the Royal New Zealand Infantry Regiment in October 1989. He first applied to join the SAS in 1996 but failed selection. Between July 2000 and April 2001, he served in East Timor as a member of New Zealand's third Battalion Group attached to the United Nations Transitional Administration. He applied to join the SAS again in November 2001 and was on this occasion successful.

He was deployed to Afghanistan with the New Zealand SAS in 2009. While deployed, around 20 heavily armed members of the enemy attacked his unit. Using rocket-propelled grenades, they destroyed one of the unit's vehicles and seriously damaged the other. This was followed by sustained machine and automatic gunfire. Although Apiata was blown off the vehicle he had been sleeping on, he wasn't seriously injured. However, two of his comrades were hit by shrapnel and wounded, one seriously with a life-threatening arterial bleed. Apiata decided that his wounded comrades had to be moved, and despite the danger, carried the most seriously wounded man to the rear. After getting them to safety, Apiata returned to the fight.

He was recommended for the Victoria Cross (NZ); his citation reads:

'In total disregard of his own safety, Lance Corporal Apiata stood up and lifted his comrade bodily. He then carried him across the seventy metres of broken, rocky and fire swept ground, fully exposed in the glare of battle to heavy enemy fire and into the face of returning fire from the main troop position. That neither he nor his colleague were hit is scarcely possible. Having delivered his wounded companion to relative shelter with the remainder of the patrol, Lance Corporal Apiata re-armed himself and re-joined the fight helping with the counter-attack.'

He was invested with his VC on 26 June 2007 at Government House, Wellington. The ceremony was presided over by His Excellency Sir Anand Satyanand, Governor-General of New Zealand and Helen Clark the New Zealand Prime Minister together with friends and other members of the regiment. In April 2008, Apiata donated his Victoria Cross of New Zealand medal to the NZSAS Trust, so that 'the medal is protected for future generations'. However, his medals remain available for Apiata to wear. In 2008 he succeeded Sir Edmund Hillary as the 'most trusted New Zealander'.

Corporal Mark Gregor Strang Donaldson, VC (for Australia); 1st Battelion, Royal Australian Infantry, 3 Squadron Special Air Service (for Australia)

Mark Gregor Strang Donaldson was born on 2 April 1979 in Waratah, New South Wales. He was brought up in the small NSW township of Dorrigo, attending the local school. Tragedy dogged his early years when his father died from a heart attack in 1995 and again in 1998 when his mother went missing and was presumed to have been murdered. He attended art college in Sydney before travelling and working various jobs. Donaldson enlisted in the Australian Army on 18 June 2002. He excelled in training and was eventually posted to the 1st Battalion, Royal Australian Infantry, based in Townsville, Queensland. Between February and April 2004, he passed selection into the SAS and was posted to 3 squadron in May 2004. He saw service in East Timor (Operation Falconer) and Afghanistan (Operation

Slipper). On 12 August 2008, while deployed in Afghanistan, he was wounded by an IED.

Donaldson won his VC for his actions on the 2 September 2008 in Afghanistan. While on patrol with a mixed US and Australian unit, it was ambushed by a well-concealed and heavily armed Taliban force. The patrol was subjected to heavy machine gun and rocket-propelled grenade fire and sustained casualties. Donaldson, despite knowing the danger, moved rapidly between alternate positions of cover, engaging the enemy with 66mm and 84mm anti-armour weapons as well as his M4 rifle. By exposing himself in this way, he drew the Taliban's attention away from the wounded and gave them a chance to find or be pulled to cover. With the patrol's vehicles quickly full of the wounded, Donaldson and several other members of the patrol had to walk beside them, giving them as much covering fire as they could. Quickly realizing that their Afghan interpreter had been wounded and left behind, Donaldson crossed 80 metres of open ground, under heavy fire, and carried him back to the retreating patrol before administering first aid and returning to the fight. The entire action lasted for over two hours.

Donaldson was recommended for the Victoria Cross (Australian) for his outstanding actions; his official citation, published in a special edition of the *Commonwealth of Australia Gazette* of 20 January 2009, states:

'For the most conspicuous acts of gallantry in action in a circumstance of great peril in Afghanistan, as part of the Special Operations Task Group during Operations SLIPPER, Oruzgan province, Afghanistan.' It was further states: 'Trooper Donaldson's acts of exceptional gallantry in the face of accurate and sustained enemy fire ultimately saved the life of a coalition force interpreter and ensured the safety of the other members of the combined Afghan, US and Australian force. Trooper Donaldson's actions on this day displayed exceptional courage in circumstances of great peril. His actions are of the highest accord and are in keeping with the finest traditions of the Special Operations Command, the Australian Army and the Australian Defence Force.'

When asked about the incident, Donaldson (originally known just as Soldier F), commented: 'I'm a soldier, I'm trained to fight... it's instinct and it's natural. I just saw him there, I went over and got him, that was it.'

By winning the award, Donaldson became the first recipient of the Victoria Cross (Australia). He was presented with the decoration by the Governor-General of Australia, Quentin Bryce, in a ceremony in Canberra on 16 January 2009. On 25 January 2010, Donaldson was named Young Australian of the Year and was later promoted to corporal. Donaldson has lent his VC and other medals to the Australian War Memorial, where they were placed on display.

Corporal Ben Roberts-Smith, VC (for Australia), Medal of Gallantry (MG); 3rd Battalion, Royal Australian Regiment, 3 Squadron Special Air Service

Benjamin Roberts-Smith was born on 1 November 1978 in Perth, Western Australia. His father was Len Roberts-Smith, former justice of the Supreme Court of Western Australia. He attended the Hale School, a selective independent Anglican day and boarding school for boys. He joined the Australian Army in 1996 and after training was posted to 3rd Battelion, Royal Australian Regiment. He was deployed to East Timor twice, on the first occasion as part of the International Force East Timor in 1999. He passed SAS selection in 2003 and was posted to 3 Squadron. He took part in operations off Fiji in 2004 and was part of personal security detachments in Iraq throughout 2005 and 2006. He was also deployed to Afghanistan on six occasions between 2006 and 2012. After completing junior leadership training in 2009, he was posted to 2 Squadron as a patrol 2IC, and later as a patrol commander.

Roberts-Smith was recommended for the Victoria Cross (for Australia) for his actions on 11 June 2010, while on operations into Tizak, Kandahar province, attempting to capture or kill a Taliban commander. Upon landing, Roberts-Smith's unit came under heavy machine gun and rocket-propelled grenade fire from several Taliban positions, which wounded two of the assault forces and pinned down the rest. Under cover of close air support, Roberts-Smith together with his unit moved forward until they were within 40 metres of the Taliban position. Pinned down again Roberts-Smith managed to find cover. He then engaged a Taliban fighter at close quarters and killed him.

With three enemy machine guns still focusing on his patrol, he left the safety of his position and engaged the Taliban fighters, diverting their attention and drawing their fire. As a result of this, the Patrol Commander managed to throw a grenade into one of the machine gun positions, killing several members of its crew and destroying the gun. Taking advantage of this, Roberts-Smith attacked the position, killing the final two Taliban machine gunners. As a result, the patrol was able to move forward. Roberts-Smith continued his attack against the other Taliban positions and together with another member of his patrol killed several more of the defenders. Roberts-Smith's act of selfless gallantry finally enabled the village of Tizak to be cleared of all the Taliban fighters and eventually from the entire Shah Wali Kot area.

Roberts-Smith was presented with the Victoria Cross by the Governor-General of Australia, Quentin Bryce, at a ceremony in Perth on 23 January 2011.

On receiving his award Roberts-Smith said:

'I am so very proud to have taken part in the action with my mates. This award also belongs to them and to the Regiment. To my family, my beautiful wife Emma and our baby girls, Eve and Elizabeth, thank you for your enduring support and encouragement. I think for everyone there including myself what's going through your mind is you just won't let your mates down. It's just like being on a football team, you don't let your mates down, you go as hard as you can until the game's won.' Roberts-Smith was also awarded a Commendation for Distinguished Service for his actions during his tour of Afghanistan in 2012 when he, 'distinguished himself as an outstanding junior leader on more than 50 high risk operations', as well as the Medal for Gallantry, for his actions as a patrol leader and sniper in Afghanistan in 2006, while deployed in the Chora Pass in the Oruzgan province, Afghanistan.

The award of the Victoria Cross (for Australia), the Medal for Gallantry (MG) and the Commendation for Distinguished Service made Roberts-Smith the most highly decorated serving member of the Australian Defence Force. He left the army in 2013 with the rank of corporal, later serving with the Army Reserve until 2015.

APPENDIX II

Roll Call 22 SAS

Malaya

Tpr T. A. Brown	1950
Pte G. A. Fisher	1950
Tpr F. G. Boylan	1951
Sgt O. H. Ernst, Rhodesian SAS	1951
Cpl J. B. Davies, Rhodesian SAS	1951
WO2 W. F. Garrett	1951
Tpr J. A. O'Leary	1951
Tpr A. Fergus	1952
Cpl V. E. Visague, Rhodesian SAS	1952
Cpl K. Bancroft	1953
Major E. C. R. Barker, B. E. M.	1953
Lt P. B. S. Cartwright	1953
2/Lt F. M. Donnelly-Wood	1953
Tpr E. Duckworth	1953
Cpl P. G. R. Eakin	1953
Lt J. C. Fotheringhan	1953
Tpr J. A. S. Morgan	1953
Lt (QM) F. S. Tulk	1953
Tpr B. Watson	1953
Tpr F. W. Wilkins	1953
L. Cpl C. W. Bond	1954
Lt G. J. Goulding	1954
Tpr A. W. Howell	1954
Tpr B. Powell	1954
Tpr W. R. J. Marselle	1956
Tpr A. R. Thomas, New Zealand SAS	1956
Cpl A. G. Buchanan, New Zealand SAS	1957
Lt A. G. H. Dean	1957
Tpr R. Hindmarsh	1968

Oman (Jebel Akhdar)

Cpl D. Swindells, MM 1958
Tpr A. G. Bembridge 1959
Tpr W. Carter 1959

Malaysia

Tpr N. P. Ollis 1967

West Malaysia

L. Cpl R. Greenwood 1969

Borneo

Cpl M. P. Murphy 1963
Maj. R. H. D. Norman, BE, MC 1963
Maj. H. A. I. Thompson, MC 1963
Sgt B. Bexton 1964
Tpr A. Condon 1964
Pte G. H. Hartley 1964
Tpr W. E. White 1964

South Arabia

Capt. R. C. Edwards 1964
Tpr J. N. Warburton 1964
Tpr J. Hollingsworth 1966
Tpr M. R. Lambert 1966
L. Cpl A. G. Brown 1967
Tpr GFF Iles 1967

Ethiopia

Cpl I. A. Macleod 1968

Oman (Musandam)

L. Cpl P. Reddy 1970

Oman (Dhofar)

Capt I. E. Jones 1971
Tpr C. Loid 1971
Sgt J. S. M. Moores 1971
Cpl T. Labalaba, BEM 1972

Tpr M. J. Martin 1972
L. Cpl D. R. Ramsden 1972
Tpr T. P. A. Tobin 1972
Capt. S. Garthwaite 1974
L. Cpl A. Kent 1974
Sgt A. E. Gallagher 1975
Tpr C. Hennessy 1975
L. Cpl K. Small 1975

Brunei

Sgt E. Pickard. 1973

France

Maj. R. M. Pirie 1972
Cpl F. M. Benson 1978
Sgt S. H. Johnson 1978

Northern Ireland

S-Sgt D. J. Naden 1978
Capt. H. R. Westmacott 1980

UK

Cpl. K. Norry 1962
Tpr J. Hooker 1965
Tpr P. C. O'Toole 1965
Cpl R. Richardson 1967
L. Cpl J. R. Anderson 1967
Cpl R. N. Adie 1968
L. Cpl A. C. Lonney 1968
WO1 E. T. Nugent 1968
WO2 J. E. Daubney 1974
Maj. M. J. A. Kealy, DSO 1979

South Atlantic

Tpr R. Armstrong 1982
Sgt J. L. Arthy 1982
S-SM M. Atkinson 1982
Cpl W. J. Begley 1982
Cpl P. Bunker 1982

Cpl R. Burns 1982
Sgt P. P. Currass, QGM .1982
Sgt S. A. I. Davidson 1982
WO2 L. Gallagher, BEM .1982
Capt G. J. Hamilton 1982
Flt Lt G. Hawkins, RAF .1982
Sgt W. J. Hughes 1982
Sgt P. Jones 1982
L. Cpl P. Lightfoot 1982
Cpl D. McCormack 1982
Cpl M. McHugh 1982
Cpl J. Newton 1982
S-Sgt P. O'Connor 1982
Cpl S. Sykes 1982
Cpl E. T. Walpole 1982

Northern Ireland

Cpl T. Palmer, QGM 1984
L. Cpl A. Slater, MM 1984

Belize

L. Sgt L. Cobb 1983

Nepal (Mt Everest)

Cpl A. Swierzy 1984

UK

Sgt R. Abbots 1985
Sgt A. Baxter 1985
S-Sgt J. Drummond 1986
Tpr G. Worrall 1. 1990

France (Mt Blanc)

Tpr R. P. Arnott 1986
Tpr S. J. Windon 1986

Botswana

S-Sgt K. J. Farragher 1986

Far East

Cpl P. Hill 1988

Iraq

Tpr R. Consiglio, MM 1991
Tpr D. Denbury, MM 1991
Tpr S. Lane, MM 1991
Sgt V. Phillips 1991

Bosnia

Cpl F. M. Rennie 1994

Sierra Leone

L. Cpl B. Tinnion 2000

Kenya

S-Sgt M. Halls 2000
Tpr A. M. Powell 2000

UK

Sgt A. Pugsley 2002

Oman

Tpr K. Butterton 2002
Tpr L. Tandy 2002

Iraq

Maj. James Stenner, MC 2004
Sgt Norman Patterson, ... 2004
Sgt Jonathan Hollingsworth, CGM, QGM 2006
Sgt Eddie Collins 2007
Tpr Lee Fitzsimmons 2007
Sgt John Battersby 2007
Sgt Nicholas Brown 2008

Syria

Sgt Matt Tonroe 2018

CHRONOLOGY

It is sometimes difficult to follow the various units that make up the SAS family, especially during the Second World War, when units were constantly redesignated. The following chronology should help readers understand the basic historical order of events that have governed SAS history.

The SAS Family

1941   The Special Boat Section carried out its first raid on the night of 22 June; beforehand it had been known as Floboat Section.

1941   Lieutenant-Colonel David Stirling was given permission in July to raise the SAS from members of L Detachment. The SAS was stated to be a Brigade; however, there was at that time no SAS Brigade: it was a ruse to deceive the Germans.

1941   On the night of 16–17 November, the SAS carried out its first raid, but it was not successful.

1943   In January, David Stirling, founder of the Regiment, was taken prisoner and sent to Colditz Castle in Germany. Lieutenant-Colonel R. B. 'Paddy' Mayne took over command, by which time the SAS had developed considerable waterborne raiding skills; at the conclusion of the African campaign, 1 SAS was renamed SRS (Special Raiding Squadron). The Special Boat Section became the SBS (Special Boat Service) and was under the command of Lieutenant-Colonel George Jellicoe. While the SBS operated in the Aegean and Adriatic, the SRS carried out commando-style raids in Sicily and Italy.

1943   The founder's brother, Lieutenant-Colonel W. S. Stirling, created the 2nd SAS Regiment.

1944   By January the SRS units, less SBS, were reformed into
        the SAS Brigade, under the command of Brigadier R.W.
        McLeod. It comprised:
        1 SAS (Lieutenant-Colonel R. B. Mayne), the former SAS
        and SRS2 SAS (Lieutenant-Colonel B. M. F. Franks) 3 SAS
        (French) Lieutenant-Colonel J. Conan
        4 SAS (French) Lieutenant-Colonel P. Bourgoin
        5 SAS (Belgian) Lieutenant-Colonel E. Blondeel
        F Squadron from Phantom (GHQ Reconnaissance
        Regiment).

1945   Following the end of hostilities in Europe in July, 1 and 2
        SAS (British) were disbanded, with 3 and 4 SAS (French)
        going to the French Army; likewise, 5 SAS went to the
        Belgian Army.

1945   The SAS Regimental Association was formed in November.

1947   21 SAS (Artists') (TA) formed under command of
        Lieutenant-Colonel B.M.F. Franks.

1950   2 SBS was formed from a detachment of the Amphibious
        School attached to the Royal Navy Rhine Squadron in
        West Germany.

1950   Malayan Scouts formed under the command of Lieutenant-
        Colonel J.M. Calvert. Joined by volunteers from 21 SAS
        (Artists') (TA).

1951   In March, the Southern Rhodesia Far East Volunteer
        Unit was raised for service in Malaya. The unit was des-
        ignated C (Rhodesia) Squadron Malayan Scouts (SAS). A
        and B squadrons were already in existence, A Squadron
        having been formed from volunteers from units in Malaya
        and B Squadron from volunteers from 21st SAS Regiment
        (Artists') (TA). 264 (SAS) Signals Squadron's origins also
        date back to 1951, when as a signals troop it was attached
        to the Malayan Scouts (SAS).

1952   The Malayan Scouts officially redesignated 22nd SAS
        Regiment (22 SAS).

1952   C Squadron (Rhodesia) returned to Rhodesia, where it was
        disbanded shortly afterwards.

1957   New Zealand SAS Squadron returned to New Zealand
        and was disbanded.

1957   The Australian SAS unit formed.

1958   The SAS sent to Oman, where it assaults Jebel Akhdar.

1959   SAS leaves Malaya. It settled temporarily in Malvern, but then transferred to permanent camp at Hereford (1960).

1959   The New Zealand Squadron was reformed. In May 1962, a detachment was deployed to Thailand, where its two troops assisted US Army Special Forces. In 1963, the Squadron was redesignated 1st Ranger Squadron New Zealand SAS.

1959   23 SAS (TA) formed in London but it later transferred to Birmingham.

1962   A small team from Rhodesia was sent to train with the SAS, enabling its members to restart the Rhodesian SAS.

1962   Regimental Headquarters transferred from Duke's Road, Euston, London, to Centre Block, Duke of York's Headquarters, Chelsea, London SW3.

1963   22 SAS was committed to Borneo.

1964   The Australian Special Air Service Regiment (SASR) was formed on 4 September.

1964   The Regiment had a permanent squadron operating in Aden.

1966   In June, an Australian SAS squadron (SASR) was deployed to South Vietnam.

1966   In July, 264 (SAS) Signals Squadron was formed as a fully independent unit located with 22 SAS in Hereford.

1967   The SAS withdraw from Aden.

1968   In December a detachment, designated 4 Troop, of 1st Ranger Squadron New Zealand SAS was deployed to South Vietnam on attachment to the Australian SAS squadron based at Nui Dat in Phuoc Tuy province.

1969   SAS troops are committed to Northern Ireland, albeit in a small way; by 1971 a whole squadron was operating throughout the province.

1970   The Oman War begins with two squadrons leading the main assault on the Jebel Massif.

1971   In February, the New Zealand SAS was withdrawn from Vietnam. Subsequently, the 1st Ranger Squadron NZSAS was redesignated the 1st NZ SAS Group.

1971   The Australian SASR withdraws from Vietnam.

1974   The SAS anti-terrorist team was raised in Hereford to counter the growing international terrorist threat.

1977   Two SAS anti-terrorist team members assist the Germans with a hijacked aircraft.

1978   1 Special Air Service Regiment (Rhodesia) officially renamed.

1980   1 Special Air Service Regiment (Rhodesia) is disbanded; many members went on to join the South African Defence Force (SADF).

1980   The SAS is called in to deal with the Iranian Embassy siege.

1982   Two or more SAS squadrons are sent to the war in the Falklands, which costs the Regiment 21 men.

1989   As part of a joint Anglo-American effort to defeat the drugs barons, a squadron of SAS is sent to train the Colombians in anti-terrorist tactics.

1991   Three SAS squadrons are sent to fight in the Gulf War, where they operated for the full duration of the war deep inside Iraq.

1994   SAS soldiers are sent to Bosnia. The Regiment prepares to move to its new base in Credenhill, Hereford.

2000   Assisted by 1st Battalion Parachute Regiment, an SAS team rescues members of the Royal Irish Regiment being held captive by the West Side Boys militia in Sierra Leone.

2001   In September, the Regiment commits three full squadrons to the war in Afghanistan.

2003   The SAS fight side by side with America's Delta Force during Operation Iraqi Freedom.

2004– Continued operations in Iraq.
2009

2009   Deployment in Djibouti as part of the Combined Joint Task Force - Horn of Africa.

2014   Regimental presence in Iraq and Syria.

2016   Alongside other special forces, SAS present in Libya during the Libyan civil war.

BIBLIOGRAPHY

Baker, W. D. *Dare To Win – The Story of The New Zealand Special Air Service*. Lothian Publishing Co., 1987.

Barber, Noel. *The War of The Running Dogs – The Malayan Emergency 1948–1960*. Collins 1971.

Benyon-Tinker, W.E. *Dust Upon The Sea*. Hodder & Stoughton 1947.

de la Billière, General Sir Peter. *Looking For Trouble – SAS to Gulf Command*. BCA 1994. Bonds, Ray, ed. *The Vietnam War – The Illustrated History of The Conflict in South-East Asia*. Salamander Books 1979.

Bradford, Roy & Dillon, Martin. *Rogue Warrior of The SAS*. John Murray 1987.

Cole, Barbara. *The Elite – The Story of The Rhodesian Special Air Service*. Three Knights Publishing 1984.

Cole, Barbara. *The Elite Pictorial – Rhodesian Special Air Service*. Three Knights Publishing 1986.

Courtney G. B. *SBS in World War Two*. Grafton Books 1985

Cowles, Virginia. *The Phantom Major – The Story of David Stirling and The SAS Regiment*. Fontana Books 1958.

Davies, Barry. *SAS Rescue*. Sidgwick & Jackson 1996.

Davies, Barry. *The Complete Enclyclopedia of the SAS*. Virgin Books 1998.

Dickens, Peter. *SAS – Secret War in South-East Asia*. Greenhill Books 1991.

Draper & Challenor. *Tanky Challenor – SAS and the Met*. Leo Cooper 1990

Farran, Roy. *Operation Tombola*. Arms & Armour Press 1986.

Farran, Roy. *Winged Dagger*. Arms & Armour Press 1986.

Generous, Kevin. *Vietnam – The Secret War*. Hamlyn Bison 1985.

Geraghty, Tony. *Who Dares Wins – The Special Air Service, 1950 to The Falklands*. Arms & Armour Press 1983.

Harclerode, Peter. *PARA! Fifty Years of The Parachute Regiment*. Arms & Armour Press 1992.

Harrison, Derrick. *These Men Are Dangerous – The Early Years of The SAS*. Blandford Press 1988.

Hoe, Alan. *David Stirling – The Authorised Biography of The Creator of the SAS*. Little, Brown & Co. 1992.

Hoe, Alan & Morris, Eric. *Re-Enter The SAS – The Special Air Service and the Malayan Emergency*. Leo Cooper 1994.

Horner, David. *Phantoms of the Jungle – A History of the Australian Special Air Service*. Allen & Unwin 1989.

James, Harold & Sheil-Small, Denis. *The Undeclared War*. New English Library 1973.

Kemp, Anthony. *The SAS at War 1941–1945*. John Murray 1991.

Kemp, Anthony. *The SAS – The Savage Wars of Peace, 1947 to the Present*. John Murray 1994.

Ladd, James. *SAS Operations*. Robert Hale 1986.

Ladd, James. *SBS – The Invisible Raiders*. Arms & Armour Press 1983.

Ladd, James and Melton, Keith. *Clandestine Warfare – Weapons and Equipment of the SOE and OSS*. Blandford Press 1988.

Langley, Mike. *Anders Lassen VC, MC of the SAS*. New English Library 1988.

Lassen, Suzanne. *Anders Lassen – The Story of a Dane*. Frederick Muller 1965.

Lodwick, John. *The Filibusters*. Methuen & Co. 1947.

Lorain, Pierre. *Secret Warfare – The Arms and Techniques of the Resistance*. Orbis Publishing 1983.

Malone, M. J. *SAS – A Pictorial History of the Australian Special Air Service 1957–1997*. Access Press 1997.

Parker, John. *SBS – The Inside Story of the Special Boat Service*. Headline 1997.

Pitt, Barrie. *Special Boat Squadron – The Story of the SBS in the Mediterranean*. Century Publishing 1983.

Pocock, Tom. *Fighting General – The Public & Private Campaigns of General Sir Walter Walker*. Collins 1973.

Ramsay, Jack. *The Soldier's Story*. Macmillan 1996.

Seligman, Adrian. *War in the Islands – Undercover Operations in the Aegean 1942–4*. Alan Sutton Publishing 1996.

Seymour, William. *British Special Forces*. Sidgwick & Jackson 1985.

Smith, E. D. *Counter-Insurgency Operations: 1 Malaya and Borneo*. Ian Allan 1985.

Warner, Philip. *The Special Air Service*. William Kimber 1971.

PICTURE CREDITS

The publishers would like to thank the following sources for their kind permission to reproduce the pictures in this book:

First plate section
Barry Davies: 8t, 8b
Imperial War Museum: 1t, 1b, 2t, 2b, 3t, 3br, 7t
TRH Pictures: 3bl
Private collection: 4, 5, 6, 7b

Second plate section
Barry Davies: 5t, 7t
Private collection: 1t, 1b, 2, 5b, 6t, 6b, 7b, 8
Peter Liddiard: 2

Every effort has been made to acknowledge correctly and contact the source and/or copyright holder of each picture, and Welbeck Non-Fiction Limited apologizes for any unintentional errors, or omissions, which will be corrected in future editions of this book.

INDEX